AUSTRALIAN LIGHT HORSE

Men of the 12th Light Horse Regiment with their mounts. George Francis collection. Courtesy of John Francis and Joan Scott.

Other books by Phillip Bradley

On Shaggy Ridge
The Battle for Wau
To Salamaua
Wau 1942–43
Hell's Battlefield
Charles Bean's Gallipoli Illustrated

PREVIOUS PAGE
Light horsemen tend their mounts by the Sea of Galilee as the 3rd Light Horse Brigade move past. Ralph Kellett collection. Courtesy of Alan Kellett.

AUSTRALIAN LIGHT HORSE

The Campaign in the Middle East, 1916–1918

Phillip Bradley

ALLEN&UNWIN
SYDNEY·MELBOURNE·AUCKLAND·LONDON

Dedicated to Cecilia Bradley—actress, poet, writer, secretary, cook, walker, knitter, bridge player, puzzle expert, ballet aficionado, faithful Catholic, wife, mother, grandmother, and friend to so many over her extraordinary 95 years

First published in 2016

Copyright © Phillip Bradley 2016

All rights reserved. No part of this book may be reproduced or transmitted in any form or by any means, electronic or mechanical, including photocopying, recording or by any information storage and retrieval system, without prior permission in writing from the publisher. The Australian *Copyright Act 1968* (the Act) allows a maximum of one chapter or 10 per cent of this book, whichever is the greater, to be photocopied by any educational institution for its educational purposes provided that the educational institution (or body that administers it) has given a remuneration notice to the Copyright Agency (Australia) under the Act.

Allen & Unwin
83 Alexander Street
Crows Nest NSW 2065
Australia
Phone: (61 2) 8425 0100
Email: info@allenandunwin.com
Web: www.allenandunwin.com

Cataloguing-in-Publication details are available
from the National Library of Australia
www.trove.nla.gov.au

ISBN 978 1 76011 189 2

Internal design by Philip Campbell Design
Maps by Keith Mitchell
Set in 11.25/16 pt Calluna by Bookhouse, Sydney
Printed by Hang Tai Printing Company Limited, China

10 9 8 7 6 5 4 3

CONTENTS

List of maps — vi
Abbreviations — vii
Metric equivalents — vii
Introduction — ix

Chapter 1: 'Soldier's hell' — 1
April to July 1916

Chapter 2: 'Come on, boys, we are making history' — 15
1–4 August 1916

Chapter 3: 'John Turk must pay for his audacity' — 31
5–12 August 1916

Chapter 4: 'Oh, you beauties' — 43
September 1916 to January 1917

Chapter 5: 'But we have Gaza' — 57
February to March 1917

Chapter 6: 'An unqualified failure' — 71
April 1917

Chapter 7: 'First-rate horse-masters' — 85
May to October 1917

Chapter 8: 'Australians will do me' — 97
October to November 1917

Chapter 9: 'In chase of Johnny' — 109
November 1917

Chapter 10: Jerusalem — 123
November 1917 to January 1918

Chapter 11: 'I can't lose half my mounted troops' 131
February to May 1918

Chapter 12: From hell to Armageddon 145
May to September 1918

Chapter 13: 'Terrified of the Bedouins' 157
September 1918

Chapter 14: 'We are going to charge the town' 165
September to December 1918

Writer biographies	178
Photo collection biographies	181
Acknowledgements	184
Bibliography	184
Notes	187
Index	193

LIST OF MAPS

Map 1	Egypt and Palestine	2
Map 2	Sinai desert	16
Map 3	First battle of Gaza	61
Map 4	The capture of Beersheba	100
Map 5	The drive north	110
Map 6	Jaffa to Jerusalem	124
Map 7	Es Salt and Amman	132
Map 8	The battle of Megiddo	151
Map 9	Syria	166

The spelling of place names throughout this book reflects the usage at the time of the Sinai and Palestine campaigns and may not match modern spellings.

Military symbols used on the maps

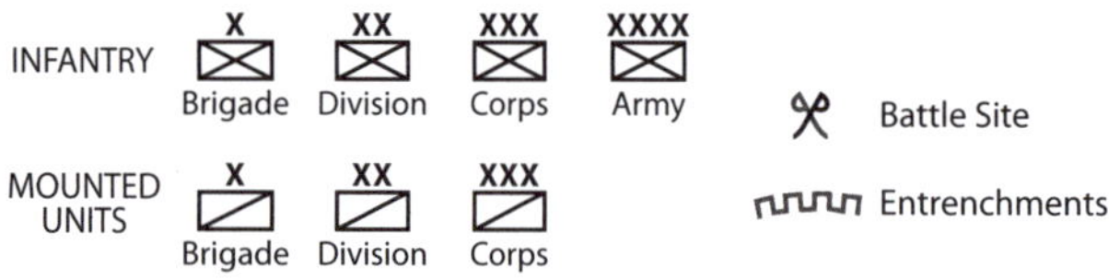

INFANTRY Brigade Division Corps Army   Battle Site

MOUNTED UNITS Brigade Division Corps   ⌐⌐⌐⌐ Entrenchments

ABBREVIATIONS

AIF	Australian Imperial Force
AWM	Australian War Memorial
DSO	Distinguished Service Order
EEF	Egyptian Expeditionary Force
HE	high explosive
HMS	His Majesty's Ship
IWM	Imperial War Museum
LH	Light Horse
MG	machine gun
NA	National Archives (United Kingdom)
NAA	National Archives of Australia
NZ	New Zealand
RHA	Royal Horse Artillery
SLNSW	State Library of New South Wales
VC	Victoria Cross

METRIC EQUIVALENTS

1 inch	2.5 centimetres
1 foot	0.3 metres
1 yard	0.9 metres
1 mile	1.6 kilometres
1 pound	450 grams

INTRODUCTION

In early October 1918, with the war in the Middle East almost over, Lieutenant General Sir Philip Chetwode wrote to Lieutenant General Sir Harry Chauvel, the Australian who had replaced Chetwode as the commander of the Desert Mounted Corps, congratulating him on the capture of Damascus. 'You have made history with a vengeance,' Chetwode wrote, 'and your performance will be talked about and quoted long after many more bloody battles in France will have been almost forgotten.' Chetwode noted that the infantry divisions had played their part but that it was Chauvel's cavalry and light horse units 'who put the lid on the Turks' aspirations for ever'.[1] Three weeks later, the Turks had surrendered and some 400 years of Ottoman rule in the Middle East were over. As Chetwode had observed, it was the mounted troops, the Australian Light Horse prominent among them, that had made victory possible on this, the most challenging of battlefields.

In August 1914 that victory was more than four years away. Australia had responded to the opening of the First World War by forming the Australian Imperial Force (AIF), which initially included a brigade of light horse mounted troops. By May 1915, another two light horse brigades had arrived in Egypt and, with the Gallipoli campaign already at a stalemate, the 1st, 2nd and 3rd Light Horse Brigades as well as the New Zealand Mounted Rifles Brigade were sent to Gallipoli to serve as infantry. In that role, the light horsemen performed with admirable courage but with little chance of breaking the Gallipoli impasse.

As the official Australian historian of the AIF's Middle Eastern campaign, Henry Gullett, observed, the light horsemen who had served at

Man and horse: Tom Bradley and Quart Pot. Godfrey Burgess collection. Courtesy of Robert Burgess.

Gallipoli had volunteered twice, once to join the AIF in Australia and once again to leave their mounts behind in Egypt to serve as infantry.[2] When the Anzacs returned to Egypt in early 1916, the AIF infantry battalions were reorganised and reinforced to create five infantry divisions to be sent to the Western Front, while the light horsemen were reunited with their horses. One light horse regiment and two-thirds of another were sent to the Western Front, but twelve light horse regiments were kept in Egypt as part of General Sir Archibald Murray's Egyptian Expeditionary Force.

Australian Light Horse covers the operations of the Australian light horse and camel troops in the Middle East from early 1916 through to the end of the war. It does so by looking at the experiences of the men who served, using their own words. Some 70 diaries or collections of correspondence from light horsemen have been used within the text,

Rowland 'Top' Hassall, 4th Machine Gun Squadron, writing home. George Francis collection.

AUSTRALIAN LIGHT HORSE

while Henry Gullett's comprehensive official history of the campaign provides the framework for their experiences.

Australian Light Horse also serves as a canvas for an outstanding collection of private photographs from those men who fought with the light horse or camel corps in the Sinai and Palestine campaigns. 'The Kodak appears to be part of the equipment of the Light Horse,' Frank Hurley, the Australian official photographer, wrote in early 1918.[3] Nearly 100 years later, many of these extraordinary photographs are published here for the first time, illuminating the journey of the light horsemen across the harshest of battlefields.

The foreground shadow marks the presence of the soldier photographer with his box brownie camera. Here Reg Dixon photographs men and horses from the 2nd Light Horse Field Ambulance. Reg Dixon collection. Courtesy of Merrien Wrighter.

INTRODUCTION

CHAPTER 1
'SOLDIER'S HELL'
April to July 1916

At the outbreak of the First World War, the boundary between the Egyptian Sinai and Ottoman-controlled Palestine ran from Rafa near the Mediterranean coast down to Akaba on the Red Sea. The line was about 150 kilometres east of the Suez Canal, but the British defences rested upon that vital waterway. Turkish forces had already made an attempt to interdict the canal in February 1915 but there had been no attempts since, the barren lands of the western Sinai proving a daunting obstacle. General Murray was nevertheless keen to push his troops out into the Sinai in order to protect the canal rather than wait for another attack on it.

Although the Australian Light Horse would earn fame in the battles from Sinai through Palestine and Syria, their first mounted operation would take place in Egypt's western desert. When Brigadier General Charles Cox's 1st Brigade[1] arrived in Egypt on 28 December 1915, it was immediately sent to the western frontier of Egypt to act as a screen against any incursion of Senussi rebels towards the Nile. Cox's brigade replaced a scratch force of light horsemen that had been given that role a month earlier. Two of Cox's three regiments were later sent to Minia, some 220 kilometres south of Cairo on the Nile, before moving to Kantara on the Suez Canal in May 1916 as the Senussi threat diminished and the Turkish threat grew.

The Anzac Mounted Division was formed in May 1916 under the command of an Australian, Major General Harry Chauvel. 'An easy natural leader,' the official historian, Henry Gullett, wrote of Chauvel, 'Reserved and aloof in manner, gentle of speech and quiet of bearing.'[2] This measured approach to command would hold Chauvel in good stead

Horace Taberner, who served with the 1st Remount Unit in Egypt, demonstrates his horsemanship. Before the war Horace had been a farm-hand in South Gippsland. Horace Taberner collection. Courtesy of Laurie Taberner.

A British warship on the Suez Canal. Note the canal defence post on the far bank. Harry Mattocks collection. Courtesy of Russ Mattocks.

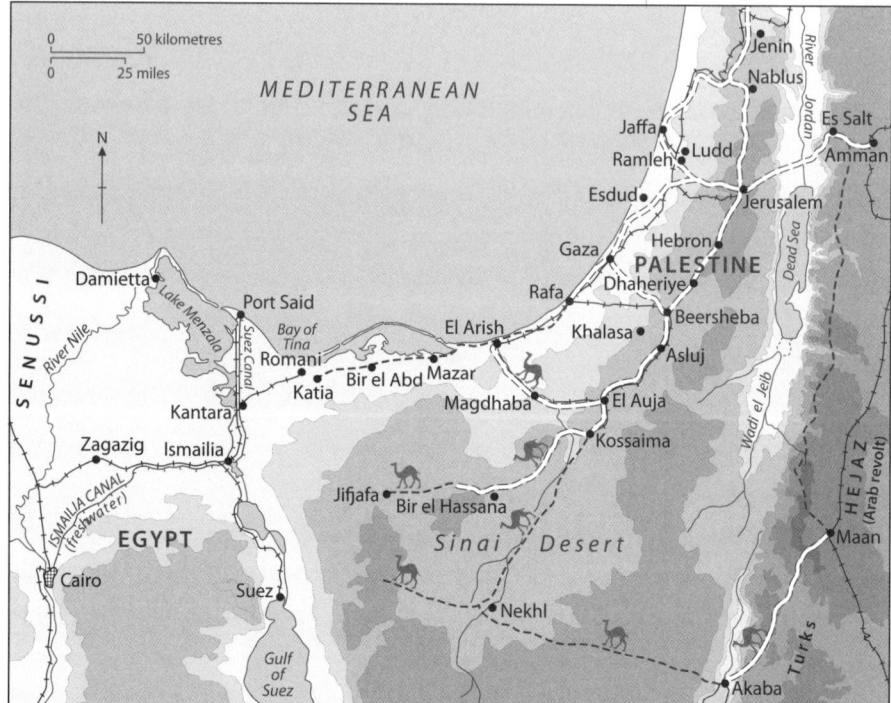

Map 1: Egypt and Palestine

throughout the war. Chauvel's division comprised four light horse brigades: the 1st under Cox, the 2nd under Brigadier General Granville Ryrie, the 3rd under Brigadier General John 'Bull' Antill and the New Zealand Mounted Rifles Brigade under Brigadier General Edward Chaytor. A battery of guns (either 13-pounder or 18-pounder types) from the Royal Horse Artillery (RHA) was attached to each brigade, namely the Leicester battery (1st Brigade), the Ayrshire battery (2nd Brigade), the Inverness battery (3rd Brigade) and the Somerset battery (New Zealand Mounted Rifles Brigade). The 11th and 12th Light Horse regiments acted as independent units.[3]

General Harry Chauvel, on the right, inspecting the Suez Canal defences at Serapeum in 1916. He looks just as the official historian later portrayed him: 'calm, debonair, crop on thigh'. The photograph was taken by General Chauvel's batman, Arthur Hitchcock. Arthur Hitchcock collection. Courtesy of Kay Alliband.

The light horsemen were not cavalrymen, though they acted in a similar way while carrying out patrol and reconnaissance work. In battle they acted more in the role of mounted infantry, using their horses to bring them rapidly to the battlefield and then normally fighting dismounted. Each brigade was of three regiments plus corps units, and each regiment had three squadrons each of four troops. Ideally, each troop was made up of ten four-man sections. One man from each section remained with the four horses during battle and therefore each light horse brigade had only 800 rifles when dismounted, which was similar to the strength of an infantry battalion. A mounted machine-gun section was attached to each squadron, though these would be consolidated into separate brigade-level machine-gun squadrons in July 1916.

Supply, particularly the supply of water, was the key consideration for any light horse operation in Egypt and beyond. Each man needed 4.5 litres of water a day, though he would often get less than a litre. A horse required more than 20 litres a day; any less than that and they soon lost condition. Each man required a kilogram of rations a day but a horse required 9 kilograms of bulky feed. With Murray's plan to establish a force of 50,000 men at Katia oasis, some 40 kilometres east of the canal, thousands of camels would be needed for supply. A railway was obviously needed, and construction soon began from the east side of the canal at Kantara towards Romani, 10 kilometres north-west of Katia.[4]

A typical light horseman. Harry Mattocks collection.

The Turks had three possible avenues of advance across the Sinai to the Suez Canal: the southern, central and northern routes. Water for the northern route could be obtained at the Katia oasis, while the central and southern routes would require wells to be sunk. The Turks had used the central route in the raid on the canal in February 1915 and had already extended the railway south from Beersheba to Asluj, where wells were sunk and water cisterns filled. A light horse raid on Jifjafa on 11 April 1916, however, destroyed a water-drilling plant, while a follow-up patrol a few months later emptied and sealed the nearby water cisterns. The Turkish force would therefore have to use the northern route via Katia for any future advance on the Suez Canal.

The British 5th Mounted Brigade under Brigadier General Edgar Wiggin reached Romani first. The brigade was a yeomanry unit made up of English farmers, with the landed gentry as their officers. Wiggin set up his headquarters at Romani with outposts out to the east at Katia, Oghratina and Hamisah (see Map 2). Ill-informed and overconfident, Wiggin took three of his mounted squadrons, one-third of his total force, out to Mageibra to chase a reported 200-strong Turkish force. Meanwhile, at dawn on 23 April, a large Turkish force struck under the cover of a heavy morning mist at Oghratina, overrunning the startled Worcester Yeomanry encamped there. Katia, held by only a squadron of Gloucester Yeomanry, was next.[5]

Guided by Bedouin scouts, the Turks were able to set up their machine guns on the sand hills surrounding the oasis where the yeomanry had set up camp under the date palms. Small mountain guns were also positioned close by. When the fog finally lifted, the 100 defenders at Katia under Captain Michael Lloyd-Baker were faced with some 600 attackers. Well-directed Turkish artillery soon opened up on the horse lines, preventing any escape.[6] Outgunned, outnumbered and unable to manoeuvre, the yeomanry fought it out from their meagre shell scrapes in the sand, holding out long enough to enable an unmounted cavalry squadron from Hamisah to join them. But two squadrons from Romani and two others under Wiggin failed to reach Katia oasis in time, and the position fell to the Turks after a bitter fight. Only nine of the defenders regained the British lines, while the wounded were left to the merciless Bedouin. A shaken Wiggin ordered his remaining men back to the canal, abandoning the Romani base. At an outpost at Dueidar, 20 kilometres east of the canal, a resolute company of some 100 Royal Scots Fusiliers from the 52nd Division, warned by an alert fox terrier as the Turks crept up to the outpost under the cover of mist, halted the Turkish advance.[7]

On the evening of 23 April, General Ryrie's 2nd Light Horse Brigade crossed the canal at Kantara and moved east into the Sinai, passing the retiring yeomanry in the night and reaching Hill 70, 11 kilometres east of the canal, around midnight. It soon became clear that the Turkish attack was only a raid, which meant that Ryrie

Scottish troops at Dueidar, June 1916. Edwin Mulford collection. Courtesy of Kerrie Ferguson.

'SOLDIER'S HELL'

was able to move his brigade forward and reoccupy Romani on 25 April, the first anniversary of the Anzac landings.

The Turks had withdrawn to Bir el Abd, 25 kilometres east of Katia. Unlike Wiggin, the canny Ryrie would keep his force concentrated and only send mobile patrols out to Katia, Oghratina and Hamisah. The first job of his brigade was to bury about 70 dead yeoman at Katia. 'We saw a lot of dead Tommies and Turks,' Joe Burgess wrote. 'They were stripped of most of their clothes and look a horrible sight . . . the horses were all lying dead, tied up to the lines.'[8] Gordon Macrae noted that 'most of the dead were stripped of their clothes and the stench was horrible. The burial party was taken from my troop and they had to wear respirators.'[9] When a party from the Worcestershire Yeomanry later went out to rebury their dead, the officer in charge found his brother, whom he recognised only by a distinctive scarf around his neck.[10]

These were dim days for British armed forces in the Middle East. In Mesopotamia (part of modern-day Iraq) the British force at Kut-el-Amara had finally surrendered to Turkish forces on 29 April after a siege that had lasted nearly five months. Meanwhile, British troop strength in Egypt was successively weakened as more and more divisions headed to France, leaving General Murray with the equivalent of three infantry divisions plus the Anzac Mounted Division and the yeomanry. The Turks had three divisions in the northern Sinai plus some 4000 Bedouin irregulars and a superior air arm, with German aircraft and pilots.

The Romani base was surrounded by sand dunes, some of them large enough to dominate the battlefield. It was upon these positions that the defence of Romani would now be based rather than on far-flung outposts. With the railway rapidly approaching Romani, it was the ideal site from which to defend the canal, as any Turkish move against it using the central or southern routes through the Sinai would leave them exposed on the right flank. But the decision to defend Katia oasis only by intermittent patrols left it open to Turkish occupation.

The railhead at Romani. George Francis collection.

6 AUSTRALIAN LIGHT HORSE

The pre-war telegraph line that ran back to Kantara could readily be tapped. On one occasion a foreign conversation was heard by the light horse signallers and a Turkish interpreter was called for. He was also puzzled, until it was realised a Scottish unit (speaking English) was in the area. Further out, heliographs (which signalled in Morse code using flashes of sunlight) were used, the mirror having to be continuously adjusted to allow for the changing angle of the sun. A signal station on a hilltop at Romani could receive Morse signals directed its way from heliographs as far away as 50 kilometres.[11]

By mid-May the heat of summer had arrived, curtailing mobile operations. As early as 25 April, Maurie Evans, serving with the 1st Light Horse Field Ambulance at Sohag, more than 500 kilometres south of Cairo on the upper Nile, wrote that 'the heat is getting beyond all reason'. It had reached 46 degrees Celsius by then and would only get worse. On 19 May, Evans was experiencing 50 degrees Celsius in the shade, with a hot wind 'that feels like a blast from the biggest furnace God ever made'.[12] As Bill Peterson, a signaller with the 2nd Light Horse, noted, heat was not

Four light horsemen at the Ramesseum, near the Valley of the Kings at Luxor. Of the fallen Ramses II statue, the English poet Percy Bysshe Shelley wrote in 'Ozymandias', 'Half sunk, a shattered visage lies.' Wilfred Baker collection. Courtesy of Joan Cupit.

the only concern at Sohag. 'It is almost impossible to lay and doze during the day for the flies,' he wrote. Peterson also noted the death of Sergeant Vernon Ware, the brigade police sergeant, who had died of pneumonia on 3 April. 'They planted him this afternoon,' he wrote. 'It seems hard to go through that Gallipoli hell of many months without a scratch and then to die . . . in some lonely spot like this.'[13]

'Work, heat, dust, sand and more work,' Robert Fell wrote in April. 'An absolute nightmare.'[14] Verner Knuckey lived in a tent where 'millions of flies came home to roost'.[15] On 6 May, Joe Burgess wrote 'it was thundering hot yesterday'. Next day he was off to Katia, where 'the sand flies nearly ate me and my horse'. By 19 May, it was 52 degrees Celsius in the ambulance tent at Romani.[16] Captain Harold Mulder wrote that 'the heat is bad enough but these flies make it nearly unbearable'. On 4 June he added, 'A beast of a day with a hot wind blowing . . . "Arab's Heaven" and soldier's hell.'[17]

Even in summer, however, the nights could be freezing, particularly if a wind came off the sea from the north. 'As cold as chastity,' Maurie Evans wrote on 31 May.[18] The two light horse brigades at Romani suffered from the heat, the blinding sun and the flies, but it was the sandstorms, the feared *khamsin* that was said to blow for 50 days from late April, that tested them to the limit. Henry Sullivan was out in the desert with the 5th Light Horse on 13 April when a sandstorm blew up. 'Saddles, rifles etc and ourselves almost buried in sand,' he wrote. 'Sand and desert awful.'[19] Verner Knuckey experienced how 'the fine sand strikes the face and hands and it feels like red hot needles'.[20]

'The country here is composed of nothing but loose sand hills,' Fred Tomlins observed, 'and most of the hills so steep that the rider has to dismount and lead his horse up and down them, and both horse and rider up to their knees going down them and is very heavy work on both.'[21] Maurie Evans wrote of the ride into Romani: 'Our last stage was across pure sand, heaped into every shape and position, terrible going for the horses. The long column of horsemen climbing up and down in and out among the enormous orange coloured sand dunes set off by the deep blue of the sky.'[22]

To aid the search for water, Lieutenant Colonel Lachlan Wilson of the 5th Light Horse introduced the spear point pump, purchased from regimental funds in defiance of headquarters. It consisted of a hollow pipe perforated above the spear-like point that could be pushed through the sand in low-lying areas to provide water for the horses quickly, without the need to dig and reinforce wells. A single spear point could raise 3500 litres per hour.[23] The horses drank the brackish well water, but water for the men came up on camels from the canal or railhead.

A 6th Light Horse reconnaissance to Bir el Bayud, some 10 kilometres south of Bir el Abd, at the height of summer on 16 May, resulted in men being hospitalised with sunstroke and heat exhaustion, and left many of the horses in a distressed condition.[24] Gordon Macrae, who was on the patrol, noted that by 11 a.m. the water the men carried with them was so hot it was undrinkable. 'Our throats were already parched and the sun being on the backs of our heads made us feel giddy,' he wrote. The patrol reached a well but the water was undrinkable. By now, some of the men were staggering and frothing at the mouth while a few had fainted. 'It seemed as though the wind was blowing off the furnaces of hell,' Macrae wrote. On returning to Romani, 28 men went straight into hospital and 500 horses needed an extended spell.[25] Joe Burgess had ridden one of them. 'My mare was wobbly and panting but the plucky little beggar kept going,' he wrote.[26] The brigade commander, Granville Ryrie, observed, 'I don't think I can stand the heat here if it gets any worse as it is sure to do . . . I hate this infernal desert, it makes me tired to look at the sand & it is everywhere.'[27]

In late May, Cox's 1st Brigade relieved Ryrie's 2nd. Bill Peterson reached Romani on 26 May. 'Great sand dunes are on all sides of the camp,' he wrote, 'and we are camped down in a hollow close to a clump of palm trees.'

A light horse camp in the desert. The horses are tethered to rope lines that have been anchored to buried sandbags. Harry Mattocks collection.

'SOLDIER'S HELL'   9

These clumps of palms among the dunes were known as hods, and water could usually be found below the surface there.[28] 'We have been living very poorly here on bully beef, bread and jam,' Fred Tomlins wrote, 'but we could not even get enough bully and at times had to make a meal of dried bread and half a pint of tea.'[29] As Bill Peterson later observed, bully beef and hard biscuits 'will soon wear the strongest constitution down'. In comparison, the Turkish rations looked like 'rolls of thin brown cardboard' containing 'dried apricots and dates reduced to suet and rolled into wide thin sheets', which were 'far in advance of our own iron rations'.[30] With the arrival of the railway at the end of May, the Lowland Scots of the 52nd Infantry Division also arrived at Romani, as did the New Zealand Mounted Rifles Brigade.

Late on 30 May, the light horse regiments moved out in columns lit only by the stars of the desert night, heading towards Hod Salmana, some 7 kilometres east of Bir el Abd. Bill Peterson wrote of how 'the whole brigade turned out at 10 o'clock last night and we took part in one of the longest and most tedious night marches I have ever participated in'.[31] Maurie Evans considered the prospects for any wounded: 'It will be hell for anyone who gets wounded badly as they have to travel by camel for over 30 miles.' On his return to Romani, Evans noted 'an overwhelming sense of irritable sleepiness unable to be appeased'.[32] At Oghratina, Fred Tomlins wrote how 'Scores of Tommies are still lying on top of the ground where they were killed.' The desert wind had blown the sand cover from their shallow graves.[33]

Four Turkish privates prepare their meal. One rolls the flatbread while another cooks it. Note the clever use of rocks to help seal the tents. Ralph Kellett collection.

10   AUSTRALIAN LIGHT HORSE

Romani camp. Arthur Reynolds collection. Courtesy of Kay Stacy.

❖

Death also came from the air. The German air detachment flew Rumpler Taube and Albatros Scout aircraft over the Sinai. The Taube, or dove, was so named for its distinctive and gracefully swept-back, dove-like wings. Bill Peterson wrote that 'she resembles a huge white transparent butterfly'.[34] At dawn on 1 June, Fred Tomlins watched as 'the burr of an aeroplane was heard coming from the south very high up . . . one glance at her dove tail convinced me she was a Taube and was out for revenge'.[35] The aircraft was high, 'so high we did not worry,' Bert Billings wrote, 'however his aim was good'. The plane dropped two bombs, then three and then another three. The third of the middle three exploded in the horse lines of the 3rd Light Horse. 'The horse lines broke under the strain and/or all horses were released to give them a chance,' Billings wrote. 'They just galloped until they dropped and were found miles away at our outposts, but many were never found.'[36] 'Every bomb exploded but they sank well into the soft sand before exploding which affected their destructive power a lot as there were hardly any splinters flying,' Fred Tomlins observed.[37] Ten men, seven from the 3rd Light Horse, were killed. 'Most of us got abroad our hacks and hit out for the open desert, where we stayed until the Taube left,' Lieutenant Stuart Macfarlane wrote. 'We all rode bare-back with only a halter, so there were several spills.'[38] The raid resulted in the death of 47 horses. A team of four camels was needed to drag each one to its grave.[39]

'Swimming our horses.' Joseph Bradshaw collection. Courtesy of Bob Smith.

The base at Romani was close to the ocean and, as Bert Billings noted, 'swims were one of the bright spots in our life ... after the swim the horses would keep on rolling in the sand'.[40] 'The surf makes a chap as love sick for the sea as a soldier leaving his girl at the old "loo" [Woolloomooloo] wharf,' Joe Burgess wrote.[41] Though involved in a world war, the men were in their own world. On 8 June, Fred Tomlins heard the news that HMS *Hampshire* had been sunk off the Orkney Islands with almost all hands lost, including Lord Kitchener, the British Secretary of State for War. 'Stiff luck for K but nobody here thinks it will affect the war much,' he wrote.[42]

On the afternoon of 10 June, the Muksheib Column, comprising the 10th Light Horse plus two squadrons of the 9th supported by some 800 camels, all under the command of Lieutenant Colonel Thomas Todd, moved out from the railhead to drain out the water in the cisterns and pools in the Wadi Um Muksheib, south of Jifjafa, 75 kilometres to the east. As General Antill observed, it 'turned out to be a bigger job than expected', taking four days to drain some 36,000,000 litres of water.[43]

Bill Peterson was on a patrol to Oghratina around the same time. 'It was a beautiful moonlight night,' he wrote, 'and the long column stretched far out upon the desert like some gigantic confusing thing [as] we wound in and out among the sand dunes.' Upon reaching the wells, the horses 'were so eager for water that they plunged their muzzles into the canvas bucket upsetting most of the contents in their eagerness,' Peterson wrote. 'My fellow drank six buckets before he cried enough.'[44]

On 22 June, a 1st Light Horse patrol got lost in the desert near Oghratina. 'The night was hot and our bottles dry and a good many lads' mouths were parched for the want of water and they were dropping off to sleep as they rode,' Fred Tomlins wrote.[45] 'It's red hot,' Burgess added. 'The

OPPOSITE, TOP
Water containers, known as fantasses, at Oghratina in July 1916. These held drinking water for the men; the horses and camels had to make do with the brackish well water. Arthur Reynolds collection.

wind must be blowing right direct off Hades itself.'[46] Such occurrences could prove fatal. On 9 July, two men from the Wellington Mounted Rifles died of exhaustion during a patrol to Salmana.[47] On 16 July, Maurie Pearce wrote that 'These long "stunts" combined with the great amount of night work we are getting, the excessive heat and bad food etc are the cause of such a great deal of sickness. We have been out of bed every morning at 3.30 a.m. ever since our arrival here.'[48] Meanwhile, the men of the 3rd Brigade had been issued with emu plumes for their hats. When the Tommies asked what bird they were from, the men would tell them they were kangaroo feathers.[49]

In July, the heavy machine guns were reorganised from a two-gun section per regiment to twelve per brigade, deployed as a separate squadron. Three Lewis light machine guns were also allocated to each regiment. One of the machine-gunners, Gordon Cooper, wrote, 'expecting some fun: Turks advancing from Oghratina'.[50]

A Vickers gun barrel stowed for travel. Colin Wells, a former boundary rider, is alongside. 'Men became extraordinarily quick at unpacking and going into action,' Henry Gullett noted. George Francis collection.

'SOLDIER'S HELL' 13

CHAPTER 2

'COME ON, BOYS, WE ARE MAKING HISTORY'

1–4 August 1916

At the start of August 1916, both light horse brigades at Romani had temporary commanders. Lieutenant Colonel John Meredith took over the command of the 1st Brigade after General Cox fell ill and was sent on leave to England. Johnny Meredith, as the troopers called him, got off to a bad start when he led the brigade astray on the night of 31 July, 'much to the disgust of the lads who were not at all pleased with the concern'.[1]

At the time, General Ryrie was in England, on leave of absence related to his standing as an Australian politician. In Ryrie's absence, Colonel Jack Royston, the commander of the 12th Light Horse, was appointed to temporary command of the 2nd Brigade. Royston was a South African who had served in the Boer War and in German West Africa in the current war. Both new commanders had dominating sand hills east of Romani named after them.

On 19 July, a Turkish advance on Katia was spotted from the air. That night, light horse patrols fired at Turkish forces near Oghratina and some prisoners were taken from the Egypt Expeditionary Force, which comprised 20,000 troops under the command of the German General Friedrich Kress von Kressenstein. The 'picturesque ruffian', Djemal Pasha, was the nominal commander-in-chief.[2] The troops were backed up by some 2500 Austro-Hungarians and Germans serving six heavy batteries of Austro-Hungarian and German artillery, plus the German 605th Machine Gun Company.

The 605th, led by Lieutenant Benkwitz with 31 men, had departed Berlin by train on 29 March 1916, reaching Constantinople on 7 April before crossing the Bosphorus and reaching Semakh on the Sea of Galilee

Lieutenant Frank 'Towser' Nivison, 12th Light Horse machine-gun section, behind a Vickers gun that has been set up with the tripod reversed for anti-aircraft purposes. Such use caused problems for both the gunner, upon whom the hot cartridge shells would fall, and the loader, who had to ensure he kept the ammunition belt at the correct angle of entry to prevent stoppages. George Francis collection.

Colonel Jack Royston at Dueidar in mid-1916. This photo was taken while he was in command of the 12th Light Horse before Romani. George Francis collection.

in early June. Here the company incorporated 67 Turkish ranks and began working with camels and carrying out field firing tests. On 22 July, the company saw its first action when the machine-gunners opened fire on a British plane at Bir el Abd.[3]

Most of the Turkish troops were from the veteran 3rd Division. Manned by Anatolian troops, this division had performed well at Gallipoli and in the earlier attack on the yeomanry at Katia. The Turkish force was some 160 kilometres from the nearest railhead and relied for supply mainly on limited camel trains, 18,000 of which would be employed on this operation. There were only a few mounted camel troops to provide any mobility to rival the manoeuvrability of the light horse.

Nevertheless, the Turkish force had very good artillery support, and this could prove critical. The aim of the operation was to advance to within artillery range of the Suez Canal and thus close the vital waterway

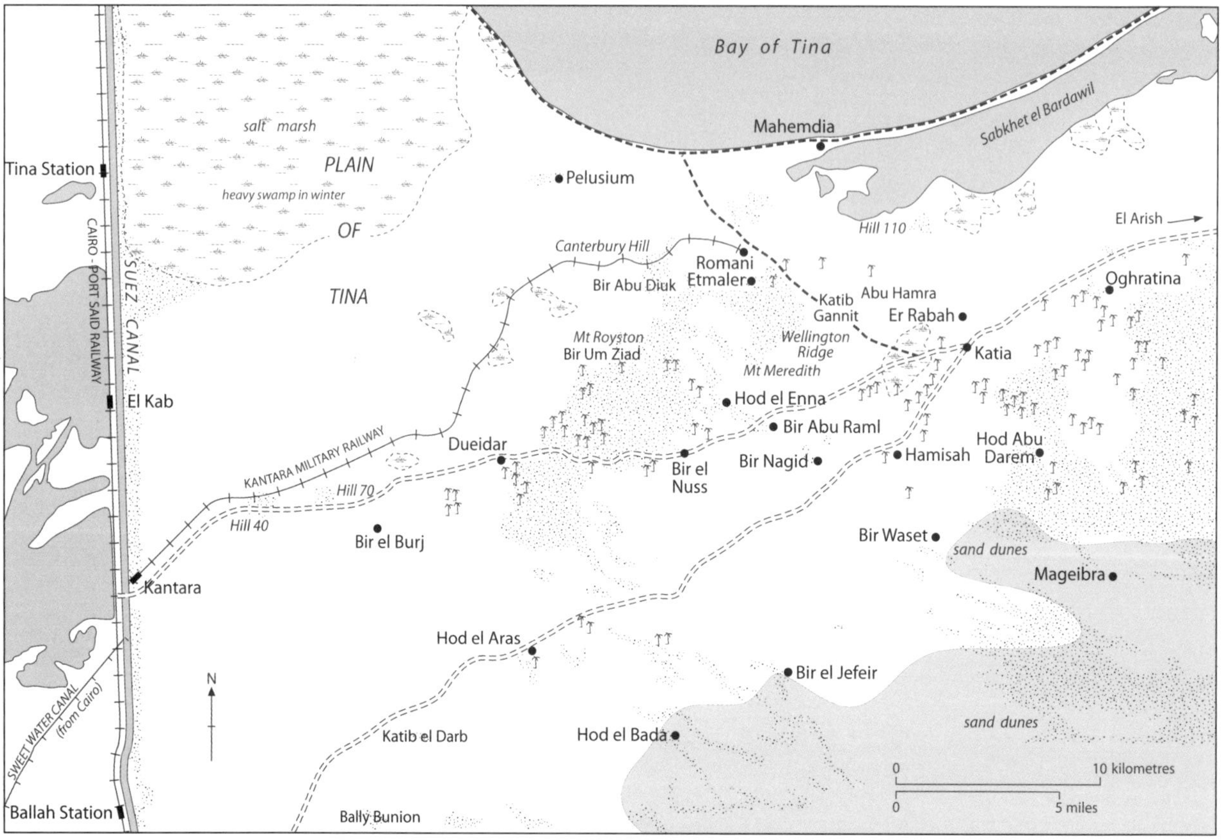

A Turkish camel train loading ammunition. George Francis collection.

to shipping. Wooden planks or lined furrows were required to move the artillery pieces across the sand. The attack would be made in the heat of summer, but to wait for cooler weather would have exacerbated the water problem. Unlike the Allied force, the Turkish troops were forced to drink the brackish water from the desert oases to survive. All movement was by night, led by Bedouin scouts, the days spent sheltering under palm groves. Oghratina was reached without incident.

Major Carl Mühlmann, serving as a German staff officer with von Kressenstein, noted that 'surprise and swiftness of execution were essential to success'. As soon as darkness fell on 3 August, the Turkish left wing advanced, aiming to outflank the Romani defences to the south before turning north to come in behind the main infantry defences in Romani. Mühlmann wrote that 'the hours of the night sped by'.[4]

The light horsemen knew the Turks were coming. General Chauvel later wrote that 'it was evident that the long threatened second attack on the Suez Canal was about to be launched'.[5] On 22 July, Captain Harold Mulder wrote, 'the whole of the Turkish 3rd Division led by a German

OPPOSITE, BOTTOM
Map 2: Sinai desert

'COME ON, BOYS, WE ARE MAKING HISTORY' 17

The 6th Light Horse on the march. Ralph Kellett collection.

general and with German machine gunners are there . . . I guess we'll smash the whole lot up.'[6] Starting on 20 July, the 1st and 2nd Brigades patrolled out from Romani on alternate days, returning at midnight but leaving out small mobile listening posts overnight. Gordon Macrae, who was with the 6th Light Horse, wrote, 'we have been going solid all week. Every alternate day we go out to meet Jacko [the Turks].'[7] The New Zealand brigade, later joined by the 3rd Brigade, patrolled the Mageibra area on the right flank. Both sides manoeuvred their forces for the coming clash.

On 26 July, Maurie Pearce wrote, 'The opinion of the heads appears to be that the Turks are preparing for a big attack on the Suez Canal . . . we are ready for them and for a spell after we have towelled them up.' Pearce got his fight on 29 July, when a troop from the 1st Light Horse on outpost duty at Katia was outflanked and nearly surrounded by the Turks. 'Bullets were very thick round us,' Pearce wrote, but 'luckily the Turks overestimated the range and the bullets went high, otherwise few of us would have got away . . . Long, Roper and Rinaldi were hit and a few horses, one [of which] had to be shot.'[8]

The commander of the Imperial force, Lieutenant General Sir Herbert Lawrence, had been ordered to hold Romani and draw in the Turks, but he also had concerns about his open right flank. Lawrence had four infantry brigades and five artillery batteries defending his supply base at Romani, with the Anzac Mounted Division out in front and covering the right

The 1st Light Horse camp at Romani. Royal New South Wales Lancers Memorial Museum collection.

flank. Another infantry division was gathering at Kantara, while two naval monitors had anchored off Oghratina to shell any enemy troop concentrations there. Lawrence's major weakness was his own location; he was content to control the battle from his headquarters at Kantara, despite General Murray urging him forward.

A camel train. Edwin Mulford collection.

Jeff Holmes, who was a horse team driver with the engineers of the 1st Field Squadron, watched the build-up at Romani. 'Trains of camels have been passing for the last few days but the longest of all passed today,' he wrote on 26 July. 'There were two thousand camels, nearly 5 miles in length and it took nearly two hours to pass by.'9

On 2 August, a Turkish deserter of Bosnian origin from the 3rd Turkish Division gave himself up at No. 8 Post at Romani. He told his captors that about 19,000 Turkish troops were advancing on Katia and Romani.[10] On the morning of 3 August, the first Turkish forces entered the Katia area, with more to the south-east. The deep wells at Katia were vital for any further advance. Bill Peterson wrote, 'Jacko is having the time of his life since occupying Qatia. He won't have a leg to stand on soon.'[11] Later in the afternoon, Peterson was sent up onto Mount Meredith to lay a phone line and was kept busy that night repairing breaks caused by passing horsemen. At 10 p.m. the first reports of gunfire came in from the outpost line and by 11 p.m. the firing had increased.

General Chauvel ordered Lieutenant Colonel Meredith's 1st Brigade to occupy the high sand dunes forward of Romani. Lieutenant Colonel David Fulton's 3rd Light Horse was on the left, from the infantry outpost to Mount Meredith, while Lieutenant Colonel George Bourne's 2nd Light Horse stretched south from Mount Meredith to Hod el Enna, with the 1st Light Horse in reserve at Romani. The light horsemen established the outpost line just after dusk and then waited.[12] Major Mick Bruxner, who was from the same fertile lands of the Upper Clarence Valley in northern New South Wales as General Chauvel, was a squadron commander with the 6th Light Horse. He later wrote of 'the tiny Cossack posts of 4 or 5 men, camouflaged behind a dune amongst the bushes', far out in front of 'the remainder of the troop sleeping, perhaps many of them their last earthly sleep, like tired giants . . . in a little hollow are the patient horses'.[13]

Just before midnight, a force of some 500 Turks was spotted near Hod el Enna, and Meredith's regiment was brought up to cover the left flank. The Turkish plan had been to follow the 2nd Brigade back to Romani. Out with the 1st Brigade's machine-gun squadron, Gordon Cooper heard the first shots fifteen minutes before midnight.[14] As Bruxner wrote, 'up and down the line comes the crackle, crackle of rifle fire and the rip-rip-rip of machine guns. This is only a feeler by John Turk.' But by 1 a.m., 'up steep slopes comes the Turk infantry, withering away under our steady fire, but always coming swiftly on'.[15] Charles Livingstone, also with the 6th, wrote, 'When I felt liquid running down my leg I thought I had been hit too, but the bullet went right through my water bottle and hit the leg of the man behind me.'[16]

Around 1 a.m. on 4 August, the Turks attacked the outpost line out of the darkness, and under a heavy exchange of fire crept closer in.

Then at about 2.30 a.m. they 'charged with fixed bayonets yelling allah, allah'.[17] 'Light Horse on Meredith Hill hard pressed urgently require reinforcements,' Bill Peterson wrote. 'Every available man up in the firing line most of my signallers are there.'[18] The 1st Light Horse moved from reserve up onto Mount Meredith but, as Peterson related, the position could not be held. 'Turks have charged with the bayonet and have taken Meredith Hill, which makes our position untenable now,' he wrote. 'The only thing to do is to withdraw to safer ground.' Peterson gave his report to Colonel Royston, who galloped off as the Turks pressed their attack. 'I hear the Turks yelling cursing and shouting and before we realised what had happened they pour over the ridge about 50 yards from us firing for all they are worth point blank,' Peterson wrote. 'Then a mad scramble for our horses . . . the bullets were like hailstones.'[19]

After two 3rd Light Horse outposts were overrun, Major Michael Shanahan found four horseless men. He got two up on the horse and with the other two hanging onto the stirrups, his mighty steed carried all five men to safety. The light horsemen held onto the wall of sand that was Mount Meredith until flanking moves forced its abandonment around

Trenches at Romani.
Arthur Reynolds collection.

'COME ON, BOYS, WE ARE MAKING HISTORY'

3 a.m. On the right, Shanahan's squadron took heavy casualties from Turkish flanking fire and also withdrew. As the retiring units reached their second line, the order rang out: 'Sections about—Action front!'[20]

Sapper John Hobbs, a signaller with the 1st Brigade, was hunkered down only 10 metres behind the firing line and under very heavy fire. 'The enemy poured rifle and machine-gun fire on us,' he wrote. 'I cast a hasty glance round and saw three of our boys being dragged out by the arms and legs.' 'Allah, allah, finish Australia,' came the cry from the Turks. The brigade held out for three hours 'until it was impossible for human flesh to stand more'. Hobbs took a wounded man back on his horse, which he led over a machine-gun-swept ridge. 'I was horribly scared and could hardly stand when we got in,' he wrote.[21]

Fred Tomlins, who was with the 1st Light Horse, got the alarm at midnight. 'Our outposts were retiring and fighting their way back,' he wrote. 'We rode up close to the Turks, dismounted for action and were soon in the thick of it just at dawn,' he continued. 'The Turks were coming up the gully in hundreds and the closest were within 100 yards of us when we opened fire and they charged yelling Allah Allah, but again Allah deserted them and they fell thick and fast.'[22]

Turkish dead in the Romani sand below one of the dominating sand ridges. When later buried, many were found stripped naked with not even an identity disc. 'That was Bedouin work,' the official historian wrote. Hugh Poate collection. Courtesy of Jim Poate.

Lloyd Corliss was also with the 1st Light Horse. 'The retreat was a lively one and we were all mixed up and no unit of the First Regt was kept together,' he wrote. 'The enemy fired many shells and done some very good shooting.'[23] Frank Willis was another 1st Light Horseman. On the previous day he had found time to write home: 'We are hard at it here at last and have had a few quite exciting little adventures lately.' Back at his family property at Crookwell in the Southern Tablelands of New South Wales, Willis's beloved dog howled throughout the night. The next morning the dog was missing, never to be seen again. By then Frank Willis lay dead on the Romani sand. He had survived the retreat and was refilling his water bottle from a water tank behind a sand bank when a stray bullet struck him in the head.[24]

At 4.20 a.m. the 2nd Brigade moved up on the right flank of the battered 1st. The 6th and 7th Light Horse occupied Wellington Ridge alongside Lieutenant Colonel William Meldrum's Wellington Mounted Rifles, which had been attached. At about the same time the Turkish guns opened up. The fighting continued until 'that fatal tinge of dawn and with it the bark of a mountain gun and the whine of the shell followed by the white puff as the shrapnel bursts over the stubborn line'.[25]

At 7.00 a.m. the Wellingtons covered the withdrawal of the 6th and 7th Light Horsemen from Wellington Ridge. The ridge was swept by shrapnel, machine-gun and rifle fire. 'The Turks have a terrible lot of machine guns,' Robert Farnes wrote.[26] Squadrons moved back in steps one at a time under covering fire, leaving none of the 80 or so wounded men behind.[27] 'Wounded come straggling in, pale, blood-stained men with the cheery smile still on their lips,' one of the light horsemen wrote. '"Pretty warm up there, boys," they remark.'[28] 'All of a sudden bullets began to whiz around, then we all took shelter,' Jeff Holmes wrote. 'The Turks opened fire with their 12-pounders and a few shells burst right over us and it is a miracle we escaped being hit.' The accompanying Somerset battery opened up in reply, 'and Jacko's guns were soon silenced'.[29]

A Royal Horse Artillery field gun in full recoil after firing. Godfrey Burgess collection.

Once dawn broke, Gordon Cooper was able to open fire with his machine gun, but the enemy reply soon came. 'The Turkish guns and artillery got onto us pretty quickly, had a very lively hour or so, had to retire and were shelled all the way back,' he wrote. 'My horse got a pellet in the neck, very close shave.'[30] 'A battery of mountain guns—manned they say by Austrians was shrapnelling us with really admirable precision,' Maurie Evans wrote. 'I haven't been so mortally frightened since Sari Bair this time last year.'[31]

Fred Tomlins was in the thick of it with the 1st Light Horse. 'The Turkish machine guns made our positions rather uncomfortable at times,' he wrote, 'and then the Turkish artillery got the range of our led horses

'COME ON, BOYS, WE ARE MAKING HISTORY'

and played havoc with them but very few of the men leading the horses were hit.' With considerable Turkish reinforcements moving up, the order to retire was given at 7 a.m. The machine-gun and shrapnel fire was very heavy as the men covered the kilometre back to their horses. After Lieutenant William Nelson was hit, Fred Tomlins helped to get him back. 'We had to lay him down frequently to spell and it was very heavy in the sand,' Tomlins wrote. 'Shrapnel and machine gun fire were cutting the ground up all around us.' After getting Nelson to the Field Ambulance, Tomlins grabbed a riderless horse and 'was glad when I felt the neddy springing along under me'.[32] When Maurie Evans and his mates got back to their horses, 'we clapped our spurs in and away we went hell for leather over the ridge and into the reset little dip and after us came the sand carts rolling and ploughing up the sand like ships in a heavy sea'.[33]

Another 1st Light Horse trooper, Corporal Austin Edwards, had been shot, the bullet passing through his left biceps and chest and then out his back. Edwards managed to reach the waiting horses, where he was able to remount his horse, Taffy, and escape the advancing Turks. He later claimed that Taffy's patience saved him, because not only was Edwards under fire when he remounted, but he could only manage it with his one good arm.[34]

'Too much this for two thin brigades,' Mick Bruxner wrote, 'but still they hold and then bang, bang, bang, bang—the good old Territorial RHA are into it. Beautiful 15-pound shrapnel bursts over the Turk, taking heavy toll, but still he comes on.' Then the light horsemen were forced to pull back. 'A grim job this getting back under fire. Men limp on or are put in front of a mate; four boys go by carrying one in a blanket; 600 yards to go and under fire all the way ... the line forms again.'[35]

Austin Edwards alongside his horse, Taffy. Austin Edwards collection. SLNSW a7206214, PXA 404/116.

❖

Meanwhile, the 6th and 7th Light Horse, temporarily under the control of the imposing 56-year-old Boer war veteran 'Galloping Jack' Royston, moved out to the right flank between Mount Royston and Etmaler, where the Turkish threat was greatest. As each of his horses tired, Royston would grab another; he supposedly wore out fourteen horses that day. 'Colonel Royston is doing some fine work, he is everywhere,' one of his signallers observed.[36] Out with the 6th Light Horse on the right flank, Major Donald Gordon Cross watched Royston approach in a cloud of dust and felt uneasy about having his horse, which was hidden behind a nearby sand hill, borrowed. 'Forward, Cross, they are surrendering in thousands. Come on, boys, we are making history,' Royston told him, before galloping off again.[37]

Colonel George Macarthur-Onslow's 7th Light Horse took up the high ground south-east of Wellington Ridge, while the 6th Light Horse moved to the south-west of the ridge. These two regiments checked the left flank of the Turkish advance before withdrawing under heavy pressure. Corporal Carrick Paul was one of the horse holders with the 6th Light Horse. During the fighting, Paul's squadron commander noticed Paul was holding his arm so asked him what was wrong with it. 'Oh nothing, just a bit of a crack,' Paul replied. He actually had had a bullet through his shoulder.[38]

Meldrum's Wellington Regiment was kept in reserve after retiring behind another ridge. After the withdrawal, the Wellingtons were on the left with the 7th and then the 6th Light Horse on their right. 'These positions were held throughout the day,' Royston later told Chaplain William Fraser.[39] One of the British generals rode up to Royston and asked, 'Can you hold them, colonel?' 'If they get through that crowd,' Royston replied, puffing on his corncob pipe and pointing to his men, 'they can have the camp.'[40] But it was a hard fight, with Royston putting every machine gun into the line and calling up two regiments of the 1st Brigade to help. Leaving their horses, the light horsemen advanced under fire some 1500 metres to their firing line. Royston 'was a great inspiration', Colonel Meldrum later wrote. 'He told me I held the key of the position and had to hold on at all costs.' Meldrum's 'Well-and-Trulies' complied. 'From dawn to dusk we were dourly defending,' Meldrum wrote. 'From 10 o'clock onwards it was impossible for either side to advance without heavy loss.' Meldrum understood the key to the battle: 'We could win by defending. The Turks had to advance or fail.'[41] Four enemy aircraft appeared over Romani at 5.15 a.m. and dropped about 30 bombs, and at 6 a.m. Turkish artillery began shelling Romani station. As day broke and the heat rose, the light horsemen fought to retain Wellington Ridge.

A camel supply train at Etmaler. Walter Smyth collection. Courtesy of Robyn Thompson.

German officer Major Mühlmann was behind the centre of the Turkish attack looking down from a high dune over Romani. He watched as the light horsemen retreated before the Turkish advance only to take up new positions further back. 'The Australian Cavalry fought in a most exemplary fashion,' Mühlmann later wrote. 'Many a time we cursed those active and agile horsemen in their big soft hats.'[42]

❖

By 7 a.m. the desperate Turks had taken Wellington Ridge and, with the wells at Etmaler less than 1 kilometre away, the threat was immediate. When the Turks on the crest of the ridge opened fire on the camps at Etmaler, the British artillery responded and cleared the crest. Jim Greatorex wrote of how the artillery 'made "Johnny" sit up and take notice'.[43] The machine-gunners also did a job on the Turkish force. Heinrich Römer-Andreae was one of the Germans in the attack that reached the heights east of Romani at about 8 a.m. 'Scarcely had we looked over the top of the range—when a tremendous machine gun fire was experienced by us,' he wrote.[44]

By extending their left flank to get in behind Romani, the Turkish force was now vulnerable to an attack on that flank. Chaytor's New Zealand Mounted Rifles Brigade and Wiggin's reformed 5th Mounted Brigade stood ready at Hill 70 for such a stroke.[45] Back at Kantara, however, General Lawrence was in no position to give Chaytor the order to strike, as communications with Romani had been cut by Turkish artillery fire. Bert Billings simply noted, 'Things serious.' When the line to 3rd Light Horse went out at 10.45 a.m., Jeff Playfoot and Billings went out to fix it 'and got peppered all the way, one big shrapnel bursting right over us and splattered all round, but missed'.[46]

Meanwhile, Turkish troops continued to advance around Chauvel's right flank and he had to extend his line to cover the railway. He also realised that if he could get his two brigades out of the line and mount them up, he could make the attack on the Turkish left flank himself. Chauvel asked that the British reserve brigade take over his lines but once again the absence of Lawrence delayed a decision.

At the enemy headquarters, Carl Mühlmann observed that 'as time passed Kress and his staff looked expectantly to his left wing where the decision depended'. Von Kressenstein had deployed two Turkish battalions on that flank alongside a mountain gun battery and some of his machine guns. When Mühlmann went to see the Turkish commander on the left, 'I found him very depressed ... troops were exhausted; heat and thirst had wrought greater havoc with them than the bullets of the enemy.' Ominously, as Mühlmann

A well in the sand hills near Romani. Royal New South Wales Lancers Memorial Museum collection.

The grim fate of a German soldier in the Sinai desert. Walter Smyth collection.

rode off he saw mounted troops moving to envelop the Turkish left wing. Scouts also reported two other mounted brigades moving up from the south. 'All hope of victory was abandoned,' he later wrote.[47]

❖

Chaytor's force had finally reached the battle in the afternoon, and the New Zealanders and yeomanry attacked Mount Royston. Colonel Lachlan Wilson's 5th Light Horse, which was attached to Chaytor's brigade, advanced around the enemy left flank and 'this proved to be the turning point'. From 4 to 5 p.m. the Turkish forces on this flank put up the white flag.[48] At 5 p.m. Bill Peterson, who was sheltering with the signal section in a palm grove, noted that 'the Turks around our flank have "imsheed" [gone away] and are apparently in retreat'.[49] By 6 p.m. the remaining defenders had surrendered. Most of the prisoners taken were desperate for water. 'We could have caught hundreds more had our horses been fresh,' Gordon Macrae wrote.[50] 'They retired at night a beaten mob,' William Burchill added.[51]

Turkish prisoners captured at Romani on 4 and 5 August 1916. Royal New South Wales Lancers Memorial Museum collection.

The Turkish force may have retreated but it had not been beaten. That evening Heinrich Römer-Andreae kept watch for the Allied advance. 'As the enemy was very bold I scarcely kept under cover,' he later wrote. A young Australian lieutenant, Alan Righetti from the 2nd Light Horse, had been killed during the day and Römer-Andreae was later brought the identification disc by a Turkish soldier. In 1920 he wrote to Alan Righetti's mother, telling her, 'Your son fell as a hero.'[52]

That night, Chauvel redeployed his light horsemen. 'In the evening all the mounted men walked round to the right flank, the infantry taking our places,' Maurie Pearce wrote. 'More infantry reinforcements arrived about dusk and lined the hills on the left flank of the Turks.'[53] There was little sleep for the signallers. 'I was kept going from midnight until about 7 am rejoining lines which were continually getting broken by rifle fire and shrapnel,' Robert Farnes wrote.[54] All night the field ambulances worked to get the wounded out to the railhead. Tragically, there was no rail stock allocated to transport them back to Kantara, though facilities for the wounded were no better there.

The British officer Lieutenant George Wallis had been severely wounded by artillery fire at Romani and was lying on a stretcher at Cairo railway station when a 'kindly Australian put his wideawake hat over my face' to shield him from the sun. When he was moved it was therefore assumed that Wallis was Australian, so he was taken to No. 3 Australian General Hospital, 'where they just would not let me die,' he later wrote. Dr Hugh Poate, who had honed his surgical skills in a cramped dusty dugout at Gallipoli, carried out eight operations on the head and arm of Wallis. In comparison the British Nazarea Hospital in Cairo 'had a foul name' and Wallis thought he 'would have died for a cert' there. Here he came under the care of the Australian nurse Beulah McMinn. She told Wallis how the nurses had heard him in a delirium talking of his wife Mollie and his newborn son 'and we just couldn't let you die'.[55]

Back at Romani the exhausted light horsemen got what rest they could in the knowledge that they would be back in the saddle well before dawn. 'We gave the bridle reins a twist around one foot and lay down anywhere and dropped off to sleep,' Fred Tomlins wrote. 'Our horses were about as tired as we were and did not disturb us.'[56]

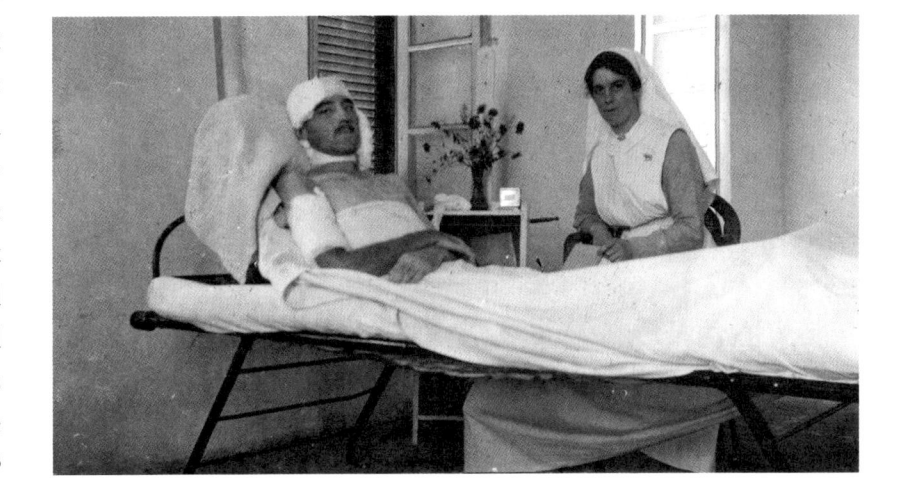

Lieutenant George Wallis and the Australian nurse Beulah McMinn at No. 3 Australian General Hospital in Cairo. 'We just couldn't let you die,' she later told him. Hugh Poate collection.

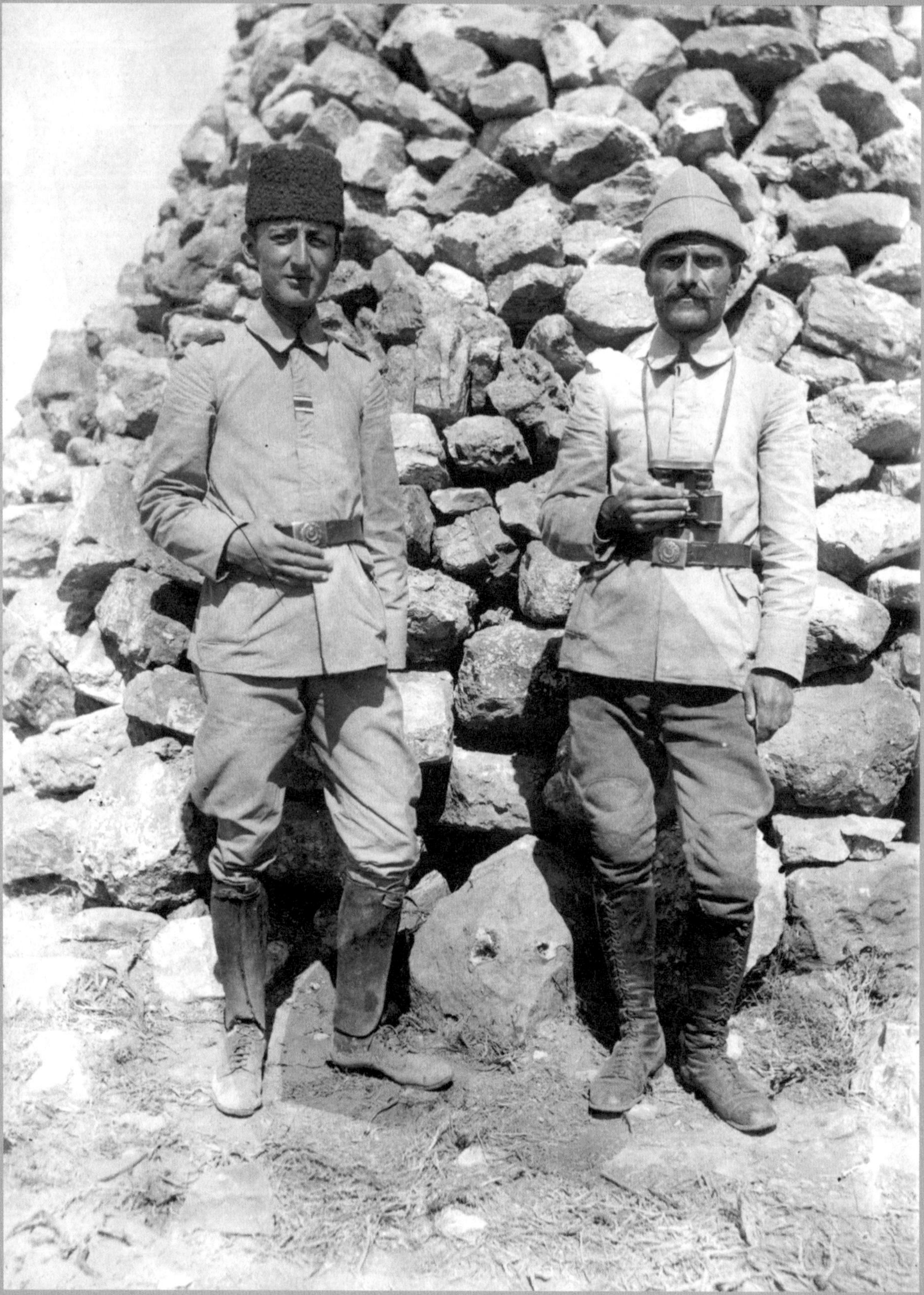

CHAPTER 3

'JOHN TURK MUST PAY FOR HIS AUDACITY'

5–12 August 1916

At 4 a.m. on 5 August 1916, the Wellington Mounted Rifles with the 7th Light Horse on their right flank and British infantry on their left attacked Wellington Ridge at bayonet point and drove the Turks off. As Colonel Royston noted in his report, 'that was the turning point . . . the enemy broke and fled in disorder'. The Turks retired to Mount Meredith and then back to Katia.[1] Bill Peterson wrote of how 'the whole line advanced dismounted, the led horses being brought along behind'. The bodies of two men killed the previous day were found. 'Lieutenant Righetti and Sergeant Jepson are lying close together,' Peterson wrote, 'both shot through the head and both stripped for their superior clothes and boots.'[2] There were 800 prisoners taken along with seven machine guns and an ammunition column. A battery of artillery was abandoned in perfect order.

At 6.15 a.m. the 1st Brigade charged the Turks on the ridges of Mount Royston. 'Absolutely cleared the Turks out and got them running,' Bert Billings wrote. 'Terrific bombardment by our 18 pounders, whole patches being subjected to terrific shelling.'[3] Ken McAulay, who was with the 2nd Light Horse, watched as the line of men 'raised a cooee and charged. It was not a charge but a drive.'[4] As Robert Farnes observed, 'the whole line advanced and cut the Turks up terribly . . . dead and dying were lying everywhere'.[5] 'The fruits of victory are not yet plucked and John Turk must pay for his audacity in full,' Mick Bruxner later wrote. 'At the first shimmer of light the long line of men went quietly into the darkness.'[6]

Fred Tomlins observed the effects of the British artillery: 'Camels were lying dead everywhere some loaded with artillery shells and others with machine guns. Amongst the dead Turks lying about were odd German

A Turkish officer alongside his German counterpart. Ralph Kellett collection.

1st Light Horse troops halt in the desert. John Gorrell collection. Courtesy of Richard Gorrell.

A horse holder. One of the men from each four-man light horse section had this task. Wilfred Baker collection.

officers, also Germans to every machine gun we came across.'[7] A complete Turkish ambulance unit of five officers and 58 other ranks, with 80 camels and drivers attached, was captured and put to work treating their own wounded.[8] 'The Jackos were coming in with pieces of white rag tied on sticks everywhere,' Lloyd Corliss wrote.[9] 'Got a few prisoners . . . who were absolutely done in,' Gordon Cooper added.[10] Mick Bruxner watched them come in: 'Turks had their hands stretched high above their heads silhouetted against the skyline of Wellington Ridge.'[11]

❖

By 8 a.m. the Turks who had managed to withdraw were in prepared positions at Katia alongside fresh troops, which had arrived to cover the retreat to Oghratina. 'Unfortunately for us the enemy did not attack us on the morning of the 5th but under cover of darkness retreated to Katia,' Maurie Pearce wrote.[12] After meeting with Meredith and Meldrum, General Chaytor ordered a combined attack on Katia that afternoon. The New Zealanders would go in on the right with the 1st Brigade in the centre and the 2nd Brigade on the left, all advancing under an umbrella of machine-gun fire. The light horsemen reached the palm fringe before dismounting under heavy fire.[13]

At 3.15 p.m. four mounted brigades moved on Katia. Maurie Evans observed that 'Everywhere the eyes could see over the desert there were mounted troops advancing on Katia.'[14] Lloyd Corliss watched as four mounted brigades lined up and galloped down a slope at the Turkish position about 3 kilometres ahead. When they came under heavy fire the men dismounted and got the horses under cover. Corliss was a horse holder, keeping the horses away from the Turkish shellfire that was searching for them.[15] Jim Greatorex was with the 1st Brigade machine-gun section. 'We attacked at 4 p.m.,' he wrote. 'Galloped a mile into action and brought gun into position to cover the advance of the dismounted troops.'[16] 'A regiment of English yeomanry attacked with swords and lost 35% of their men and did no good,' Fred Tomlins observed. 'Their machine gun fire was too hot.'[17]

Brigadier General Antill's 3rd Brigade had left Dueidar at dawn on 5 August and 'marched under a boiling sun all the morning'.[18] At 1.30 p.m. the 9th Light Horse moved off to attack followed by the 10th Light Horse and the supporting gun battery. Stan Parkes remained at the oasis in charge of the dressing station. An hour later the first of fourteen men wounded in the attacks came back on sand carts. While the 9th attacked with two squadrons, the 10th moved around the enemy left flank. 'By this time the enemy could be seen to be falling back as fast as possible,' Parkes wrote. But the German machine-gunners stayed at their guns.[19] 'After some 2 hours fighting enemy hoisted white flag.'[20] Some 500 prisoners, including some Austrians and Germans, were captured, the latter rather surly.[21] 'We have quite a number of German prisoners, mostly officers and machine gun crews,' Maurie Evans wrote. 'The Turks fought well but say the Germans turned the machine guns on them when they started to retire or surrender.'[22] Bill Peterson later wrote of a 'German officer found dead outside Katia with a *Turkish* bayonet right through him'.[23]

At 5.30 p.m. the battle was at its height. 'They have been at it hard since 2 o'clock . . . the fighting is terrific,' Bill Peterson wrote. 'Machine guns by the dozen are going as fast as they can feed them with belts of ammunition,' he added. 'Shells of all calibres are bursting around. Even shells from the monitors away out in the Med are heaving them in.' One hour later, Peterson continued, 'the sun is fast disappearing over the horizon as if ashamed to shed this glorious light on such a ghastly scene as this'.[24]

Gordon Macrae was with the 6th Light Horse. 'I never felt so done in all my life,' he wrote. 'I could no more run than I could fly and I don't think I cared whether I got hit or not. My tongue and mouth was so swollen I could not chew a biscuit.'[25] 'Our horses have been 48 hours without a drink and are just about beat,' another 6th trooper, William Burchill, wrote.[26]

Turkish prisoners escorted by Indian guards. The tall prisoner at the front is an Austrian. Joseph Bradshaw collection.

Maurie Evans noted that 'we had I think bitten off a bit more than we could chew'.[27] 'Enemy tried hard to get our horses with shells,' Lieutenant Stuart Macfarlane wrote. 'This was the worst experience I have ever had, we only had one bottle of water for 35 hours and we all had an awful time from thirst. The horses were for 56 hours without water and for 44 hours in the saddle.'[28]

The position was too formidable to take before nightfall, and without the water from the Katia wells the horses had to be taken back to Romani. The troops retired at 6.30 p.m. as dusk fell. 'Under cover of darkness we withdrew to Romani, our horses and men being completely knocked up, hungry and thirsty after the two days strenuous battle,' Maurie Pearce wrote.[29] Back at Romani that night, the men and horses were fighting at the troughs to get the brackish water.[30] Bill Peterson returned to Romani with the 2nd Light Horse at 11.30 p.m. 'Dead dog tired, hungry and weary after being in the saddle for two days and nights,' he wrote. Only some 135 men remained in the regiment.[31]

12th Light Horse troopers saddling up. George Francis collection.

34   AUSTRALIAN LIGHT HORSE

The next day, 6 August, Fred Tomlins wrote, 'we cannot get water today and are living on what tea we are issued with and some of the lads are drinking the salt water, dead horses are lying everywhere and are beginning to hum some'.[32] Maurie Evans concurred. 'To the west of the camp the air is heavy with the scent of dead horse,' he wrote.[33] Jeff Holmes watched the British infantry units moving up to Katia. 'All transport is done by camels and it is marvellous how the water, tucker, horse feed etc is kept up to so many soldiers,' he wrote. 'There must be fully 10 thousand to 15 thousand troops around Katea and 5 thousand or more horses . . . this campaign is a mounted man's place and an infantry man is really out of place.'[34] In temperatures around 44 degrees Celsius, the infantry occupied Katia on 7 August following the phased withdrawal of the Turkish force. 'On the trail of Jacko,' Harry Bostock wrote.[35]

On 7 August, the 11th Light Horse attacked at the gallop over some exposed low ground. After dismounting, the men ran up the sand ridges where, as Pelham Jackson related, the troopers 'lined the crest and opened fire on the Turks'. As the Turks retreated under the covering fire of their rearguards, the light horsemen called up their horses and headed off in

Supply carts at Katia oasis on 11 August 1916. Arthur Reynolds collection.

pursuit. But when the horsemen came over a low sand hill, the Turks opened fire from new positions. As 'we raced along the side of the hill to get under cover', Jackson was hit, the bullet grazing his right temple. 'Just like a kick from a horse,' he wrote. Pulling on the reins in shock, he fell to the sand with his horse across his legs, both man and beast pinned to the slope. Blinded by the blood and sand, Jackson lay helpless as more shots whistled by. After about fifteen minutes he was able to move aside and allow his horse to roll down the hill before staggering away. Next day, Jackson was back in action.[36]

At 3 p.m. the 8th Light Horse moved out, following the 'thousands of foot tracks in the soft sand' of the retreating Turks, and was in touch with them all night. Early the next morning, the regiment drew rations for man and horse—about ten double handfuls of barley for the horse and six biscuits and a tin of bully beef for the man plus some section rations. Only one bottle of fresh water was allocated per man. To water the horses, one man drew the water from the well while another carried the buckets to the horses.[37]

The 8th Light Horse was soon in contact and 'the firing was pretty brisk'. Verner Knuckey was behind the top of a sand hill but was being fired on from the flank. The first thing he knew there was 'a vicious "zip" and sand rose about two feet to my right'. When the second shot hit the same distance to his left, Knuckey knew it was time to move and sure enough the third bullet hit the ground where he had been lying. His squadron retired soon thereafter, the light horsemen suffering terribly in the heat. 'The only shade was what the horse threw,' Knuckey wrote. In the middle of the day, each man would try to sleep under their horse, which would not move an inch.[38] That day, Arthur Hogan wrote home to his mother about his 'first fight with Johnny the Turk': 'I was fighting for 36 hours with the bullets flying around me the

A well in the desert. Fred Horsley collection. Courtesy of Cliff Horsley.

Three light horsemen asleep in the shade of their horses. George Francis collection.

whole time. 'I was expecting to get hit every minute but Johnny wasn't as lucky as me & he couldn't shoot straight.'³⁹

General Chauvel knew his mounted brigades were at the end of their tether but he was desperate to defeat the Turkish force before it could withdraw. He ordered a general attack on Bir el Abd for 9 August. The objective was to get behind the town and cut off any remaining Turks, but the enemy force was well entrenched, with strong redoubts that extended 24 kilometres inland from the coast. Some 6000 men were defending the position and they were well supported by artillery. During the night of 8–9 August, the 1st and 2nd Brigades moved north, with the 3rd Brigade and the New Zealanders bearing south. Chauvel, who had only about 3000 men, deployed the 1st Brigade on the left flank, the 2nd to its right, then the New Zealand Mounted Rifles and 3rd Brigades.

The 8th Light Horse attacked first followed by the 9th but, as Verner Knuckey noted, 'it proved impossible to turn the enemy's left', despite support from seven machine guns and the Inverness battery. 'The feeling was glorious, bullets hissing around us in open formation galloping forward,' he wrote. One horse was shot in the front leg yet kept going with the mob, 'screaming like a human being' until 'one of the men led the horse away and shot him'. The regiment dismounted and crossed the ground under machine-gun fire through a hail of lead. 'One could almost feel them going past,' Knuckey wrote.[40]

'The Turks opened the show by putting a couple of shells right amongst our horses before we dismounted for action,' Fred Tomlins wrote, 'but got none of us.' The 1st Light Horse mounts were moved behind a steep sand hill for safety while the light horsemen took up positions on the hill above. 'The Turkish infantry welcomed us with a burst of rifle fire from the ridge opposite and the fun commenced,' Tomlins wrote.[41]

After the Ayrshire battery opened up, 'they then gave us what oh!' Bert Billings wrote. The Turkish artillery got onto the four 13-pounder guns, which were out in the open. At 12.35 p.m. a shell hit the led horses, killing four men and wounding about fifteen others. Many horses were also killed.[42] The Turkish artillery fire took a terrific toll. 'It was a pitiful sight to see the horses, the shells were landing right in amongst them,' Robert Farnes wrote.[43] Yet, as Bill Peterson observed, 'the four guns of the RHA kept on barking . . . the noise was ear splitting'.[44] Fred Tomlins, who was working with the battery as a signaller, 'saw some of the finest artillery shooting I have ever seen wiping out a camel train and cutting up Turkish troops advancing across an open stretch of country to reinforce their men'.[45]

The 1st Brigade leaving Etmaler for the attack on Bir el Abd, 8 August 1916. George Francis collection.

Soon after noon the Turks opened up with two 6-inch howitzers on the RHA battery. Low on ammunition, the battery soon retired. The Turks then fired on the horses and men. 'It was concentrated hell for a while and was the hottest corner I have ever been in,' Jim Greatorex wrote.[46] The Ayrshire battery fired from 7.15 a.m. to 2 p.m. when the guns were ordered back, but it was rendered immobile by the loss of horses. Reserves from 2nd and 3rd Light Horse were sent to the extreme left to hold back the Turks and provide horses to enable the artillery to escape.[47]

At 2.15 p.m. the men of Colonel Bourne's 2nd Light Horse had mounted and gone out to the left flank. 'Jacko opened up with everything,' Bill Peterson wrote, 'horses going down like nine pins . . . bleeding and limping some were lying and struggling where they were struck down, numbers of them killed and some literally blown to pieces'.[48] The farrier quartermaster sergeant had perhaps the most difficult role of all: shooting the wounded horses.

At 3 p.m. the machine guns moved up in support to fire over the heads of the light horsemen, but this attracted shellfire from all around. 'The next hour was agony for us,' Verner Knuckey wrote. Five Echuca boys copped it and only two survived to be invalided home. Knuckey's tent mate and great friend, Dick Chambers, was one of those killed, along with twelve horses. 'Poor brutes,' Knuckey wrote. 'There are no half measures about shrapnel pellets.'[49] 'Most of the casualties were from shrapnel,' Fred Tomlins added. 'Our horses suffered badly.' Fortunately, many of the Turkish howitzer shells sank well into the sand before exploding. Tomlins wrote that 'they made big holes and knocked scores of men down from the shock but hit no one . . . my body was paralysed at times from the explosions'.[50]

The heat was merciless, the temperature 44 degrees Celsius in the shade, 'which does not exist'.[51] 'If ever the sun burnt it did that day,' Knuckey wrote. 'The hot sand scorched our skin.' Wounded men would crawl off for help. 'In several cases I saw them crawling on one hand and the other arm practically blown off, blood was everywhere and at last we knew what war meant.'[52] Serving with the 3rd Light Horse Field Ambulance, Stan Parkes helped treat 50 wounded men, some terribly mutilated. Five of them soon died of wounds while the others were evacuated on camels. 'It has been a very hard day for our men and they have had a severe check, and badly knocked about,' Parkes wrote.[53] During the day, Lance Sergeant John Flockhart, who was attached to the 8th Light Horse, brought in seven severely wounded men from the firing line on horseback while under fire. He was recommended for the Victoria Cross but awarded a Military Medal. Flockhart had done similar work during the fighting at Bir Nagid two days earlier.

When the Turkish infantry advanced, the RHA battery was ordered to use rapid fire but only had twenty rounds left and had to hold onto them. At 3.45 p.m. the 2nd Light Horse retired in sections through 'a tornado of shells and bullets'. By 5 p.m. the whole column was heading back to Hod ed Debabis, 7 kilometres west of Bir el Abd. The horses drank their fill despite the water being 'particularly vile' and at 8.30 p.m. the 2nd Light Horse was back at Oghratina. 'Jacko made the pace exceptionally hot to make up for his smashing defeat at Romani,' Bill Peterson wrote.[54] Harry Maddrell noted how it was 'all open fighting . . . only cover was what nature provided and I can tell you the Turks didn't forget to use their artillery'.[55]

Maurie Pearce wrote that 'it was a bad day for us, one of our best tent pals poor little Nobbs killed . . . "Nobby" died wonderfully game, he was hit in the side by a piece of shell and also had his arm badly gashed.' He died in the sand cart on the way back to Romani. 'Before he died he merely remarked that it was the fortune of war,' Pearce wrote. 'He was only 21.'[56]

With considerable Turkish reinforcements moving up and artillery ammunition low, Chauvel's men pulled out. When the 1st Light Horse retired at 4 p.m., Harry Bostock was one of the last to go. 'Laid in a little hole all day in the burning sun with bullets flying round,' he wrote. 'I had a most strenuous time. No rations or water all day.'[57]

By late afternoon the light horsemen were 'nearly mad for water'. As darkness fell, Lieutenant William McGrath pulled his 8th Light Horse troopers out, covered by the 10th Light Horse, which held back a Turkish counterattack. Most of the men and horses had gone for more than 24 hours without water.[58] Henry Langtip watched the wounded come back to Romani 'on sand carts and camels'. 'It must be terrible to be out in the desert for days,' he wrote.[59] Trooper Gordon McCook knew it. Three days later they found him still out there on the battlefield, shot through both legs and unable to move, barely alive. The Turks had found him first, made him comfortable and left him a full water bottle. That was only half the story. Ron Ross said that all McCook's money and clothes had been stolen.[60] McCook would die of his wounds eleven days later.

The battle of Romani was as much a triumph for the horses as the men. 'Until Romani our horses had never been really tested,' Don Cross

Water troughs set up at a desert hod. Arthur Reynolds collection.

A church service at Romani in the shadow of one of the sand ridges. William and Francis Woods collection. Courtesy of Elizabeth Woods.

wrote. 'Now they certainly were—ploughing through sand in the middle of an Egyptian summer with an average of [125 kilograms] on their backs, they went for 56 hours without water ... on the last day they were so weary that at each brief halt they would lie down and stretch out, until the time came to move again.'[61] 'The fights at Bir el Abd and Bir Bayud spelt the end of the pursuit,' Major Carl Mühlmann wrote. 'We could not consider attempting a new attack. But the worse was that our unsuccessful attacks had clearly revealed to the enemy our weakness.'[62]

A dozen light horse officers who had been wounded at Romani recuperating at No. 3 Australian General Hospital in Cairo. Hugh Poate collection.

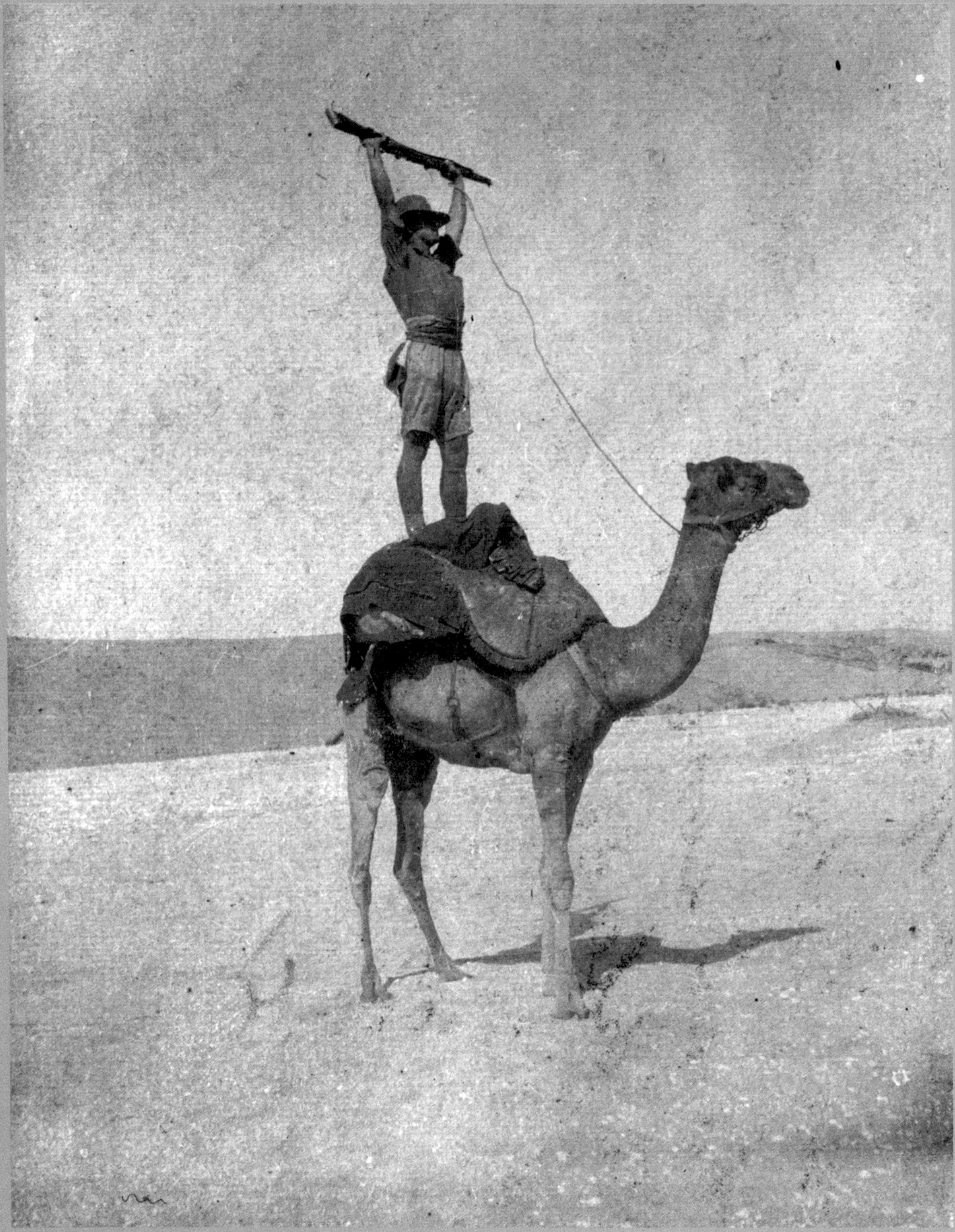

CHAPTER 4

'OH, YOU BEAUTIES'

September 1916 to January 1917

Following the failure to take Romani, the Turkish forces had withdrawn to El Arish with a forward detachment on the coast at Mazar. Any further Allied advance was dependent on how quickly the railway line and water-supply pipeline could be pushed forward from Romani. Meanwhile, General Murray had returned to Cairo and Major General Charles Dobell had taken over command of operations in the Sinai from General Lawrence.

On 16 and 17 September 1916, General Chauvel advanced with his 2nd and 3rd Brigades, the latter now under the command of Brigadier General Royston, and a detachment from the Imperial Camel Corps under Captain George Langley, with three artillery batteries in support. But the Camel Brigade and two of the artillery batteries failed to arrive and, under orders not to attack if there was resistance, Chauvel called it off. If the aim had been to capture Mazar, Chauvel's non-attack had the desired effect; the Turks abandoned the place two days later.

As always, the issue of water supply dictated Chauvel's actions. Although 64,000 litres of water was supplied for the two brigades, the ineffective use of pumps and troughs meant that many horses went without. The quality of fodder was also poor and, as Michael Minahan wrote, the men fared little better. 'Since we left Romani on October 18 our daily rations have been Bacon, Meat, Potatoes, Onion, Bread, Jam. Cheese occasionally. Figs very, very seldom,' he wrote. 'Not enough to fatten a rat.'[1]

The Allied forces, now composed of Chauvel's Anzac Division, the Imperial Camel Corps and four understrength and inexperienced infantry divisions, were now formed into the Desert Column under the command of

Bronco the circus rider, now serving with the Imperial Camel Corps but still performing. A well-handled camel could endure five days without water and carry considerably more weight than a horse. Joseph Bradshaw collection.

Returning to Bir el Bayud for water. George Francis collection.

OPPOSITE, TOP

An enemy mine washed up on a Palestinian beach. Harry Mattocks collection.

Lieutenant General Sir Philip Chetwode. Of the Australians, Chetwode observed: 'Your men not only fail to salute but as I passed along they laughed aloud at my orderlies.'[2] The Turkish forces arrayed against Chetwode were limited to about 25,000 by their need to hold strong forces in Syria to guard against an amphibious operation. The shadow of Gallipoli lingered.

As Chauvel prepared to attack El Arish, air reconnaissance showed that the Turks were retiring north. On 20 December, Chauvel sent four brigades on a 40-kilometre night march to intercept the retirement. The ride meant leaving the harsh sandy desert behind for firmer ground; the official historian noted that 'No night ride in the whole campaign gave the light horsemen so much satisfaction.'[3] Not all were satisfied. Robert Fell, who was with the 10th Light Horse, wrote how the men 'pushed on thru the night. Awful journey (rough). Fell down sand hill with camel.'[4]

On the morning of 21 December, Maurie Pearce wrote of how 'the brigadier drew a cordon around the town and commenced searching the houses and inhabitants'.[5] The Turks had gone, but not far. The Allied force split, heading north to prepared positions at Rafa and east to Magdhaba. Of El Arish, Tom Baker wrote, 'fairly large town built of limestone bricks in the Egyptian style, very happy at having got here at last, and without firing a shot'.[6] Holding El Arish would enable limited supplies to be shipped up the coast, but to forestall this the Turks had laid mines along the foreshore before withdrawing. At least one of the sea mines had drifted ashore or had been purposefully placed on the beach. Two inquisitive 1st Light Horsemen who had gone for a swim came into contact with it. 'The biggest part of them that could be found would be as small as a man's hand,' Lloyd Corliss wrote.[7] 'The vagaries of fortune,' Maurie Evans added. 'Blown to atoms.'[8]

After aircraft had confirmed the Turks were there, Chetwode directed Chauvel to the fortified railhead town of Magdhaba while his infantry held the new base at El Arish. The brigades left El Arish on the night of 22 December. It was another night march, 30 kilometres along the Wadi el Arish that ran south, but again over firm ground. 'Good hard track all the way,' Tom Baker wrote.⁹ The dry riverbed of the ancient wadi was 2–5 kilometres wide and covered with fine white clay that rose in a cloud of dust under the hooves of the passing column. The wadi ran all the way to Magdhaba and well beyond. At the rear of the column, Major Horace Robertson, second-in-command of the 10th Light Horse, found the pace varied from slow to a gallop, causing a 'continual concertina motion' within the column. For most of the light horsemen it was their third night without sleep.¹⁰ Every hour the men would ride for 40 minutes, lead the horses for ten minutes in order to warm themselves up in the bitter cold and then rest for ten minutes. On arrival at about 4 a.m., the whole force formed up in parade-ground order about 3 kilometres from the enemy positions.¹¹ 'It was like a billiard table except here and there where water courses lay, and gullies had been washed out,' Jeff Holmes wrote.¹²

Chauvel scouted the defences and made his plans in the predawn light. Aircraft appeared at 6.30 a.m., drawing fire from the Turks and giving away their positions to Chauvel's keen eye. The planes also landed so the airmen could report their observations directly to Chauvel. 'It was a queer sight to see the airmen in their flying togs galloping about on horses for a change,' Fred Tomlins wrote.¹³ As always, water was the key consideration. The wells at Lahfan, midway between El Arish and Magdhaba, had been destroyed by the Turks, so if Magdhaba could not be captured before dusk Chauvel would need to pull his mounted force back to the coast.

Light horsemen on the move through the barren hills. Fred Horsley collection.

'OH, YOU BEAUTIES'   45

Light Horse desert camp. Joseph Bradshaw collection.

The Australians attacked Magdhaba from the front and flanks at about 9.30 a.m. on 23 December. As Fred Tomlins, who was with the 1st Light Horse in reserve, wrote, 'The New Zealanders and the 3rd Brigade commenced the ball rolling.'[14] Royston's 3rd Brigade was sent to the south, where Lieutenant Colonel Leslie Maygar's 8th Light Horse and Lieutenant Colonel William Scott's 9th were given orders 'to storm and take trenches'. General Royston accompanied his third regiment, Lieutenant Colonel Thomas Todd's 10th, which was sent out to block a Turkish camel train seen moving south. As Royston later noted, '[Todd] cut off the fugitives.'[15] Meanwhile, General Chaytor attacked at the wadi and took Hill 345, and then Chauvel, acting on aerial reports that the Turks were pulling out, launched Cox's 1st Brigade at Magdhaba.

Despite coming under artillery fire, Cox's brigade galloped on until stopped by heavy machine-gun fire. Cox had his men dismount some 1800 metres from No. 2 Redoubt. The New Zealanders and Brigadier General Clement Smith's Imperial Camel Brigade were also held up by the Turkish fire. 'The redoubts were all round works,' Arthur Mills wrote. 'The Turks could fire in any direction . . . with about 2½ miles flat country to fire over.'[16] Another cameleer, Joe Bolger wrote, 'Fierce fighting all day, very hot, had no dinner, nearly hit a number of times.'[17] Cox sent Lieutenant Colonel David Fulton's 3rd Light Horse to help in the attack on No. 2 Redoubt, but just before the attack Chauvel ordered a general withdrawal. When Cox saw the order he told the messenger to 'Take that damned thing away and let me see it for the first time in half-an-hour.'[18] The redoubt soon fell, with three officers and 92 men captured, and from it Fulton was able to direct effective fire onto the next one. Harry Bostock, who was with Fulton's regiment, wrote, 'After dismounting for action three times on three ridges we came in close quarters.'[19]

Fred Tomlins, who was with the 1st Light Horse, wrote that 'The Turks fought well from the redoubts.' At midday, Tomlins noted, when the ambulance wagons galloped up to the front line, 'Abdul gave us another instance of fair fighting as he stopped firing in the direction of the ambulance.' Tomlins's C Squadron then joined another squadron from each regiment in capturing the guns in the hills to the south.[20] 'In the afternoon the artillery made the trenches untenable and our fellows advanced and took them,' Jeff Holmes wrote of the action.[21]

Soon after midday, Royston informed Major Robertson that Colonel Todd had been injured in a horse fall and Robertson was now in command of the regiment. Royston then told him to push forward. 'I well remember him riding over to me at Magdhaba to tell me that I was in command of the regiment,' Robertson later wrote. 'He was gone almost before I recovered speech.'[22]

Robertson got his regiment mounted up and the light horsemen advanced in an extended line over a flat riverbed 'as bare as one's hand' into the enemy fire. The fire came from the south-west, to Robertson's right front, so his regiment swept further east, raising dust that screened them. The pace varied between a trot and canter, rising to a gallop as they neared the main wadi channel. Here the regiment cut off a group of 300 retreating Turks, capturing the lot. Robertson now swung north to cut off any further enemy escape and also to press the rear of the redoubts. 'I put one squadron against each,' Robertson later

A 2nd Light Horse Field Ambulance cart at Rafa. Reg Dixon collection.

Three Camel Corps riflemen take shelter in a captured trench. John Davidson collection. Courtesy of Rob Davidson.

'OH, YOU BEAUTIES' 47

recounted. With 30 to 40 men, Lieutenant Fred Cox and Lieutenant Alex Martin rushed a redoubt of some 350 defenders, galloping past. When Martin's horse was shot out from under him, Fred Cox went back and rescued him. The 10th Light Horse captured 722 prisoners, including the chief engineer of the Turkish Army.[23] Five had come from a trench captured by the imposing General Royston. 'I yelled something in Zulu to them,' he told the official historian.[24]

The men of the 2nd Light Horse were also prominent. Major Gilbert Birkbeck led a squadron at the same redoubt that Cox and Martin had attacked, the light horsemen shooting from their saddles and breaking the Turk defence. 'Birkbeck's force charged over ground littered with their horses and some men,' Henry Gullett wrote. The charge put Birkbeck's men across the Turks' line of retreat 'and this made them very jumpy'.[25] Meanwhile, No. 1 Redoubt fell at about 4 p.m. and the Magdhaba commander, Khadir Bey, was among those captured. No. 3 Redoubt soon followed.

The 8th and 9th Light Horse made another dismounted advance, but under the added weight of a second bandolier this was difficult. The extra ammunition soon proved its worth, however. Though overall casualties were light, the 8th lost three of its officers killed and another wounded. Around 4.15 p.m., the defenders 'threw in the sponge'.[26] The 8th watered their horses at the captured hospital and, as Ron Ross related, spent the next day 'cleaning and burying the dead, burning everything that would burn'. The 8th returned to El Arish with the camels dragging the wounded on sand carts.[27]

During the ride back to El Arish, Fred Tomlins watched 'men dropping off to sleep as they rode along'. In the congested wadi 'it was very amusing to see someone wake up and ask where he was, to find himself with the wrong brigade'.[28] Meanwhile, the Scottish infantry used camels to carry water and horse feed out to meet the column 11 kilometres from El Arish. As Tom Baker noted, 'very tired horses had no water for 30 hours'.[29]

Many prisoners were captured, including—mistakenly—the protesting French military attaché Captain Count St Quentin. Aside from the 1282 prisoners, the Turks had lost 92 dead and about 300 wounded. Among those captured were the men and guns of the German 603rd Machine Gun Company. Chauvel's men had lost 22 men killed and 124 wounded. The mud huts at Magdhaba were turned into hospitals. 'We moved into the Turkish hospital with our wounded,' Leo Hanly wrote. 'Some very bad cases came through our hands.'[30] 'In the redoubts the dead and dying were lying everywhere,' Fred Tomlins wrote. 'Scores of Turks were found standing in the firing position leaning on the parapet with a bullet hole through the forehead.'[31]

A train of 150 camels, each carrying two wounded men on cacolets—covered platforms that were slung either side of a camel—made its way back to El Arish in the cold and dust. With the railhead still 50 kilometres away and sea transport disorganised, it would be more than a week before the wounded reached hospitals. The stoicism of these wounded men stood in direct contrast to the inefficiency of the British rear-area staff. Next day, Leo Hanly went out with camels to collect Turkish wounded who had been out there all night. 'Got seven but one died,' he wrote. 'Cacolets no good for wounded.'[32] 'A hideous night,' Henry Gullett wrote, with 'groaning men.'[33]

On 26 December, the twelve men of the mobile ambulance section of the 3rd Light Horse

Light Horse camp at El Arish. Wilfred Baker collection.

Dead Turk at Magdhaba. Royal New South Wales Lancers Memorial Museum collection.

Field Ambulance had 250 wounded in their hospital, including 60 Turks. Two captured Syrian doctors helped out. 'We have the whole of the casualties from Magdhaba,' Stan Parkes wrote. 'We hope to evacuate the poor devils tomorrow.' They got 60 out on sand carts to the railhead the next day and the rest the day after.[34] The prisoners were also on their way back from Magdhaba, and Jeff Holmes watched them pass: 'Such a non-descript lot you never set eyes upon.'[35]

On 26 December, after making them wait for two hours, General Chetwode addressed the men and told them it was the first time he had seen mounted men assault and capture trenches. Meanwhile, El Arish was being rapidly developed as a supply base. Maurie Evans, who watched a supply ship landing stores on the shore, observed, 'The place will soon be like Anzac.'[36] Fred Tomlins wrote that 'an army of natives had the unenviable job of pushing the boats off from the shores into the breakers'.[37]

On 1 January 1917, Bill Peterson wrote, 'we buried poor old 1916 at 12 o'clock'.[38] Fred Tomlins enjoyed the first rum issue since Gallipoli but it

Landing stores on the coast. William and Francis Woods collection.

was miserable the next day, biting cold with a violent sandstorm blowing up and then rain at sundown and 'not even a tent for the CO'.[39] 'Terrific wind blowing,' Robert Fell wrote. 'Had the coldest swim I ever had . . . rumours of big battle to come off at Rafa.'[40]

❖

After General Murray had come forward to El Arish and met with General Chetwode to press for a further advance, General Chauvel's Desert Column was soon on the move again. On 8 January, Chauvel rode out of El Arish with the 1st and 3rd Brigades, the New Zealand Mounted Rifles Brigade and most of the Imperial Camel Brigade. As the column closed in on the small frontier post of Magruntein, 2 kilometres south of Rafa, the horses found grass for the first time since leaving the Nile Delta. Further on, the Turks were in a strong elevated position at Rafa, marked by redoubts at three corners and the dominating Hill 255 at the fourth. 'An excellent position with no cover for advancing troops,' Stan Parkes observed.[41] But as Jeff Holmes wrote, 'this time there were more troops than the Magdhaba stunt'.[42] The attack would be made on 9 January.

With the attack going in over open ground, a task more suited to infantry than mounted troops, artillery support would be critical. Once the RHA gun batteries opened up, Chaytor's New Zealanders moved in from the east while Cox's 1st Brigade approached from the south-east. Cox sent the 1st Light Horse in at 9.45 a.m., covered by four machine guns. The town of Rafa was outside the Turkish fortress, and at 10.40 a.m. troops from the Canterbury Mounted Rifles occupied it. The Turkish headquarters at Rafa Police Post was captured along with eight officers, six of them German, as well as 163 other ranks.[43]

'We just dropped off sand onto green pastures,' John Davidson observed. Harry Mattocks collection.

With the New Zealanders on their right, the light horsemen advanced to within 1800 metres and dismounted, moving in short stretches across open ground under fire until they reached a sunken road 700 metres east of the enemy positions. The ground ahead 'was as level as a tennis court, and afforded no protection'.[44] 'Very little cover for us,' Lloyd Corliss wrote. 'In fact it was murder to ask men to advance across such country ... we had to advance in short rushes.' The last rush left the men sheltering along the sunken road. 'A good many men were wounded while there, but we made things warm for the Turks and most of them cleared further back,' Corliss wrote.[45] Stuart Macfarlane was a Lewis gunner with the 1st Light Horse. 'The Lewis gun worked splendidly,' he wrote. 'We managed to keep her right up with the line and only had one stoppage.'[46] At 11 a.m. Cox sent his other two regiments forward, the 2nd Light Horse to the right and the 3rd to the left. The advance came under enfilade fire from the Turkish redoubts, heaviest against the 3rd on the left.

Turkish trenches at Rafa. Reg Dixon collection.

Jim Greatorex had only arrived at El Arish on 6 January, having come up from Kantara with his section from the 1st Machine Gun Squadron on the previous day. He left camp on the afternoon of 8 January and after riding all night, 'got to bizz' at about 10 a.m. 'Got good position for gun in trench,' he wrote. With his gun he was able to give covering fire to the troopers advancing on the main redoubt before moving up onto a ridge to fire into the rear of the Turkish trenches.[47] 'We can see the Turks going in all directions,' Gordon Cooper wrote. Cooper's machine-gun section 'charged across ploughed fields for about a mile then dismounted and advanced over ploughed ground for over a mile'.[48]

The 3rd Brigade and the 5th Mounted Brigade (Yeomanry) entered the battle at about 11 a.m. Robert Fell was with the 3rd Brigade. 'We then went into action dismounted. Fighting very hot. Our men dropping fast,' he wrote. Fell, who was in charge of a Lewis gun, had his gunner shot in the right arm and was himself wounded. 'Got a bullet through my tunic singlet and cardigan—just grazed my right shoulder,' he wrote.[49]

At 2 p.m. the Turkish position was surrounded but still unbroken. Royston was able to gallop around the fortress but could find no obvious point of weakness in its defences. 'Our batteries now poured shrapnel in as fast as they could,' John Stephen wrote. 'Meanwhile the regiments were advancing by short rushes towards trenches under heavy fire.'[50] As the day progressed, however, some of the Allied machine guns and artillery pieces ran out of ammunition, easing the pressure on the approximately 2000 defenders, who with the benefit of the higher ground were able to fire on Allied troops with little or no cover.[51] As Harry Bostock wrote, it was a 'hard fight all day over level bare ground'.[52]

The decisive thrusts came from the cameleers in the south and the New Zealanders in the north. But with some 2500 enemy reinforcements reported to be approaching the battlefield from the east, General Chetwode ordered a withdrawal at 4.25 p.m. and rode off with the 5th Mounted Brigade. As Royston observed, 'things were looking rather black about 4 p.m. . . . orders were given for all forces to retire'.[53] The Anzac commanders, however, remembered Magdhaba and, with the troops already advancing, ignored the withdrawal order. 'Order reached NZ Brigade too late,' Michael Minahan wrote. 'They were at Jacko with the bayonet.'[54] At 4.30 p.m. the New Zealanders swept forward up an open grassy slope, under the cover of their brigade machine-gun squadron and Lewis gun teams against the main redoubt on Hill 255 in the north. That support 'made the redoubt appear like a smoking furnace, and kept the Turks' fire down'. From their new position they were able to fire on the rear of the other redoubts, unhinging the Turkish defence.[55]

'NZ brigade coming on with a rush on our right flank took main redoubt,' Jim Greatorex wrote.[56] Les Horder was also with the machine guns. 'Several times we ran out of ammunition and water as we were using rapid fire,' he wrote. The New Zealanders 'hopped out and attacked with fixed bayonets'.[57] After seeing the New Zealanders advancing over the skyline, the 9th Light Horse joined them in that final attack. 'It was a marvellous sight to see them,' John Stephen wrote, 'with bayonets fixed and cheering like mad, rush the position. Jacko flew white flag then but our boys made it warm.'[58] 'They had no shelter whatever while covering fully a thousand yards in front of the trenches,' Jeff Holmes wrote of the attackers. The machine guns kept the Turkish heads down and 'kept them from being wiped out'.[59]

The men of the Imperial Camel Brigade dismounted at dawn. 'There we stood, broad daylight, in full view of the Turkish position,' John Davidson wrote. 'We dismounted and handed over camels, eight to a man.' The cameleers then advanced on foot from the south. 'We moved off in 3 lines of open order,' John Davidson continued. 'Jacko pumped his shells at us in rapid succession.'[60] Joe Bolger was with them and wrote at noon, 'Battle in full swing. Rifle fire and MG and cannon fire deafening.'[61] Despite orders to retire, the line of men in the 3rd Camel Battalion advanced in rushes led by Major Hubert Huddleston, a 'great giant of a man waving a stick'. In the late afternoon, Huddleston's cameleers made a bayonet charge over open ground with Huddleston's words ringing in their ears: 'Into them, lads!' he shouted. The charge left the men exhausted but scared the fight out of the defenders, who readily surrendered. 'The Turk, they took their shirts off and threw their shirts away,' John Davidson recounted. 'They were afraid of the bayonet.' The 3rd Battalion of cameleers had made the key breakthrough.[62]

With the defences broken, the light horse regiments also took up the advance. 'It was all over (including the shouting) in 15 minutes,' Jim Greatorex wrote.[63] 'Turks in trenches did not wait for the bayonet,' General Cox later told Henry Gullett. 'As our fellows appeared on parapet they jumped out and shook hands.'[64] The Turks surrendered at 4.45 p.m. 'Enemy trenches were full of dead and wounded while ours were still on the field,' John Stephen wrote.[65] As the 1st Light Horse headed back with a swag of prisoners, General Chetwode rode up, 'his face as red as fire'. 'Oh, you beauties,' he roared and shook some of the men's hands.[66]

Dead horses following the battle at Rafa. Reg Dixon collection.

It was midnight before the field ambulances had brought all the wounded to the Casualty Clearing Station 3 kilometres west of Rafa.[67] 'Every available sand cart was requisitioned—still 120 wounded men were left on the field,' Colonel Royston said. Flesh-wound cases were offloaded midway to El Arish and the sand carts sent back to Rafa for more, but the wounded were not cleared until 9 a.m. the next day. Royston pulled his men out at 10 a.m. 'By this time the Bedouin started to strip our dead,' he later said.[68] As the official historian noted, 'afterwards it was found that even the graves had been opened'.[69]

Of Chauvel's brigades, 71 men were killed and 415 wounded during the Rafa action. The Turks had 200 killed, 168 wounded and lost 1434 prisoners along with four mountain guns.[70] Robert Fell arrived back at El Arish the day after the battle, 'dead weary and hungry. Had no sleep for 58 hours and nil food.'[71] Gullett later called Magdhaba and Rafa 'sparkling little victories'.[72]

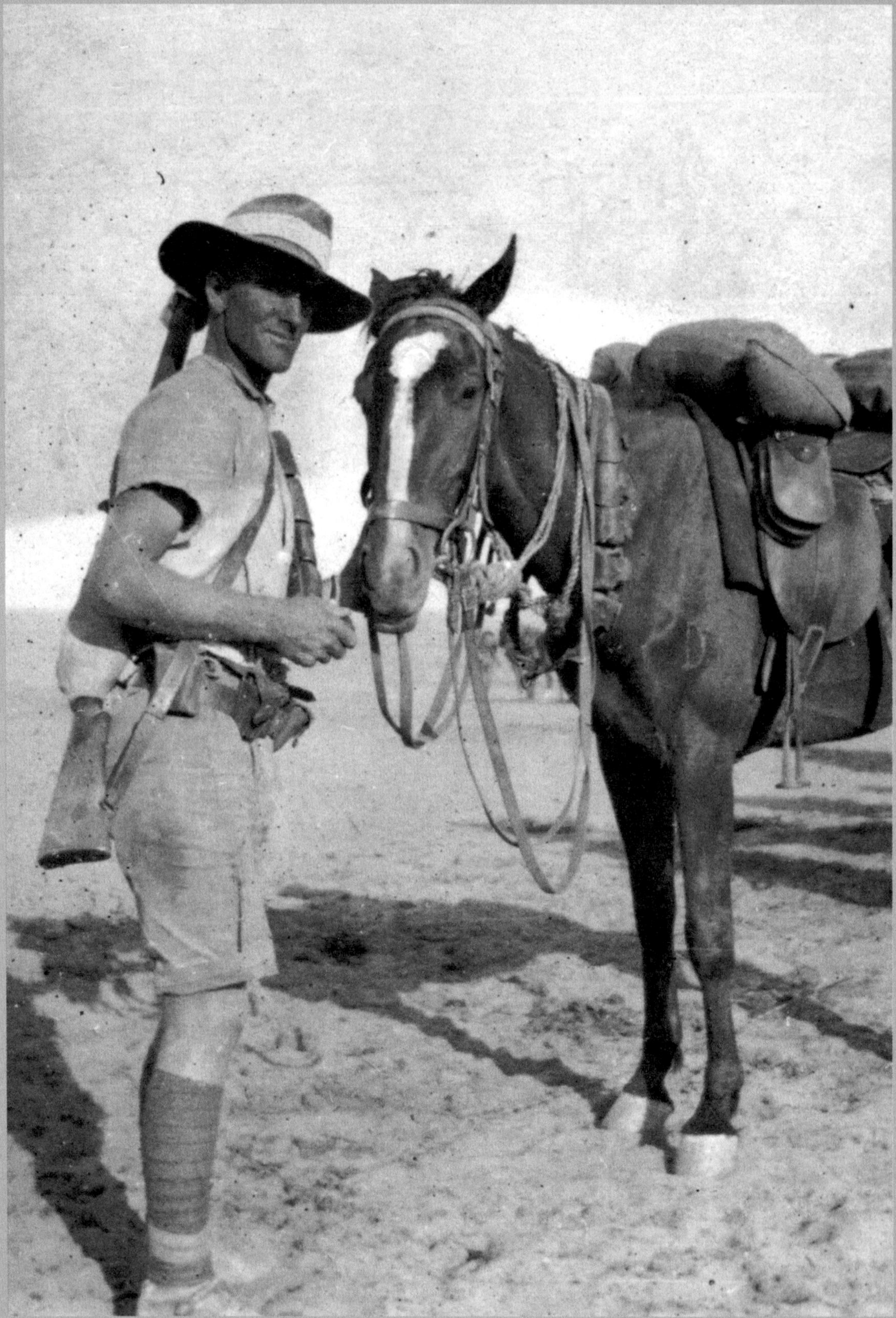

CHAPTER 5

'BUT WE HAVE GAZA'

February to March 1917

The railhead from Kantara was now approaching El Arish, though it would require constant attention from labour gangs to clear drifting sand from the rails. As always, water was the most vital necessity, and three pumping plants at Kantara forced drinking water up the 12-inch pipeline towards El Arish. Concrete reservoirs had been constructed at Romani, Bir el Abd and Mazar, and another was under construction at El Arish.[1] Large-scale military operations were not possible once the fierce summer weather arrived around May, so a build-up of forces forward of El Arish quickly got under way.

General Murray now had four infantry divisions available for operations and a second mounted division was being formed. Now that they were out of the desert dunes of the Sinai, the infantry could be more easily employed and the slow camel supply trains could be replaced by more efficient wheeled transport. Unfortunately, Murray chose to remain in Cairo, and the lack of a dynamic commander-in-chief at the front would hinder the upcoming campaigns. The Anzac troops certainly had little respect for unseen generals.[2]

The remaining enemy outposts south of the Gaza–Beersheba line were soon captured. As soon as the soldiers of the small garrison at Nekhl saw the men of the 11th Light Horse approaching, they fled into the hills to the east. Bir el Hassana fell the following day. By early March, Murray was ready to attack Gaza, the Arabian Dehliz el Moulk or 'threshold of the kingdom'. 'Latest furph [rumour], a stunt to Gaza is coming off shortly,' Stan Parkes wrote on 3 February 1917. 'Infantry have been arriving here by the hundreds.'[3]

Cecil Ferris, 1st Light Horse Regiment. John Gorrell collection.

Egyptian labourers move the railhead forward. 'They are very slow workers but the work goes on through sheer excess of numbers,' Frank Hurley wrote. Harry Mattocks collection.

Gaza's defences were strong. Some 15,000 Turkish troops were covering the Gaza–Beersheba line, with about 4000 in Gaza itself. These defenders were well dug in behind a maze of imposing cactus hedges, with steep sand dunes protecting the coastal flank. About 3 kilometres to the south of the Gaza–Beersheba line, the imposing Wadi Ghuzze, the 'river of Gaza', cut across the plain parallel to the Turkish front line. 'This wadi is very rough and deep being a mile across in places, and is only fordable where roads cross,' Jeff Holmes wrote.[4]

Major General Dobell would use two infantry divisions at Gaza, the 53rd Welsh and 54th East Anglian. He also had available the Anzac Mounted Division (comprising the 1st and 2nd Light Horse Brigades alongside the New Zealand Mounted Rifles and 22nd Yeomanry Brigades) and Major General Henry Hodgson's newly formed Imperial Mounted Division (comprising the 3rd and 4th Light Horse Brigades alongside the 5th and 6th Yeomanry Brigades). The failure to keep the four Australian light horse brigades together as an Australian mounted division was typical of the approach of the British commanders to Australian units. The British were always happiest in both world wars to integrate Australian brigades, divisions and corps into higher British (or imperial) formations, be they divisions, corps or armies. Staff appointments to the new division followed the same disrespectful formula. Hodgson appointed seventeen British staff officers to his divisional headquarters but only two Australians, one a junior staff officer and the other the veterinary officer. The Imperial Camel Corps brigade, three-quarters Anzacs, had British staff officers exclusively. Such a narrow-minded policy led to, as Henry Gullett called it, 'evil results'.[5]

Life in the desert continued to test the light horsemen. After a sandstorm hit on 11 March, Robert Farnes wrote of 'a terrible night . . . the wind and sand is awful . . . all the bivvies [bivouacs] are blown away'.[6] Michael Minahan also copped it. 'Bivvie down again. Pouring rain. Wet to the bone,' he wrote. 'Bugger of a day. Blowing awful.'[7] 'The sand is showering on top of me like rain,' Joe Burgess wrote, adding 'it's the limit'.[8]

On 16 March, Stan Parkes's unit crossed the border and arrived at Khan Yunis, 'a quaint little village of mud huts'. This was a different world, a 'promised land' as Parkes saw it, with 'beautiful fertile plains which stretched out in front of us as far as you could see'.[9] After the desolate wastes of the Sinai, Robert Farnes was also impressed: 'A very large village surrounded by orchards, it doesn't look a bad place from the outside.' He was less impressed that 'a large well with an engine and pump had been blown up by the Turks'.[10]

On 21 March there was a Desert Column race meeting at Rafa. Robert Farnes noted that 'the Australians won five out of the six races they were

OPPOSITE, BOTTOM
A light horse camp in the Sinai, 29 January 1917. Arthur Reynolds collection.

The daily water issue to the women of Khan Yunis, 'where Delilah lived and was born'. William and Francis Woods collection.

allowed to start in'.[11] Tom Baker probably spoke for the majority, writing, 'could not pick a winner but did not lose much'.[12] It was a chance for the men to enjoy a drink and a smoke away from the normal campaign rigours, although, as Bill Rose observed, 'one doesn't know the horrors of war until one has to smoke issue tobacco'.[13]

❖

In the lead-up to the attack on Gaza the Australian Flying Corps was busy. On 20 March, planes from No. 1 Squadron carried out a bombing raid on Junction Station, north of Gaza. Damaging the Turkish supply line to Gaza would play an important part in the upcoming battle. Aerial bombing was in its infancy at this stage of the war, and the bomb that Lieutenant Frank McNamara's Martinsyde aircraft carried reflected that. The bomb was actually a modified 4.5-inch artillery shell and it detonated prematurely when released, wounding McNamara in the leg. As he turned back for his base at El Arish, however, McNamara spotted another plane in trouble, a B.E.2. As Fred Tomlins noted, 'Our B.E.2 planes are too slow for fighting machines and are used for bomb dropping.'[14]

Captain David Rutherford had been forced to land his B.E.2 due to engine trouble. Though McNamara could see Rutherford's plane below, he could also see enemy cavalry in the distance. Nonetheless, he turned his plane back and landed next to Rutherford's B.E.2. The prognosis was not good. Though the B.E.2 was a two-seater, McNamara's Martinsyde was only a single-seat aircraft, so Rutherford scrambled up onto the Martinsyde's wing and McNamara began to take off. But the extra weight unbalanced the plane and with McNamara's wound making effective rudder use difficult, the aircraft crashed during the take-off run. Fortunately, both men were all right, but the Martinsyde was no longer flyable, so the two airmen set it alight to prevent its capture and headed back to the B.E.2.

Some Turkish cavalrymen had now appeared, and while Rutherford worked on the B.E.2 engine, McNamara fired his revolver at the approaching horsemen. Overhead, some of the

A Royal Flying Corps B.E.2, the same type of aircraft flown by Frank McNamara during the action for which he was awarded the Victoria Cross. Roy Millar collection. Courtesy of Paul Batman.

other planes of the squadron circled over the downed planes and were able to help keep the cavalry at bay with their machine guns. Meanwhile, Rutherford had managed to get the engine started and after both men climbed aboard, the wounded McNamara piloted the aircraft back to El Arish. For his bravery, Frank McNamara was awarded the Victoria Cross, the only such award made to an Australian during the desert campaigns.

The headquarters of the Desert Column and the Eastern Force were grouped together at Deir el Belah, which was on the edge of the coastal sand dunes some 10 kilometres beyond Khan Yunis and 16 kilometres south-west of Gaza. From here the 3rd Brigade moved out to reconnoitre the Gaza defences on 25 March. The long El Sire ridge, running north–south about 1100 metres east of Gaza, was the key terrain, and its crowning knoll of Ali Muntar was the critical point. 'It is believed that Gaza is not strongly held,' the operation orders stated, 'and it is therefore intended to push the attack with great vigour.'[15] 'We have to get Gaza tomorrow and by all accounts we are going to have a tough problem,' Joe Burgess wrote. 'There is a chance of us being sandwiched as we go the other side of Gaza and hoe into reinforcements while the infantry tear into Gaza.' Burgess's final comment was prescient—'I hope they get it quick or we'll be up a tree,' he wrote.[16]

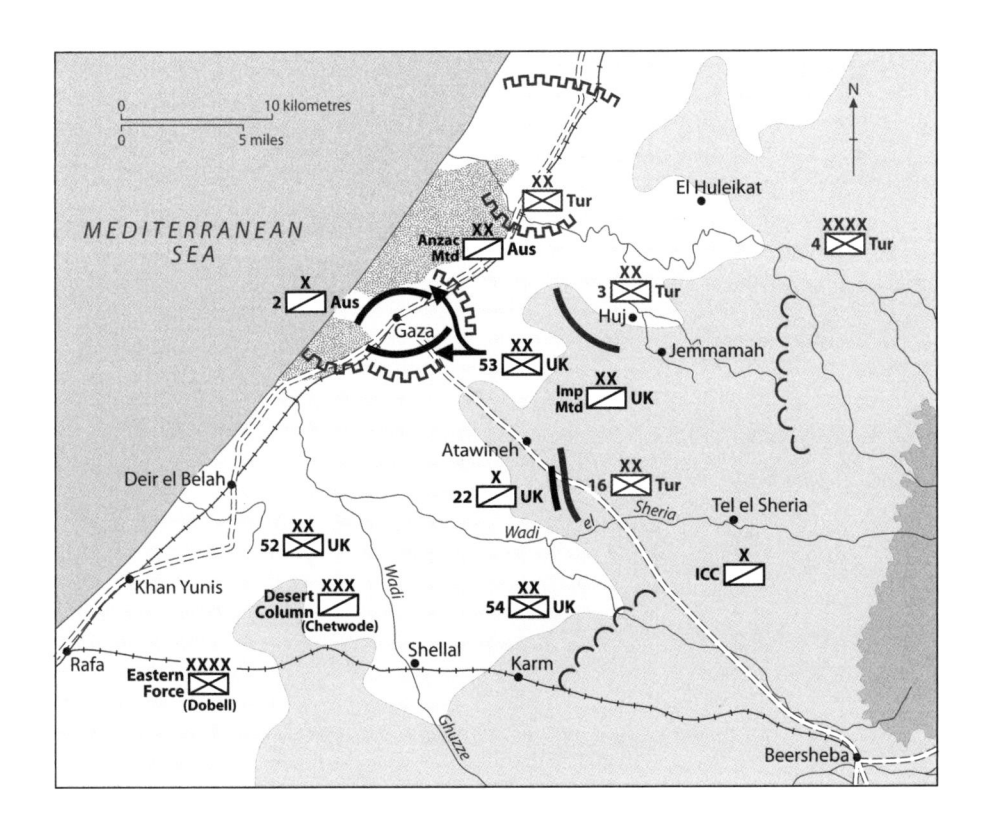

Map 3: First battle of Gaza

The signaller's tools—a heliograph, a telescope and sunlight. Wilfred Baker collection.

The Allied forces would have to be well directed and would have to fight well to win this battle. Chetwode sent the 53rd Division against Gaza from the south-east while directing Chauvel's mounted division to move around the town to the north-east and then north as far as the coast. Hodgson's mounted division and the Camel Brigade would take up a blocking position east of Gaza to stymie any Turkish reinforcements. The 54th Division was in reserve behind the 53rd.[17]

Chauvel's division crossed the Wadi Ghuzze in the early morning darkness of 26 March while the infantry and artillery moved up to the start line. 'Infantry and artillery passed through Khan Yunus all night,' Harry Bostock wrote.[18] A heavy morning fog covered any Allied movements from the Turkish observers until it began to lift at 8 a.m.[19] 'About daylight a heavy fog came up, and by the time it had lifted, we had a great screen for our movements,' Jeff Holmes wrote.[20] The fog also hindered the light horsemen, making it difficult to keep the columns on the right track. 'About 4 am a thick blanket of fog screened everything and progress was very slow,' Gordon Macrae wrote. 'Several times the column almost got away from us.'[21] By the time Stan Parkes moved off with the 3rd Light Horse Field Ambulance at 5 a.m. 'a dense fog obscured everything'.[22]

The troopers of the 7th Light Horse got in close enough to charge an enemy aerodrome, where two German aircraft just managed to get into the air before the horsemen arrived. 'If it hadn't have been for a couple of camel men who fired their rifles we could have got them on the ground,' Robert Farnes wrote.[23] The troopers galloped on, crossing the Gaza–Beersheba road, cutting the phone wires as they went. A Turkish general, the commander of the Turkish 53rd Division, who was on his way to take over the defence of Gaza, was captured along with three of his staff officers. The general offered a smoke from his gold cigarette case to his captors, one of whom produced a half-smoked example in return.[24] The general was 'very upset at being taken prisoner, more so because the fellows laughed at him,' Farnes wrote.[25] As Gordon Macrae described it, the light horsemen 'pushed right in behind Gaza cutting off all communication and capturing more prisoners. The whole fight seemed more like a big parade ground movement.'[26] Jeff Holmes noted that 'to surround Jacko we had travelled fully 15 mile'.[27] 'We made a wide semi-circle,' was how Joe Burgess put it.[28] Robert Farnes wrote, 'we were not allowed to push on into Gaza', but the light horsemen 'gave the Turks a very warm time as they were coming out and we annihilated about a company of them'.[29] With Gaza now sealed off, it was up to the infantry to capture it.

❖

Major General Alister Dallas should have had his 53rd Division troops across the Wadi Ghuzze by dawn. After marching up from Khan Yunis, the 158th Brigade had left Deir el Belah at 1 a.m. but the guide lost his way and the brigade only reached Wadi Ghuzze just before dawn at 4.30 a.m. It was not until 5.45 a.m. that the lead battalion, the 1/5th Royal Welsh Fusiliers, reached the start line for the attack, only to be held up by the fog. When the fog began to lift at 7.45 a.m., two enemy aeroplanes took off from Gaza and warning bugles sounded out from the Turkish lines. The two-hour delay in the main attack was costly. Despite Chetwode's orders to get the attack going, Dallas now brought further delays upon his troops by insisting they wait until his artillery spotters could see their targets. This cost the British troops any chance of surprise or utilising the fog cover, and they would pay dearly. By 12 p.m. the infantry reached the cactus garden about 700 metres from Ali Muntar, where they came under heavy fire both from Ali Muntar and from Green Hill on the left flank.[30] A battalion was sent to attack Green Hill in support of the main assault on Ali Muntar. 'It was a great sight; but they had a large number of casualties,' Robert Farnes wrote.[31]

At midday the infantry attack finally got underway when two brigades, the 158th and 160th, began their advance. With more than 3 kilometres of open ground to cover against forewarned defenders in strong and dominant positions, it was a considerable challenge. At a range of about 1 kilometre, the rifle and machine-gun fire cracked out across the open plain and the infantry in their long textbook lines were mown down. The Turkish artillery added to the slaughter and the attack stalled about 500 metres short of Ali Muntar. After the 159th Brigade moved up at 2 p.m. some of the lower-level British officers began to show the sense their seniors sorely lacked and advanced their men in rushes.

A small party of infantry managed to get into the Turkish defences among the cactus hedges and the position was consolidated by 6.10 p.m. By now the guns had been brought up to within 1500 metres of Ali Muntar, and their well-directed fire helped break down the defences. 'The whole battle was like a medieval affair,' Lieutenant Colonel Fred Wollaston wrote.[32]

Further back, Joe Bolger lay in the shade of his camel and watched the assault. 'I can see the shrapnel shells fired by the Turks a few miles away,' he wrote. 'They are firing into the Scotties infantry, they are putting it in fairly thick too.'[33] The infantry had no shade from the frightful heat. Joe Burgess watched the battle from north of the town. 'The little Tommies went at it bravely,' he wrote, 'and for hours fought in perfectly open country . . . it looked and sounded very dinkum.'[34]

A Turkish machine-gun section keeps a low profile on a barren plain typical of many on the Sinai and Palestine battlefields.
Clarence Reid collection. Courtesy of Lyndall Caldwell.

The infantry that had reached the maze of cactus hedges below Ali Muntar found further progress difficult. 'All the orchards in villages have a hedge of prickly pear which would take a good deal of negotiating and it is in these orchards behind prickly pear the Turks have their positions in Gaza,' Fred Tomlins wrote. 'I'd rather face barbed wire.'[35] With flanking fire from Green Hill cutting into the infantry ranks, Dallas threw the 161st Brigade against the position and, despite heavy casualties, both Green Hill and Ali Muntar were finally taken. Although time was running out, the sun sinking closer to the sea, Dallas's men were spent and could not exploit their success.

Cactus hedgerows near Gaza. 'Masses of small fields enclosed with great wide cactus hedges which made fine cover,' Henry Gullett wrote. Arthur Hitchcock collection.

❖

By midafternoon, Chetwode was desperate to take Gaza, and with no sight of enemy reinforcements, he ordered the two mounted divisions, with Chauvel in command, to close on Gaza to support the infantry attack if and when it came. At 2 p.m. Chauvel was ordered to use the Anzac Mounted Division against Gaza while the Imperial Mounted Division acted as the screening force. After some complex manoeuvres to reposition these screening forces, Chauvel began the mounted attack on Gaza at 4 p.m.[36]

At the end of the line, Captain John Cain's 2nd Brigade machine guns had to cut gaps in the cactus hedges for the troopers to get through. 'The whole place is full of prickly pear hedges along the roads and streets and the Turks were concealed behind them,' Robert Farnes wrote. 'Our fellows drove them out and gave them a very rough time. The Turks went right back into the town.'[37] Lieutenant Fred Waite's 5th Light Horse troop 'kept to their horses, jumped the hedges and got amongst them still mounted'. Waite fired his revolver from the saddle until thrice wounded.[38] Major Arch Bolingbroke led two other troops from the 5th Light Horse into the cactus on foot, the men hacking their way through with bayonets. 'Our men were sniping as at rabbits at Turks running in and out of hedges.'[39] Granville Ryrie used the same analogy: 'Some of our fellows were shooting off their horses like shooting rabbits, they said they could see them better from up there, they charged the Turks with the bayonet and killed a great many.'[40]

As night fell, troopers from the 7th Light Horse dashed into the outskirts of Gaza. The New Zealanders came in from the east before dismounting and entering the town. Gordon Macrae watched from a hill behind Gaza as the New Zealanders 'galloped across an open grass plain and dismounted and charged with bayonets. It was a great sight.'[41] Michael Minahan wrote of how Chaytor's New Zealanders and Ryrie's 2nd Brigade 'went into the Turks with fixed bayonets about 4 pm and advanced about two miles capturing 360 prisoners and 2 guns. Our casualties very light.'[42] By 5 p.m. the New Zealand brigade had 'effected lodgement in the outer houses of Gaza'.[43]

At 6 p.m. General Dobell, despite Chauvel's protests, ordered a withdrawal. 'But we have Gaza!' Chauvel told Dobell. 'Yes; but the Turkish reinforcements are all over you,' Dobell replied down the phone line.[44] Aware that some 10,000 enemy reinforcements were on the way to Gaza, Chetwode, who had the final say, agreed to the withdrawal. With about half his mounted forces diverted to Gaza from the screening force, Chetwode believed there was a serious threat of a Turkish counterattack. What he didn't realise was that resistance in Gaza had crumbled and the town was there for the taking.

Gaza. Walter Smyth collection.

When Ryrie and Chaytor, whose brigades had cracked open the back door to Gaza, received the withdrawal order they were dumbfounded. The troops were simply disgusted. Ryrie's brigade had had only one man killed and five wounded, Chaytor's only two killed and 29 wounded. General Dallas, who had initially mishandled the operation only to be saved by the drive of his Welshmen, was equally astonished at the order. The sacrifice of his brave infantrymen had been for naught. It was said that when the Turkish commander Tala Bey was told of the withdrawal he 'laughed for a long time'.[45] Whether true or not, the story spread throughout the ranks, whose faith in their higher commanders plummeted. Turkish morale moved in the other direction and many more Allied troops would die before Gaza was secured. The often misused phrase 'lions led by donkeys' was never more appropriate than in this case. 'Just as it was getting dark we got orders to withdraw,' Robert Farnes wrote. 'Nobody cared whether they got out or not, another two hours and [we'd] have had Gaza . . . it was 2300 before we got away from Gaza, everybody very wild and a fair number wounded.'[46] 'We had to retire as the Tommies had heaved in the towel, it was a crook feeling,' Joe Burgess wrote. 'If they had only known that we were imshying the Turks would have had us on toast.'[47]

To Brigadier General H.A. Vernon, the 158th Brigade commander, the withdrawal 'appeared to be out of the question', but the retirement of the infantry from the hard-won heights commenced at midnight. Later it was ascertained that advanced parties from Vernon's brigade had pushed on into Gaza and made contact with some of the Anzac mounted troops before retiring at dawn.[48] Colonel J.W. Wintringham was in command of the 18th Machine Gun Squadron, attached to the 22nd Yeomanry Brigade. 'We had them completely surrounded,' he wrote. 'The New Zealanders were in the streets . . . it seemed almost unbelievable to be told to pack up and retire.' Some of the Turks were trying to break out. 'They started coming through a

Generals Granville Ryrie, seated, and Charles Cox, standing alongside. John Gorrell collection.

native cemetery and our MGs were laying them out neatly among the tombstones,' Wintringham wrote. 'We would only have to turn our guns north if a relieving force came.'[49]

For the light horse regiments north of Gaza, getting out of the town was a nightmare. The troopers of the 7th Light Horse were about 6 kilometres from their horses when they got the order. 'It was a very terrible ride back,' Robert Farnes wrote. 'We got to the Wadi Ghuzze about daylight ... it was almost impossible to keep awake.'[50] Tom Baker simply wrote, 'Left for Belah midnight and rode all night.'[51] 'Remained out all night ... very tired, no sleep, hungry, horses hungry and thirsty,' Stan Parkes wrote. 'General opinion, if a division of "Scotties" had attacked with the Australians, Gaza would have fallen.'[52] Joe Burgess came back with the 6th Light Horse, the troopers finally reaching Deir el Belah 'with empty stomachs, empty haversacks and empty water bottles'.[53]

The light horsemen were into their third night without sleep and 'all ranks were almost comatose from exhaustion' during the withdrawal.[54] 'Our eyes were like burnt holes in a blanket,' Granville Ryrie wrote.[55] Michael Minahan added, '8000 Turk reinforcements attacking our rear, 3rd Brigade holding them until we clear out.'[56] Royston's brigade was indeed holding them. The 9th Light Horse stayed out to the east of Gaza until 3 a.m. and saw Turkish troops moving up that night. Gordon Macrae noted that 'the 3rd Brigade gave them a warm time and stopped them from reaching Gaza till next morning'.[57] 'Enemy on all sides except one small outlet which we used,' Harry Bostock wrote. 'Retired under rifle and gun fire at the double.'[58] Robert Fell, who was with the 10th Light Horse, was 'almost surrounded and captured' but 'got back safely thanks to Gen Royston's leadership.' Ron Ross, who was with the 12th Light Horse, wrote, 'The Brig takes us off at a gallop to engage Turkish reinforcements coming from the east. About 4 am move right out of it with artillery following us up with rifle fire half in front of us ... We were lucky to get out of it so light.'[59] A detachment of armoured cars helped cover the withdrawal of Royston's brigade.

❖

Dobell and Chetwode obviously conferred for their later reports, both mentioning the need to withdraw to water the horses. But Chauvel, who had been made aware from a Turkish deserter that all but three of the wells in Gaza had been destroyed, had certainly not brought it up as an issue at the time.[60] He was simply aghast at the order. As Jeff Holmes had observed, there was ample water in and around Gaza: 'Along the flat where we stopped that day, we found several water holes and feed was in abundance for our horses.'[61] The official historian, Henry Gullett, could find no message to the Desert Column or Eastern Force recording a particular concern about the Turkish reinforcements, though there were general reports. Tom Baker, who was a signaller with 3th Brigade headquarters, had noted, for example, '3000 Turks reported to be on the east'.[62]

General Murray tried to cover up the disaster by telling the War Office his troops had advanced from Rafa to Wadi Ghuzze to cover the extension of the railway line, using the excuse that 'The fog and waterless nature of the country just sav[ed] the enemy from complete disaster.'[63] Jeff Holmes saw through the fog: 'At one time we had them surrounded, and the Turks completely cut off, and then to let them and the reinforcements get away there must have been a big bloomer and someone will have to suffer.'[64] Stan Parkes knew that 'a great opportunity has been lost and the Turks are in great strength now . . . it is quite evident there has been a lot of bungling . . . everybody is disgusted with the display'. He said what all the Anzac troopers knew—it was 'a big blunder from start to finish thanks to the Tommies in charge'.[65]

Watering horses in the Wadi Ghuzze. Each of the five pumps shown here provided water to a separate trough. Walter Smyth collection.

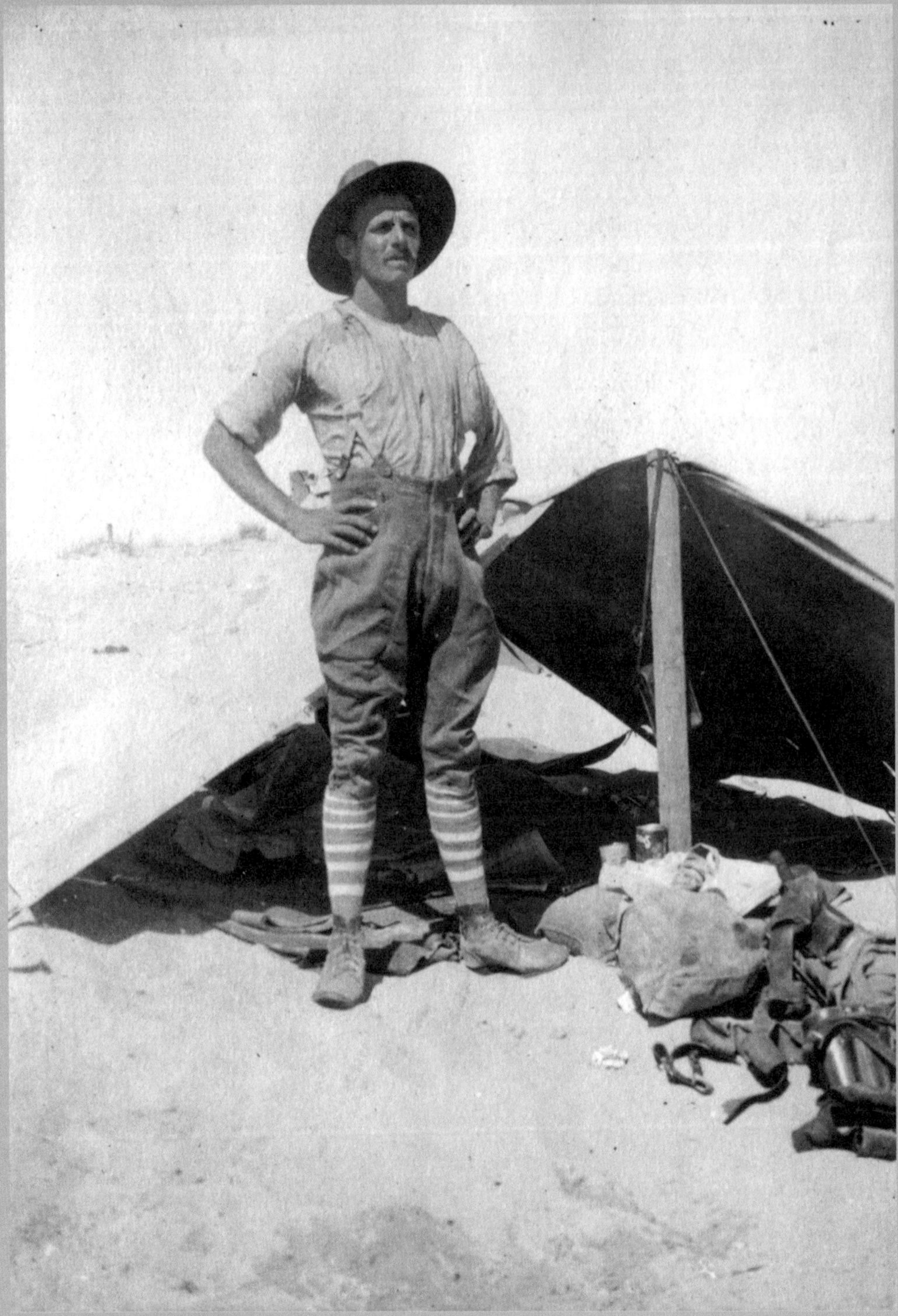

CHAPTER 6

'AN UNQUALIFIED FAILURE'

April 1917

The quickest way for Generals Murray, Dobell and Chetwode to cover up the fiasco that was First Gaza was to recapture the town but this time hold on to it. Murray had little choice; on 30 March 1917 the British War Cabinet directed him to advance on Jerusalem. As normally occurs in warfare, the failure to take advantage of the surprise and shock value of the initial attack invariably results in the second, more deliberate attack meeting much greater resistance and almost inevitable failure. The first attack had shown where the Gaza defences were weakest, and the defenders worked hard to improve those positions, particularly around the critical heights of Ali Muntar. 'Those 3 weeks had given the Turks time to dig a very strong trench system reinforced with miles of barbed wire,' Colonel Wintringham wrote.[1] 'There are miles and miles of trenches and machine gun positions and deep underground places to get away from the shelling,' Granville Ryrie added.[2]

On 9 April, Maurie Pearce was at Khan Yunis. 'We have a big army here now,' he wrote. 'Today I saw something like 30,000 horses in various camps, some thousands of camels, all kinds of motor transports and some of the famous "tanks" which have made such a name for themselves in France.'[3] The railway had now reached Deir el Belah, and new water reservoirs were being built there, supplied by the water pipeline from Kantara.

The new attack on Gaza would use new weapons of war. Tanks would be employed and 2000 gas shells had been brought forward. As Australian troops at Bullecourt on the Western Front would also soon discover, relying on a small number of tanks was a dangerous thing to do. On 3 April, Robert Fell watched the tanks arrive. 'Great secrecy observed,'

Bruce Lester, one of the Mudgee boys with the 6th Light Horse, outside the 'Palestine home' he shared with Ralph Kellett. Ralph Kellett collection.

His Majesty's Land Ship Pincher, *one of the Mark I 'male' tanks at Deir el Belah, before Second Gaza.* Walter Smyth collection.

OPPOSITE, TOP

Gas drill: troops line up in their gas masks to pass through a cloud of gas. Arthur Reynolds collection.

OPPOSITE, BOTTOM

Crossing the Wadi Ghuzze at Shellal. Arthur Reynolds collection.

he wrote. 'They are well covered.'[4] On 12 April, Maurie Evans observed, 'I have just been watching the tanks. They started up for the first time tonight taking hedges and ditches and even railway lines in their stride.' After a closer look Evans observed, 'Inside rather like the cab of an engine, 6 pounder guns are mounted in barbettes sticking out each side.'[5] Tom Baker thought 'they will be useful out here'[6] while Michael Minahan wrote that they were 'very complicated'.[7] Joe Burgess simply saw them as 'great relentless queer things'.[8]

The eight Mark I tanks, a mix of male (two 6-pounder guns) and female (four machine guns) types with names including *Tiger*, *Nutty*, *War Baby*, *Sir Archibald*, *Pincher* and *Kia-Ora*, were commanded by Major Norman Nutt. On the battlefield they would operate in widely separated pairs. As Maurie Evans wrote, the conditions for the men inside were horrific: 'One of the crew told me that the temp inside even in England reached 115° [46 degrees Celsius]!'[9] Sand also got in everywhere and readily accrued to the grease used on the tracks. This soon built up on the sprockets, causing tanks to throw off their tracks. Joe Burgess wrote that 'two got stuck in swampy ground on the way up and it was midnight when they got out'.[10]

The troops were also instructed in the use of gas. Gas helmets were issued and gas drills took place only days before the attack. On 13 April,

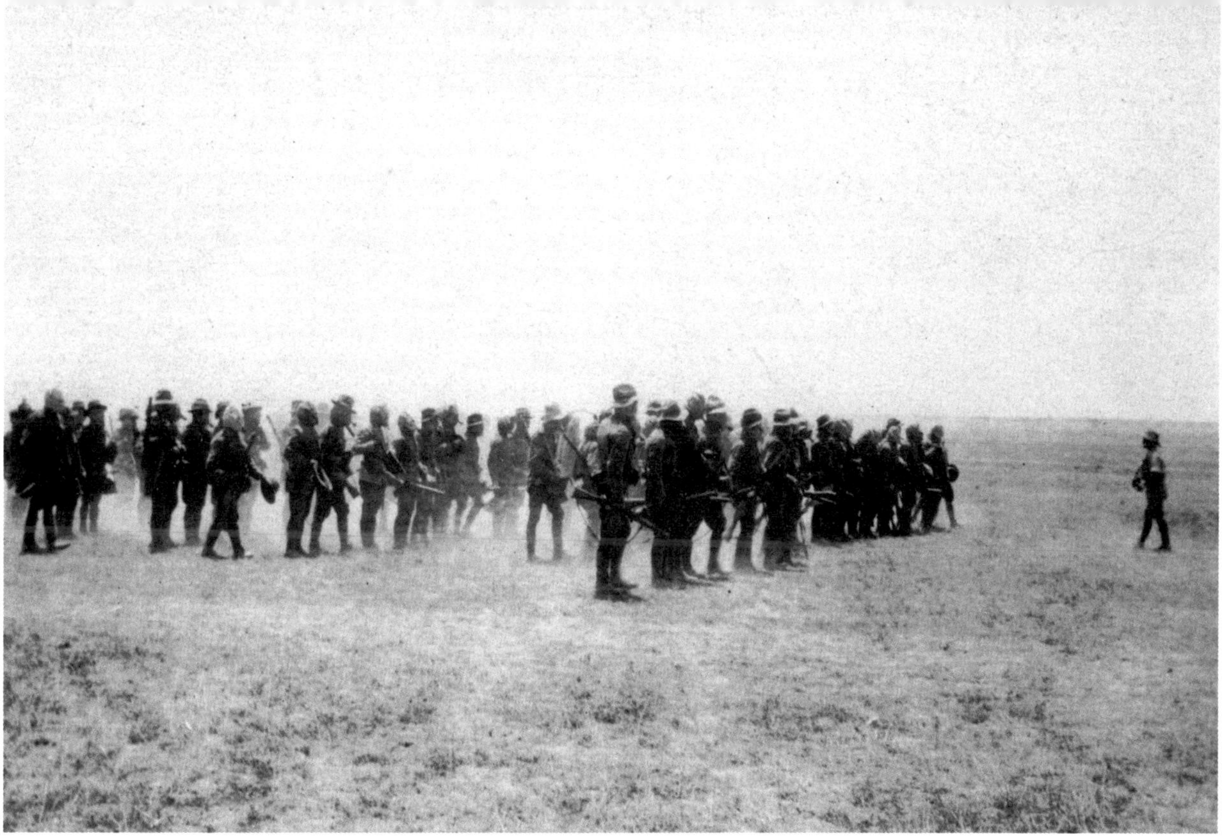

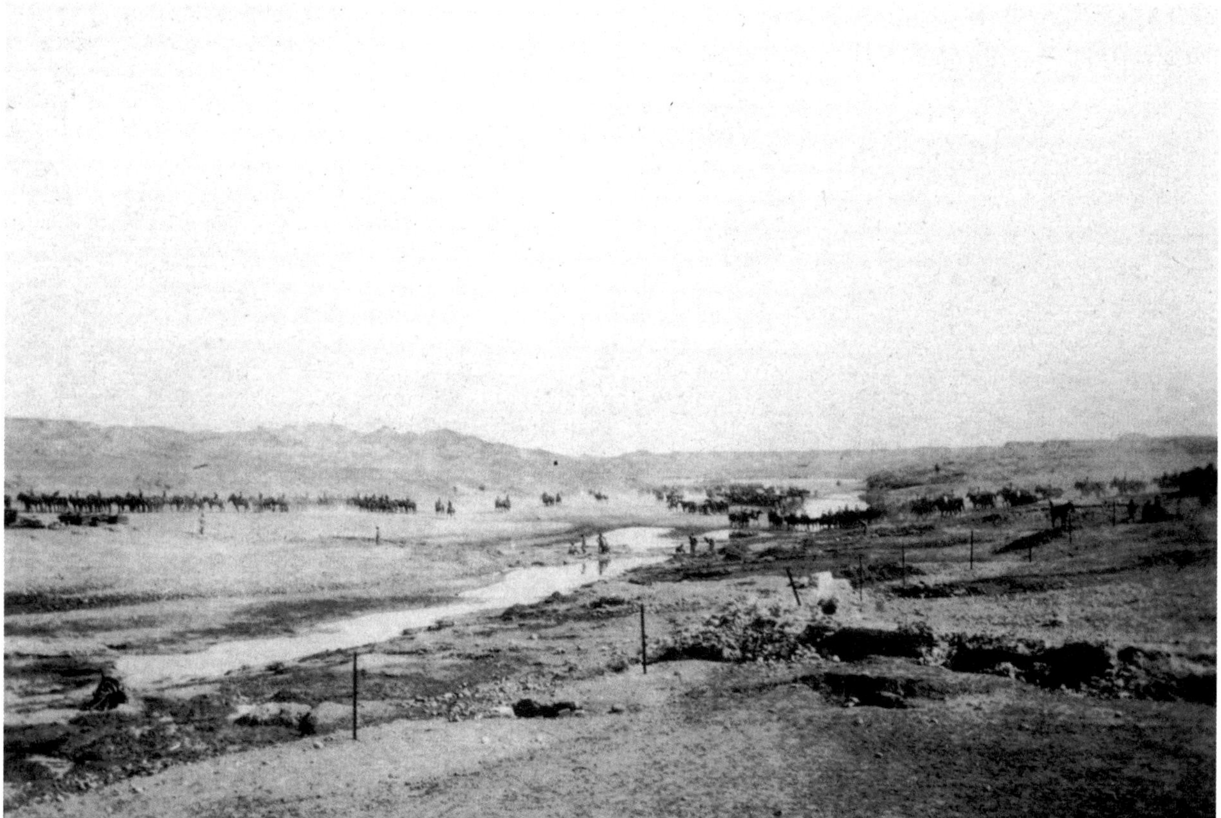

Michael Minahan wrote, 'Received gas helmets, we are going to use gas shells.'[11] Maurie Pearce added that 'they are most unpleasant things to have to wear'.[12]

Ignoring the extraordinary success of the mounted troops at First Gaza, Dobell's tactics for the second battle were straight from the Western Front. He planned an infantry assault against prepared positions over open ground, tactics that in France had led to catastrophic losses. At least on the Western Front there was plentiful artillery to batter the above-ground defences before such an attack, but at Gaza Dobell had limited artillery both in quantity and quality. Maurie Evans thought the outlook positive, writing, 'If it is not muddled up we ought to take the place.'[13]

❖

On 17 April it 'was very hot with hardly a breath of air' as the bombardment of Gaza began.[14] Under this cover, the infantry moved across Wadi Ghuzze to establish intermediate jump-off positions in front of the Gaza defences. Robert Fell, who was with the 10th Light Horse, wrote, 'Dismounted in a wadi and moved up to a ridge position before daylight. Turks opened fire at daylight . . . enemy frontal and enfilade fire . . . had to run to a wadi for our lives under fire and shells.'[15] Lieutenant Frank Throssell was one of those killed. His brother Hugo, who had been awarded the Victoria Cross at Gallipoli, was wounded. So was Lieutenant Arthur Adams, who was with the 12th Light Horse and wrote, 'Dismounted, handed horses over and waited dawn. Foley first man hit, help bandage him up . . . men knocked all round . . . got hit 3 places myself at 8 am . . . enemy very strong.'[16]

On the right flank, the mounted divisions formed outpost lines to isolate Gaza from the east. 'We left after tea for Shellal,' John MacNamara wrote. 'The whole division went out. Travelled all night.'[17] An enemy air raid on 2nd Brigade lines killed six and wounded thirteen men, while seventeen horses were killed and thirteen wounded.[18] Robert Farnes, whose groom was killed, wrote, 'We had just got clear of the place when a plane came over and dropped three bombs in quick succession.'[19] When a British six-gun battery moved up, another Taube dropped a smoke bomb next to them and they were then heavily shelled. The guns were quickly moved. 'It was great to see the way the teams came up at the gallop, swung round, limbered up and away in about 3 or 4 seconds, under heavy shell fire,' MacNamara wrote.[20] Fred Tomlins added that 'it was a fine sight to see the Tommies get their guns away at the gallop'.[21]

❖

The attack resumed two days later. At 5.30 a.m. on 19 April, the British artillery opened up a two-hour bombardment. It included the much-vaunted gas shells but they had little effect in the hot, dry atmosphere and sea breezes. Most of the enemy gun batteries were also left untouched. The infantrymen from both the 52nd and 54th Divisions lost heavily upon leaving the trenches. 'The Turks seemed to have reserved their machine-gun fire for certain places,' wrote Colonel Fred Wollaston, a battalion commander in the 54th. 'The troops were caught by this fire from every direction and on coming to these selected spots they were simply mown down.'[22]

The 52nd headed for Ali Muntar on the left while the 54th made good progress towards what became known as Tank Redoubt on the right. Scattered as they were, the tanks gathered infantrymen around them and that attracted concentrated artillery fire. 'The tanks then crawled along the ridge followed by every sort of Turkish shell until one was hit and destroyed,' Fred Wollaston wrote. 'It was a pitiable sight to see it burning and all the crew were casualties.'[23]

The remains of Nutty *at Tank Redoubt. When Arthur Mills saw it nine months later, he wrote, 'the enemy big guns had given her a bad time of it. She had got right up to the enemy trenches.'* Walter Smyth collection.

The Camel Brigade moved in to support the attack from the right flank. Two companies of the 1st Camel Battalion dismounted some 4 kilometres away and advanced towards Tank Redoubt in support of the 54th Division infantry. 'We advanced smartly,' Joe Bolger wrote. 'The shrapnel just mowed everything . . . a tank in action, it did not last long . . . we dug ourselves in and laid there all day. The heat was frightful.'[24] Despite being hit by shellfire, the crew of the tank *Nutty*, 'sticking to their infernal posts, drove it bang into the redoubt'.[25] Here it 'caused great havoc amongst the enemy' before being 'brewed up'.[26] 'This tank got into one redoubt,' Fred Wollaston wrote, 'but it was knocked out a few minutes later and the crew came out of it burning.'[27]

Under cover of six Lewis guns, the Australians rushed the redoubt, but casualties increased as they got closer and copped much of the shellfire directed towards *Nutty* and the small Union Jack that fluttered from it. 'We got it in the neck,' John Davidson wrote. 'Curse the tank!'[28] Of the two Australian camel battalions, only some 100 men remained to make the final charge at the redoubt and only a remnant of about 30 under Lieutenant Archie Campbell made it, joining about twenty British infantrymen who had also succeeded. Some 500 Turkish defenders had been put to flight and another 40 captured. The Australians hung on for two hours before being forced out. The six Lewis gunners were mighty, fighting to the end, five dying gamely by their guns and the sixth, William Barry, having his right arm shattered. Barry continued to operate the gun until Campbell told him to save his life as best as he could. 'What about my gun, sir?' Barry asked and then, after Campbell told him to leave the gun behind, said, 'I think I can carry it.' Barry then carried it out over his left shoulder. Of the 102 men Campbell had taken into action, 92 were casualties.[29]

Meanwhile, the 3rd Camel Battalion, joined by some 11th Light Horsemen, had advanced on the right, crossing the Beersheba road. With his company commander wounded, Lieutenant John Davidson was at the heart of the single company trying to hang on but finally having to retire. 'Enemy shells crashed in our rear,' he

'Three of my gunners,' John Davidson wrote on the caption. 'Two on right killed.' Very few of the Australian Lewis gunners who took part in Second Gaza survived. John Davidson collection.

wrote. 'Rifle and machine gun fire in front.'[30] Robert Farnes got it right when he wrote, 'The Camel Corps got cut up badly.'[31]

❖

General Hodgson's orders were to 'demonstrate strongly against' the Atawineh defences. The official historian called Royston impetuous in advancing his brigade earlier than the 7.30 a.m. scheduled start time, but Royston knew that once dawn broke his men would be easy targets for the Turkish machine guns and artillery. Royston's brigade therefore got ahead of Meredith's 4th Brigade on the left and the 5th Yeomanry Brigade on the right.[32]

General Meredith deployed Lieutenant Colonel William Grant's 11th Light Horse and Lieutenant Colonel Harold McIntosh's 12th Light Horse in the attack. The 11th dismounted about 4 kilometres from Atawineh redoubt and the men advanced in columns through the fields of barley, soon overrunning an enemy outpost. The Turkish artillery opened up with shrapnel fire, which was soon followed by heavy machine-gun and rifle fire. The two regiments went to ground about 500 metres from the redoubt with no prospect of getting closer without severe losses. McIntosh was one of those hit, a shrapnel ball severing an artery in his groin. Although he was evacuated, he died a few days later at El Arish after his wound reopened. By 10 a.m. every officer in one of the squadrons was a casualty. One of them called out, 'Stretcher bearer here, I have got one in the leg,' but when he sat up he was killed by shrapnel.[33] 'When the shrapnel hit the ground, dust would be flung up and, to me, it looked like rain pouncing on the ground,' Bill Smyth wrote.[34] 'Our lads advanced in open order. Turkish HE and shrapnel coming over all the time,' Pat Hamilton added. 'Wounded all up and down wadi. A hot corner. A tank in flames.'[35] After holding their line all day, the 11th and 12th Light Horse withdrew at 7.30 p.m.

'Hanging on at Gaza,' John Davidson wrote on the caption. John Davidson collection.

This photo 'was taken during the biggest battle in Palestine' according to Joe Bradshaw. For the Australian cameleers that was Second Gaza. 'All these men are wounded,' Bradshaw added. 'The poor fellow who is lying down had his knee cap blown off. He is now a prisoner of war.' Joseph Bradshaw collection.

In Royston's brigade the 9th and 10th Light Horse advanced up the slope. When dawn broke, the men lay down in the barley before advancing to within 500 metres of the Atawineh redoubt. After reaching the Beersheba road, there was a bare slope ahead with no chance of getting closer. Lieutenant Colonel Leslie Maygar's 8th Light Horse had no cover and suffered heavily, but Maygar, a Victoria Cross recipient from the Boer War, inspired his men to hang on. 'I had my charger Dick shot from under me,' Maygar, who had lost his other horse at Romani, wrote. 'I can tell you Jack the Turk is a good fighter . . . we will have some hard hitting before we get to Jerusalem and Damascus.'[36] 'Our horses suffered heavily. The shells used to drop amongst them and give the horse holders all they knew to keep them from stampeding,' John Stephen noted.[37] 'The biggest battle the 10th ever in. Lasted all day,' Robert Fell wrote. 'I had three narrow escapes . . . watch saved me from stomach wound.'[38] Ron Kemp, who was also with the 3rd Brigade wrote, 'I had the escape of my life. One of the coal boxes [howitzer shells] lobbed at my feet, killed the two horses I was holding, wounded Bill Hall, 50 yards away, but didn't touch me.' The brigade retired at sunset after 'many of our old mates were killed'.[39] As always, Royston was an inspiration. Stan Parkes wrote that 'the "old brig" must have a charmed life; he was galloping up and down the firing line all day'.[40] 'Our Brigadier Royston as usual worked splendidly and is admired by all,' Leo Hanly added.[41]

General Royston (standing at left) with a signals section. Wilfred Baker collection.

Captain Wilfred Evans, helped by four orderlies from the 3rd Light Horse Field Ambulance, treated 240 wounded men that day. 'We had only six sand carts to do all the work, but we got in all the wounded,' Stan Parkes wrote.[42] 'It was the worst cutting up since Gallipoli this brigade had had,' John Stephen observed of the effect on his 3rd Brigade.[43] Pelham Jackson, who was with the 11th Light Horse, was killed on 19 April while helping to carry a comrade to safety. Jackson's mother later received a letter from Major Jim Loynes, the commander of A Squadron, who apologised for not having written earlier; he had had two bullets in his shoulder from the same battle.[44] As the official historian later noted 'The day's offensive had been an unqualified failure'.[45]

Further out on the right flank, Chauvel's as yet uncommitted mounted division moved from Shellal against the Hareira redoubt. Though there were some clashes with Turkish cavalry, German aircraft caused the greater damage. At 11 a.m. on 20 April, four aircraft dropped sixteen bombs on light horse lines west of Shellal, causing 32 casualties among the men and killing 53 horses. As Fred Tomlins put it, 'Four Taubes came over and gave us a fine exhibition of bomb dropping.'[46] John MacNamara thought one Taube had spotted the brigade and then, 'half an hour later four more came up one behind the other and dropped 16 bombs on us. We did not have time to scatter so just got off our horses and laid down as flat as one could get.' Following this attack, the 2nd Brigade adopted a new 'Taube formation', which maintained greater distance between each troop.[47]

Turkish cavalry on parade near Kuneitra. The Turkish cavalry 'never on one occasion charged light horse or even waited if our men rode at them,' Henry Gullett wrote. Arthur Mills described the Turkish ponies as 'little fellows but very strong and wiry'. Royal New South Wales Lancers Memorial Museum collection.

The graves of Sergeant Robert Thomson (2nd Light Horse Field Ambulance), Lance Corporal Charles Austin (Provost Corps), Trooper Leo Ussher (6th Light Horse) and Private Herbert Thorpe (2nd Brigade Headquarters), who were buried alongside the interpreter Armenac Kemkemian, who was working with the Australians. All were killed on the morning of 17 April 1917 during a bombing raid on the 2nd Brigade camp at Shellal. The bombing also killed seventeen horses. Harry Mattocks collection.

The light horse outposts kept any Turkish cavalry at bay. On 24 April, the 7th Light Horse captured a complete troop of Turkish lancers comprising one officer and seventeen other ranks.[48] 'No shots were fired and every one was captured,' Robert Farnes wrote. 'Our fellows had a great time chasing them, they simply charged into them and knocked their horses over.'[49] Tom Baker watched the prisoners being brought in. 'They were well equipped and armed with lance, sword and carbine,' he wrote, 'but their horses were in poor condition.'[50]

As John MacNamara observed, 'The attack over Gaza way had not done well at all . . . a very severe knock back.'[51] 'Our attack has blown out,' Maurie Evans added. 'Our people seem to have a habit of putting two and two together expecting to make five and then find out that they only achieve three.'[52] Jeff Holmes summed it up: 'Jacko has entrenched in a very strong position and will take some routing out.'[53]

General Dobell abandoned the offensive with Gaza still in enemy hands and with 5900 of his men casualties. Coming on top of the failure of the Arras offensive in France, this did not go down well in London. 'Gaza appears to be a second Gallipoli,' was the general opinion there.[54] There were ramifications. Dobell was replaced by Chetwode and Chauvel took over Chetwode's role at the head of the Desert Column. Chaytor moved up to command the Anzac Mounted Division. In a short time, General Murray would also be replaced.

❖

When a black-and-white mosaic with a Nabatean inscription had been discovered on a hill at Rafa at the end of March 1917, Chaplain Reverend William Maitland Woods, a keen amateur archaeologist and a man of the cloth, clearly understood the value of the discovery. 'I saw it for a moment, returned to take a copy of the inscription after the lapse of a few days, to find that the troops in the district, who at that time were sweeping over the country, had taken up every single stone with bayonets and [jack knives].'[55]

Only weeks later, on 6 April 1917, another mosaic was uncovered on a hill at Shellal above the Wadi Ghuzze, which the Turks had evacuated in early March. The mosaic, partly damaged by Turkish trenches, lay across a ruined church floor and dated from the reign of the Roman emperor Justinian. Woods considered the mosaic of immense value due to the inscription and the date thereon (AD561–62). 'I recognized this as soon as I saw it in situ,' Woods later wrote to the Australian Official First World War Historian, Charles Bean. Woods, with the incident at Rafa still fresh in his mind, also realised the danger of leaving the mosaic in situ at Shellal. As Woods wrote, on this occasion, 'I raised a successful howl, a guard was put on, and a great portion of it was saved.'[56] Robert Fell visited the site, now known as Mosaic Hill, on 5 June and wrote how the floor was 'beautifully inlaid in mosaic with coloured stone . . . Bones of some cleric named George discovered under floor.'[57]

It took more than fourteen days to complete the 'delicate and laborious operation' to remove the mosaic. At the request of the new Egyptian Expeditionary Force commander, General Edmund Allenby, Woods later went to Cairo and had some of the crates opened to show him and a collection of imperial staff officers this 'most wonderful piece of work, some 1400 years old'. A move then developed to take the mosaic to Europe, 'where the savants of the world could see it,' Woods noted sarcastically. 'I was told to go and pack it up for England,' he told Bean. Fortunately, the food controller in Egypt declined to take the crated mosaic on board a steamer leaving for England as 'it was not food'. Aware of his own lack of influence, Woods hoped that Australia would prevent the move to England. 'The value was created only when the Australian forces had

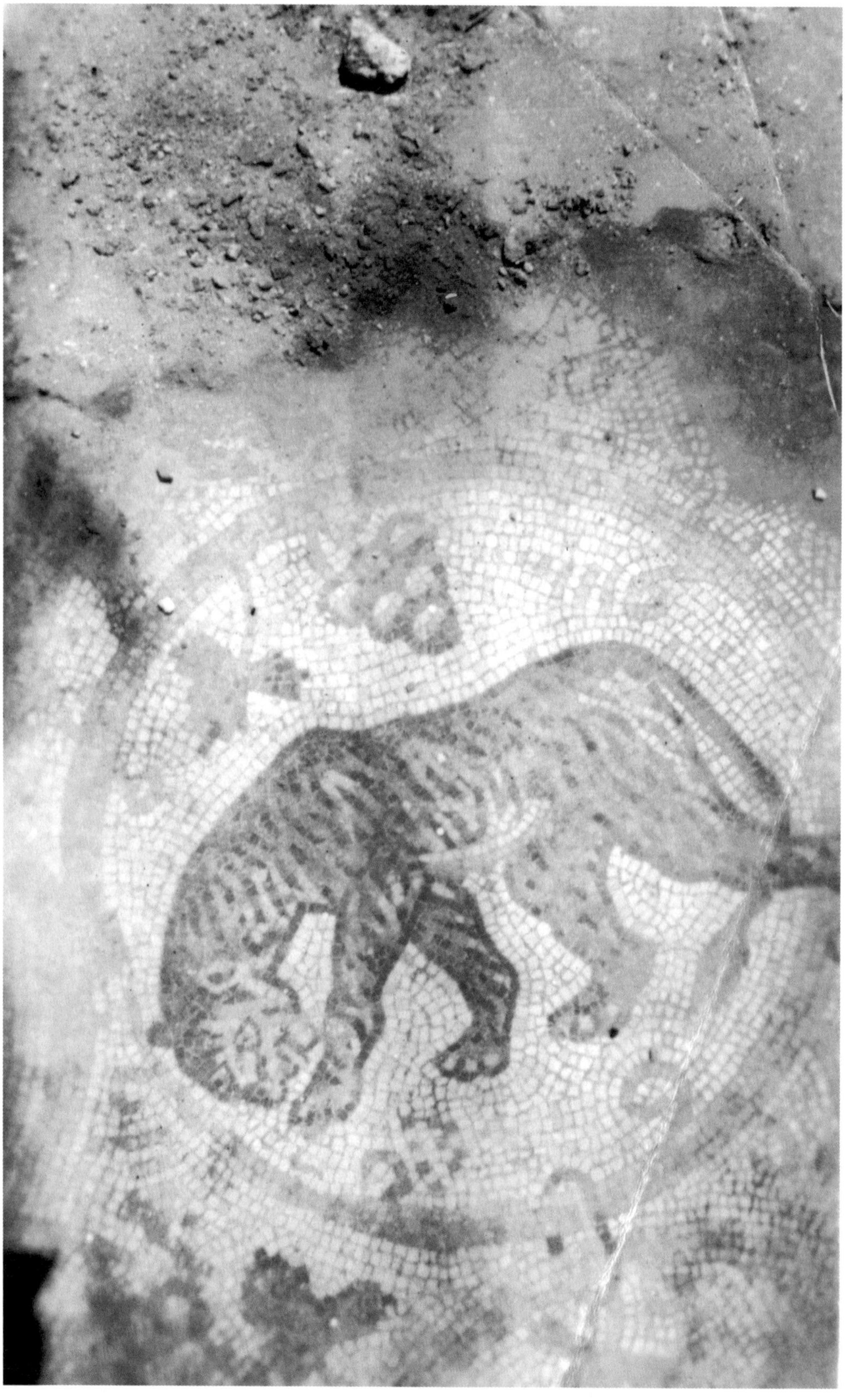

removed it out of danger, and possible destruction, such as had happened to the Rafa mosaic,' Woods wrote. 'It should become the property of future generations of Australians . . . there is nothing else like it in the world.'⁵⁸ The Shellal mosaic was brought to Australia and is today displayed at the Australian War Memorial, an enduring monument to the Australian Light Horse.

❖

Operations now wound down for the summer. Stan Parkes wrote on 24 April that the 'weather is warming up and the dust is something awful, the grass has all disappeared and the ground is like powder'.⁵⁹ The next day, Les Horder noted that it was 'Still hot with a scorching wind, must be 130 [54 degrees Celsius] in the shade.'⁶⁰ Henry Langtip also felt it, writing, 'It is terrible hot day and only a bottle of water.'⁶¹

Part of the 'Anzac mosaic', as Reverend Woods captioned it, before it was removed. 'We unearthed a wonderful piece of ancient work here on top of a hill, it has evidently been the floor of a Temple, there are lions & tigers & birds & dogs chasing rabbits & peacocks and all sorts of things,' Granville Ryrie wrote. 'It is done in different coloured little square stones set in cement.' William and Francis Woods collection.

The ruined church where the Shellal mosaic was found. William and Francis Woods collection.

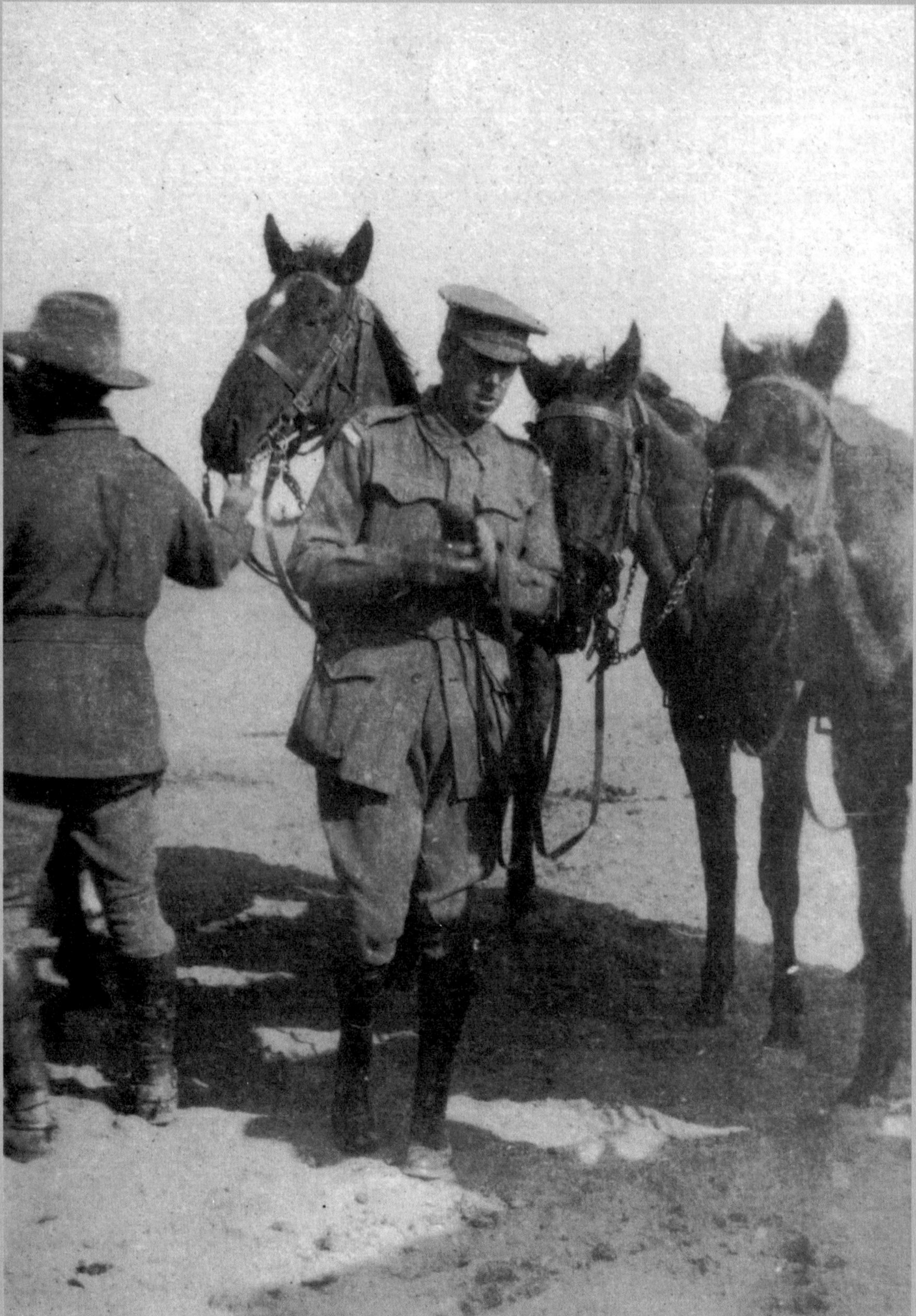

CHAPTER 7
'FIRST-RATE HORSE-MASTERS'
May to October 1917

From Gaza to Hareira the Turks had built a series of strong redoubts, but between Hareira and Beersheba there was a 7-kilometre unfortified gap. The lack of water in the area for any attacking force provided the security. General Chetwode had replaced the bungling Dobell and set about regaining the confidence of the men who had been so badly let down by their higher command (including Chetwode) during both Gaza battles. With the addition of Major General George de Symons Barrow's Yeomanry Mounted Division, Chetwode now had three mounted divisions, and his planning focused on utilising the priceless advantage their mobility offered. The Desert Column now became the Desert Mounted Corps, and the three divisions of the corps rotated, each spending a month patrolling the inland flank, a month training at Abasan el Kebir and a month resting at Deir el Belah. The heat, dust and a constant lack of water and good food made it a difficult summer to survive for man and horse alike.

Trooper Ted Dengate, who arrived at the front in mid-May 1917, found the frequent sandstorms a problem, writing home to his wife, 'Bullets won't be as bad as the sand which is blowing about here.' Dengate was from Molong in the Central West of New South Wales, one of five 'Molongites' in the 12th Light Horse. He was trained as a Hotchkiss gunner. 'Rather a complicated affair,' he wrote of the gun. 'I am going to take one of them back to Australia to shoot foxes with.'[1]

To protect the Allied right flank, engineers were escorted out to Asluj, 25 kilometres south of Beersheba, to destroy the Turkish railway. The ride out was tough going. 'We were blinded with dust and the night was horribly sultry,' Joe Burgess wrote.[2] The party reached the railway

Smoko. Arthur Reynolds *collection.*

TOP

Godfrey Burgess and Tom Bradley, two of the 12th Light Horse 'Molongites', reading the Molong news at Tel el Fara in 1917. Godfrey Burgess collection.

ABOVE

A Hotchkiss machine gun. The gun was fed by 30-round metal strips, and twelve guns were allocated to each light horse regiment in April 1917. They were usually deployed on the flanks of the line, thus providing enfilading fire against any enemy attackers or defenders. Reg Dixon collection.

line the next morning, 23 May. 'The engineers immediately got to work and in two hours' time had blown up two railway bridges and fifteen miles of railway line,' Maurie Pearce wrote. 'At 10.30 a.m. we set off on the return trip home and we did not reach home till midnight,' he continued. 'These night treks are something to live in dread of.' The only opposition encountered during the operation were Bedouin snipers, so haystacks and crops were burned on the way back in retaliation.[3] The troops had been 34 hours in the saddle and Joe Burgess felt it: 'The ride back seemed never ending and I was as saddle sore as could be.'[4] John MacNamara concurred: 'For the last 10 miles or so I could not sit in one position in the saddle for more than 5 minutes as I was so sore.'[5]

Maurie Evans saw the two sides of life in the desert. 'In the twinkling of an eye the glow fades, the stars rush out, and the . . . darkness of an eastern night descends on land, sky and sea,' he observed on 22 June. Two days later he wrote, 'During the last day or two, apparently out of the void, has come upon us a plague of black crickets.'[6] After moving from the coast up to Abasan el Kebir, Joe Burgess wrote, 'this is absolutely the dirtiest and dustiest hole of a camp we have ever struck yet . . . I was weeping mud tears. The whole country is like hot ashes in consistency for about six inches in depth.'[7] Such conditions drove the men underground. 'Living in dugouts below ground—on account of heat, dust and flies,' Robert Fell wrote.[8]

On 13 August, John MacNamara was out on a stunt with the 1st Light Horse. The light horsemen crossed the railway line and then went on about 1500 metres to Hill 1160, where they were engaged at long range by Turkish small-arms fire and then shelled. 'After about 2 minutes everyone was off the hill with the exception of my mate & myself,' he wrote. MacNamara, who was sending a message on a heliograph at the time, was later awarded a Military Medal for his devotion to duty. 'You could have knocked me down with a feather,' he wrote on being told of the award.⁹

Upon his arrival in Egypt on 27 June, the new commander of the Egyptian Expeditionary Force, General Edmund Allenby, immediately set to the task of planning the next offensive. Allenby had directions from the British War Office to drive into Palestine, and his recent experience on the Western Front with cavalry and infantry made him an ideal appointment. By moving his headquarters from the Savoy Hotel in Cairo to Rafa in Palestine, Allenby made an immediate impression on the officers and men under his command. As Henry Gullett wrote, 'He went through the hot dusty camps of his army like a strong, fresh, reviving wind.'¹⁰

'The wreck.' How the Australians left the Asluj viaduct. Ralph Kellett collection.

The light horsemen gather. Claude Ballard collection. Courtesy of Carol Whiteside.

'FIRST-RATE HORSE-MASTERS'

General Allenby, on the left, reviewing troops in Cairo. His 'big hard dial' impressed those with whom he came into contact. Reg Dixon collection.

Allenby impressed the light horsemen. Joe Burgess wrote that 'he looks a pretty capable sort of cove, he has a big hard dial with lips that twist in a flinty sort of way when he is amused'.[11] Granville Ryrie, who had a low opinion of the British commanders following the Gaza shemozzle, wrote, 'I met the new C in C [commander-in-chief] Gen Allenby and I think it will be a great improvement.'[12] The locals were told Allenby was Allah el Nebi, the 'prophet of God'.[13] The Australian light horsemen also impressed Allenby. He later wrote of them as 'tanned by the eastern sun and the parching desert wind; lean, but in hard condition; light horsemen in verity; well mounted, and first-rate horse-masters'.[14]

In addition to the mounted corps, Allenby now had seven divisions of infantry plus two separate mounted brigades, one on camels. He planned to strike in late October and reach Jerusalem before the late-November rains brought movements to a halt. Following Chetwode's well-thought-out plan, Allenby would strike on the inland flank with the four divisions

The rail bridge at Wadi Ghuzze. Arthur Hitchcock collection.

AUSTRALIAN LIGHT HORSE

of XX Infantry Corps alongside two divisions of Chauvel's Desert Mounted Corps. The orders were issued on 22 October.

By this stage the railhead had reached Deir el Belah, with a branch railway built towards Gamli. The vital water pipeline was now at Rafa, with an extension to Shellal and on to Imara. Additional wells had been sunk on the coast at Khan Yunis and Deir el Belah. Material to extend both the railway and pipeline was brought forward to Wadi Ghuzze in anticipation of the advance, and camels were gathered to carry the water forward on the heels of the troops.[15] On 18 August, John MacNamara passed through Shellal for the first time in three months. 'There is a big railway bridge over the wadi,' he wrote. 'Also a traffic bridge for the wet season and a big dam with a pumping plant on the bank of the water.'[16]

The build-up continued. 'Starting from Kantara one could see remarkable changes around about here in railways, camps, dumps, roads and many other things,' Edwin Brown wrote on 29 August. 'During the trip down artillery, munitions, troops, transports of all kinds, great supplies of rations, fodder, equipment, railway material etc etc were to be seen passing on up to the front.'[17] 'There is great activity now and it is quite evident a push is going to take place shortly,' Maurie Pearce observed in late September. 'Thousands of camels are camped all around us and a tremendous dump has been established at Shellal Junction station.'[18] The construction crews were 'full up to the brim with tales of wonderful big guns, miles upon miles of light railways for shell carrying, hundreds of guns, millions of gas shells, dozens of tanks, flame throwers galore etc etc,' Maurie Evans wrote on 11 October.[19]

❖

On the Turkish side, the Turkish commander, Djemal Pasha, was at odds with General Erich von Falkenhayn, the former Chief of the General Staff of the German Army. Following the failure of his bloodletting strategy at Verdun on the Western Front, von Falkenhayn had fallen from grace and after a stint on the Eastern Front had been sent to Palestine. The defensive successes at Gaza had lulled Djemal into believing a passive defence was all that was required on the Palestine front, while von Falkenhayn believed that an active defence based on spoiling attacks was necessary. At the front, General von Kressenstein, the 4th Army commander, was faced with the difficulty of maintaining a cohesive army. Desertions were a major problem, exacerbated by a breakdown in the supply system. Only about half the requested supplies were getting through to the front, due

General Erich von Falkenhayn, on the left, alongside Djemal Pasha in the back of a staff car. Clarence Reid collection.

to the paucity of supply animals and the poor condition of those that were available. With the wet season approaching, further supply problems were inevitable.[20]

The Turkish command expected Gaza would again be the target, and the main reserve of two infantry divisions was deployed there. Imaginative deception schemes by Allenby's intelligence officer, Colonel Richard Meinertzhagen, helped reinforce that false impression. But Allenby would strike on the inland flank, at Beersheba, attacking from three directions with six divisions. On the coast, Lieutenant General Edward Bulfin's XXI Corps would simultaneously pressure Gaza, first with artillery and later from the monitors and battleships operating offshore. The navy would also manoeuvre its smaller craft around to create the impression of an amphibious landing on the coast north of Gaza. Further afield, a military camp on Cyprus would be expanded to bluff the Turks into believing troops were gathering for another landing in Syria, thus keeping the Turkish garrison there in place.[21] Although the 1915 operation at Gallipoli had failed, it had left the Turkish command wary of another such venture.

There was considerable Allied air activity in that last week of October to try to keep the German aircraft from observing the build-up on the right flank. 'There are some splendid aeroplanes here now and they ought to shake Jacko up a bit,' Gordon Macrae wrote.[22] On 6 September, Robert Farnes got a ride in one of them: 'When we were doing the nose dive it feels as if your inside is going to your head and when you shoot straight up again it feels as if it is going to your boots.'[23]

The new British planes got good results. On 8 October, Maurie Pearce observed a German Albatros Scout landing in Allied lines due to a pierced petrol tank.[24] The plane was captured intact along with the pilot, Lieutenant Gustav Dittmar. Dittmar was unfortunate, as he was due to take home leave in a few days after three years in the Middle East.[25] But as Jeff Holmes observed on 18 October, some enemy planes had less gentle

landings. 'The enemy plane was seen to dive, then right itself, and then it seemed as if the pilot lost all control,' he wrote, 'and the plane came hurtling to the ground from a terrific height . . . the plane caught fire as it was descending.'[26] Joe Burgess saw the grim result, with 'the plane and man smashed beyond recognition'.[27]

❖

Lieutenant Gustav Dittmar's captured German Albatros Scout. As John MacNamara noted, 'it was the first [intact] Hun machine to be brought down in our lines'. Ralph Kellett collection.

Meanwhile, another battle was being fought in the Hejaz region to the south—the Arab revolt. On 15 June 1916, the Arabs had revolted against the Turkish occupation, capturing Mecca from the Turks six days later. Although the Arabs had a nominal leader in Sharif Ali Ibn Hussein, they were from many disparate tribes, with all the traditional intertribal hatreds and mistrust between them. The tribal Arabian lands stretched from the Red Sea to Damascus, and if the tribes could be brought together as one nation, this part of the Ottoman Empire would be untenable for the Turkish armies deployed there. The British saw the opportunity but it would take the extraordinary diplomatic and military skills of a small number of British officers, not to mention a considerable amount of gold, to make it happen. Following the fall of Mecca, Medina became the Turkish forward base, connected by the artery of the Hejaz railway to Amman and Deraa in the north.

It was not until the Allied advance into the northern Sinai that the Arabs had a chance to carry out operations against the inland areas without bringing down an overwhelming enemy force onto them. With most of their forces drawn to the Gaza–Beersheba line in the north, the Turks maintained only garrison troops to cover the vast inland area. Into this situation was thrust the British intelligence officer Major T.E. Lawrence, who would help bring the Arab tribes together and forge an effective strategy for the use of the Arab army. The first test for Lawrence was at Akaba in June 1917, when he brought together a disparate Arab force and boldly captured the important Red Sea port from the inland side. As the actions developed, Turkish forces and supplies had to be shifted inland from Palestine, and this convinced the British command that more resources should be allocated to support the Arabs of the Hejaz.

With the expansion of the AIF, the training of soldiers in modern weaponry was one of the most vital tasks at this stage of the war. After a period of service with the light horse, by mid-1917 Sergeant Charles Yells was serving as a weapons instructor in Egypt at the grandly titled Imperial School of Instruction. On 10 August, Yells, a Lewis gun specialist, was detached for special duty to train the Arab irregulars in how to use modern automatic weapons in their fight against the Turks in the Hejaz. The following day, 'the forceful sergeant-instructor' embarked at Suez bound for Akaba.

With Yells went Corporal Walter Brook from the Royal Welsh Fusiliers, who was an instructor on the Stokes mortar. Colonel Lawrence soon christened the men Lewis and Stokes, 'after their jealously-loved tools'.[28]

Colonel T.E. Lawrence, the legendary 'Lawrence of Arabia'. Australian War Memorial AWM B02170.

He described Yells as 'long, thin and sinuous, his supple body lounging in unmilitary curves. His hard face, arched eyebrows, and predatory nose set off the peculiarly Australian air of reckless willingness and capacity to do something very soon.' In comparison, Lawrence saw Brook as 'a stocky English yeoman, workmanlike and silent; always watching for an order to obey'.[29] The American war correspondent Lowell Thomas said of Yells that 'he was a glutton for punishment and a tiger in a fight'.[30] Once they reached Akaba, Yells and Brook would have little time to instruct. With his Arab army growing by the day as more tribes joined him at Akaba, Lawrence was keen to take the fight to the Turks as soon as possible.

Yells approached Lawrence, requesting that he and Brook join a proposed raiding party. Lawrence said that 'if they went they would lose their British Army comfort and privilege'. Yells, whose brother had been killed in France five months earlier, told him 'that he was looking for just this strangeness of life'. Lawrence agreed to the request and lent them two of his best camels.[31] When Lawrence moved his force out of Akaba, Yells and Brook rode with them.

At dawn on 16 September, Lawrence's raiding party left Wadi Rum, some 50 kilometres south-east of Akaba. With 25 Nowasera tribesmen riding alongside Lawrence, the other tribal groups followed in their own bands, unwilling to ride or even speak with the other tribes. As Lawrence observed, 'the rest of our party strayed like a broken necklace'. Lawrence had to spend more time directing the tribes than planning the raid.[32]

Mudawwarah was an isolated station on the Hejaz railway about 130 kilometres south of Maan. It had a deep well, the only one on the line south of Maan, and if that well could be destroyed it would paralyse operations on the Hejaz line. After a night reconnaissance, however, Lawrence ruled out a direct assault on the station, which had a garrison of some 300 men to his fractured 150. He took his raiders further south, where he mined a two-arched railway bridge and positioned his men, including 'Lewis and Stokes', on a nearby spur. 'The sergeants set up their toys on a terrace,' Lawrence wrote.[33]

Two Lewis gunners at work in the desert. John Davidson collection.

When a train of two engines pulling ten wagons approached from the south, the mine was blown under the second engine. 'The line vanished from sight behind a spouting column of black dust,' Lawrence observed. As the dust cleared, Yells opened fire with his Lewis gun and Brook fired two mortar bombs, the second of which fell in the gully below the bridge where the Turks from the derailed wagons were sheltering, making 'a shambles of the place'. The survivors fled in panic, straight into the line of sight of the two Lewis guns, one manned by Yells. 'The sergeant grimly traversed with drum after drum, till the open sand was littered with bodies,' Lawrence wrote.[34] Some 90 enemy troops were killed and 70 were taken prisoner. Yells was said to have accounted for between 30 and 40 of them with his Lewis gun. When he later insisted on his share of the loot from the train, Lawrence gave Yells a Turkish carpet and a cavalry sword.[35]

On 28 September, Charles Yells returned to Suez, and both he and Brook were awarded the Distinguished Conduct Medal for their part in the railway raid and the 'great destruction wrought'. Four months later, Yells returned to active service with the 3rd Light Horse Machine Gun Squadron.

The Turks responded to the attacks on the Hejaz railway by using armoured train wagons. This example was captured by the 1st Light Horse in September 1918. Harry Mattocks collection.

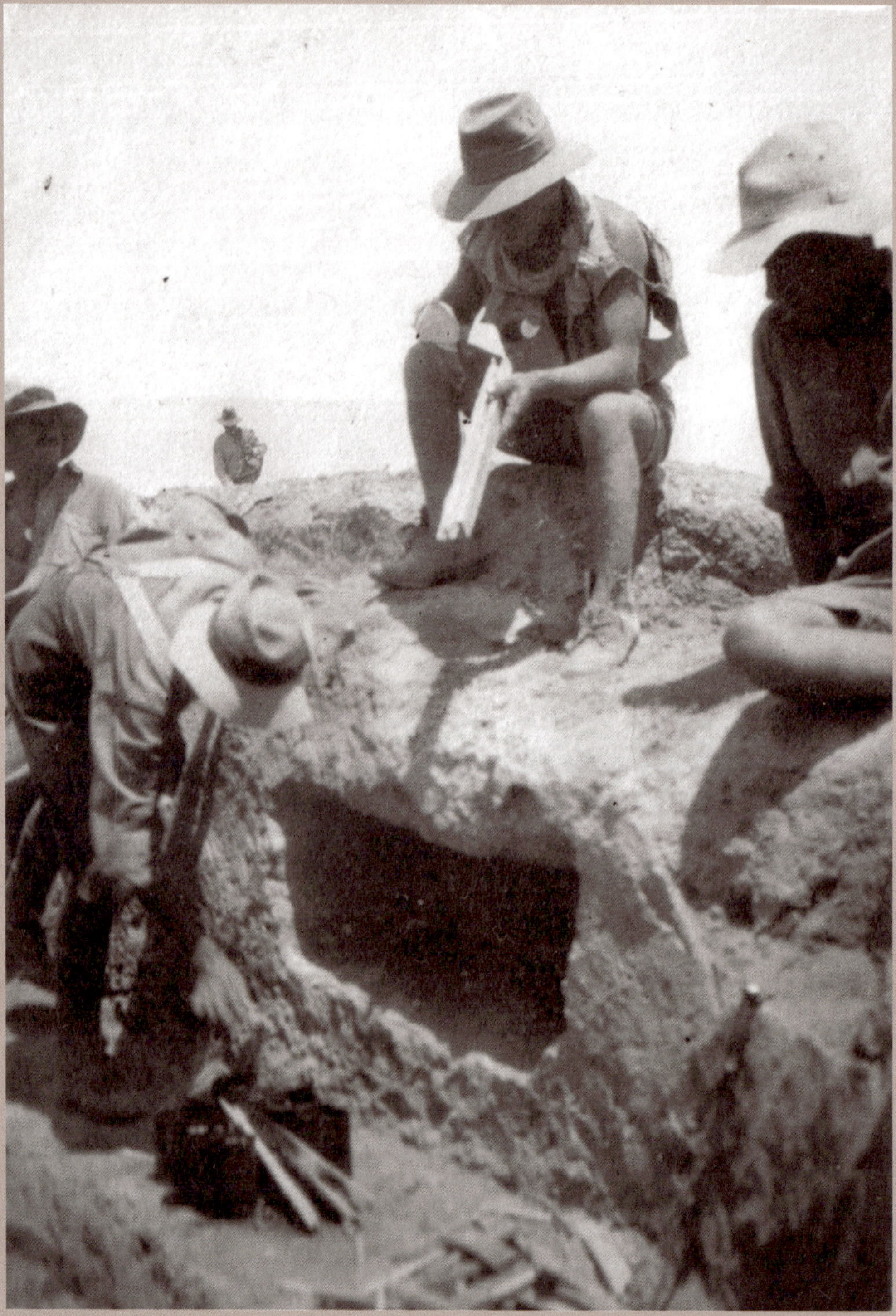

CHAPTER 8
'AUSTRALIANS WILL DO ME'
October to November 1917

This land was hard on the commanders. Generals Meredith and Royston, both older men, had moved on and the 4th Brigade was now commanded by Brigadier General William Grant, while Brigadier General Lachlan Wilson had taken over the 3rd Brigade.

In the lead-up to General Allenby's offensive, the 8th Light Horse captured a series of hills facing the enemy positions at Hareira on 25 October 1917. Two days later, the Turks counterattacked the position, now held by the Middlesex Yeomanry, and during fierce fighting many were killed or wounded.[1] John Stephen wrote, 'Jacko had attacked our outpost and had surrounded two squadrons of Yeomanry . . . found 14 dead Yeo all stripped of clothing and equipment.'[2] Things were hotting up. Robert Fell went into action with the 10th Light Horse on the afternoon of 27 October at El Buggar ridge, out past Shellal. 'Rifles and machine guns very hot,' he wrote. 'We had to lie flat, could not lift our heads.'[3]

For the attack on Beersheba, the infantry would take their water with them on 30,000 camels, each carrying two water containers, but Chauvel's divisions would have to find water in the field. They would march southeast from Shellal to Esani and thence Khalasa and Asluj. General Cox's 1st Brigade left Abasan el Kebir on 26 October and rode via Esani to Khalasa. 'A cow of a dusty day, shifted out at 5,' Les Horder wrote. 'A rotten trip to Esani getting there at midnight.'[4] Of Khalasa, Maurie Evans wrote, 'Now there is just a stone house or two vault like in appearance which has I think been built by the Turk for his frontier defence.'[5] John Stephen left for Khalasa with the 3rd Brigade on 28 October. 'Saddled up (horses carrying tremendous load) and moved off at 1600.'[6] With water the key

Boiling up the billy in a captured Turkish trench. Ralph Kellett collection.

Drawing water from an underground cistern in the Wadi Ghuzze. Two men work the lever on each hand pump. Engineers were able to extract about 1,300,000 litres a day from the Wadi Ghuzze springs, and this was stored in a 2,200,000-litre reservoir. Royal New South Wales Lancers Memorial Museum collection.

consideration, Harry Bostock noted that on 30 October there were 'Two wells with engines pumping all day and night at Khalasa in wadi.'[7]

Moving a mounted division was a massive operation. 'Our Div transport train was 4 miles long,' Harold Mulder recorded.[8] Behind Chauvel's brigades, the supply line stretched back for some 10 kilometres; there were thousands of camels in the convoys. As Gordon Cooper wrote, 29 October was a 'beautifully clear moonlight night'.[9] The next stop was Asluj, which Maurie Evans observed was 'a queer little place ringed in with hills. It has wells, barracks and a small mosque.'[10] Joe Burgess saw Asluj as 'a few solid stone buildings' among 'the flint covered hard barren hills'.[11]

Ryrie's 2nd Brigade had reached Asluj on 25 October. After the hard ride, the men then had the task of clearing the water cisterns and sinking new wells. The Australians would use the same great circular stone wells from which Moses and the Israelites had drawn water in their earthenware jars. Some of the top stones had cuts worn into them as much as 20 centimetres deep, from the ropes of thousands of years of Bedouins drawing water from the well. 'We got here without old Jacko taking a tumble at all but one of his Taubes has just been over,' Ion Idriess wrote.[12]

Jeff Holmes was with the engineers at Asluj on 26 October. 'Three wells and several large reservoirs, and around these were stone troughs,

Horses from the 1st Light Horse feeding during the move to Khalasa on 29 October 1917. Royal New South Wales Lancers Memorial Museum collection.

98 AUSTRALIAN LIGHT HORSE

one being nearly a hundred yards in length,' he wrote. A pipe ran from the reservoirs to the troughs. The engineers had to clear the wells and troughs out and rig up oil engines and pumps.[13] 'On arrival there we found that all the wells had been blown up and were full to the top with rocks & rubbish,' Granville Ryrie wrote. 'We had the engineers with us and set to work to clean them out.'[14]

By 29 October, a good water supply was available and when General Allenby turned up to inspect the work the men knew how important their task had been.[15] General Chetwode's plan was for three infantry divisions to attack the outer defences of Beersheba from the south-west, with the aim of drawing the main strength of the Turkish defenders onto them. The preliminary artillery bombardment from some 100 guns opened at 5.55 a.m. on 31 October and soon raised a pall of dust and smoke over Beersheba. The artillery included two batteries of 60-pounder guns plus two batteries of 6-inch siege howitzers and a battery of 4.5-inch howitzers. 'The enemy must have got a big surprise when our heavy guns opened out,' John MacNamara wrote.[16] 'Over the redoubts around Beersheba were the shrapnel clouds from our shells,' Ion Idriess observed. 'Black clouds of smoke and thick dust marked the bursting of high explosive shells.'[17] Chetwode's main attack went in just after midday, and under cover of the dust pall the infantrymen cut the barbed wire and captured some key outer positions.

Meanwhile, Chauvel's two mounted divisions had moved out of Asluj on the night of 30 October. 'It took from 1700 to 2400 for them to pass,' Harold Mulder wrote. 'A dandy metal road runs through it to Beersheba,' Mulder added. 'The first metal road we've seen this side of the Canal.'[18] 'Rode solid all night to some ten miles round and past Beersheba and turned in at daybreak,' Les Horder recorded.[19] Just before he rode out, John Stephen pondered, 'I wonder what tomorrow holds for us.'[20]

On the morning of 31 October, John Stephen got an idea of what the day might bring: 'Dawn broke with the sound of battle.'[21] From a nearby hill, Pat Hamilton 'could see Beersheba clearly with naked eye. A fine looking town.' His field ambulance had ridden 'right round behind it'.[22] Ion Idriess noted that the town was 'closed in by its big grey Judean hills'.[23]

Clearing out the spoil from the blocked wells at Asluj. The engineers 'had working parties of 250 men and they worked like demons,' Granville Ryrie wrote. 'There was hundreds of tons of stuff to take out of them as they were 12 ft across and 40 ft deep.' Royal New South Wales Lancers Memorial Museum collection.

1st Light Horse troops on the move near Asluj. Royal New South Wales Lancers Memorial Museum collection.

The objective of Ryrie's brigade was to cut the Beersheba–Hebron road to the north-east. Lieutenant Colonel George Macarthur-Onslow's 7th Light Horse led the way over tough ground, reaching the Hebron road only to run into strong enemy positions in the hills. 'We raced across the

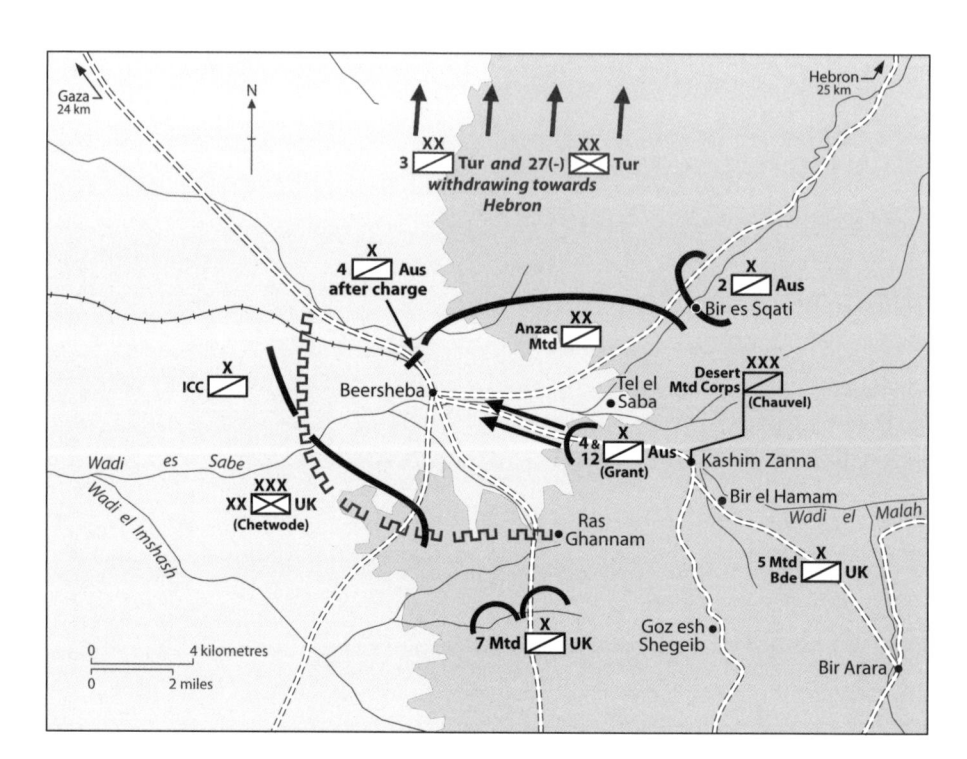

Map 4: The capture of Beersheba

100 AUSTRALIAN LIGHT HORSE

open & soon the Turks started a barrage of shells across our front but we never stopped,' Ryrie wrote.[24] Ion Idriess was with the 5th Light Horse in the foothills, firing up at the Turks on the higher ground. 'We could see the Turkish machine-gun bullets splattering the dust up merrily all up around the chaps in the seventh,' he wrote from the shelter of a wadi beside the road.[25]

Five kilometres to the east of Beersheba was the redoubt of Tel el Saba. Its steep sides and boulder-strewn top represented a formidable obstacle to any approach. General Chaytor's New Zealand brigade and General Cox's 1st Brigade got the job of taking it. The Somerset and Inverness gun batteries provided support as the New Zealanders went in alongside Lieutenant Colonel George Bell's 3rd Light Horse. Bell's men, with the 2nd Light Horse in support, moved around the southern side of the position while the New Zealanders moved in from the north.[26] One of Bell's men, Corporal Roy Dunk, watched as 'they advanced at the gallop until they reached a zone of heavy fire', where the horses 'were checked, cleared and galloped by the horse holders' back to suitable cover. The enemy artillery

Turkish troops parade at the opening of Beersheba railway station. Clarence Reid collection.

targeted the retiring horses, unaware the riders had dismounted.[27] The British artillery fought back, directed by flag signals at the Turkish machine-gun positions. It was the New Zealanders who finally took the crucial Tel el Saba heights at bayonet point, the Auckland Mounted Rifles capturing 132 prisoners and four machine guns as the rest of the defenders fled to Beersheba through a curtain of fire from the 2nd and 3rd Light Horse. It was now 3 p.m.[28]

Meanwhile, Chauvel had sent Wilson's 3rd Brigade to the east of Tel el Saba, where the Turks were still in strength on some broken ground. But the day was getting on and Chauvel knew he would need to act promptly and decisively if he was to have Beersheba before nightfall. A set-piece ground attack would not achieve the result in time, and with Grant pleading his case to allow the 4th Brigade to go for the town at the gallop, Chauvel made the crucial decision of the battle. 'Put Grant straight at it,' he told General Hodgson, Grant's divisional commander.[29] Hodgson then told Grant to 'go right in and take the town before dark'.[30] It was 4.15 p.m. and only about an hour of daylight remained.[31]

With the 11th Light Horse on outpost duty, Grant had only two regiments at hand, Lieutenant Colonel Murray Bourchier's 4th and Lieutenant Colonel Don Cameron's 12th Light Horse. David Harris was with the 12th Light Horse when word came through. 'Tighten up all your gear,' the men were told. 'In ten minutes we're going into Beersheba to water.'[32] With the regiments spread out as a precaution against air attack, it was 4.30 p.m. before they were ready, lined up on either side of the road about 6 kilometres south-east of Beersheba. The 12th were on the left and the 4th on the right. The charge would be over an open, gentle slope to the enemy trenches somewhere east of the town. Crucially, Grant knew the trenches were not protected by wire or ditches, though he was not certain exactly where they were.

'On the Beersheba stunt.' George Francis collection.

Lines of light horsemen manoeuvre for the attack on Beersheba. The attack was 'clearly seen by other brigades at the start,' Henry Gullett was later told, 'but soon obscured in dusk and dust.' George Francis collection.

The regiments formed up in three lines, each of one squadron with 5 metres between each horseman. Without sword or lance, the men held their bayonets in hand so the defenders would see the glint of them as the horsemen approached. Grant and his brigade major, Ken McKenzie, led the attack, with Bourchier and Cameron at the head of their regiments. Major James Lawson led the first squadron of the 4th, Major Eric Hyman the lead squadron of the 12th. Machine-gun fire came from the left but, despite the encroaching darkness, it was swiftly nullified by gunfire from the supporting Notts gun battery. The horsemen galloped on. 'Our pace became terrific,' David Harris wrote. 'We were galloping towards a strongly held crescent-shaped redoubt.'[33] As Henry Gullett later wrote, 'These Australian countrymen had never in all their riding at home ridden a race like this . . . all rode for victory and for Australia.'[34]

Lawson's troopers took the first trench in their stride and then crossed the main trench before dismounting amid an enemy encampment. The lead squadron of the 12th also got across the trenches, dismounted and joined with Lawson's men attacking the main trench from the rear. Lieutenants Frank Burton and Ben Meredith, both from the 4th, were killed. The recently promoted Burton was a Gallipoli veteran, as were

This photo is captioned 'Charge of the 4th Brigade on Gaza'. A re-enactment of the Beersheba charge took place using 4th Brigade light horsemen on 7 February 1918 near Gaza. Official photographer Frank Hurley wrote, 'I sensed the excitement myself, for the charge was directed against the position which I occupied.' John Gorrell collection.

'AUSTRALIANS WILL DO ME'

the four troopers who died beside him. The ruthless light horsemen got to work with the bayonet and after about 30 Turks fell, the rest put their hands up in surrender. Hyman's men also got amongst it, killing some 60 enemy defenders. Behind Hyman, Major Cuthbert Fetherstonhaugh at the head of the second squadron had his horse hit and was then hit himself as he charged on into the trenches. Observing an enemy machine-gun setting up behind a wadi on the flank, Staff Sergeant Arthur 'Jack' Cox turned his horse 90 degrees and charged the group with only his revolver as a weapon, taking all 40 Turks as prisoners. The stretcher-bearers were close behind the assault troops, the test cricketer Albert 'Tibby' Cotter among them. He died as he tried to save others.[35]

Ted Dengate was in the charge. 'Lined up along the brow of a hill, paused a moment, and then went at em,' he wrote to his wife. 'The ground was none too smooth which caused our line to get twisted a bit, but we all knew where we had to go and we did go. We spurred our horses and yelled . . . three or four horses came down, others with no riders on still going, the saddles splashed with blood . . . I could see the Turks' heads over the edge of their trenches squinting along their rifles, a lot of the fellows dismounted at that point . . . most of us kept straight on . . . some of the chaps jumped clear over the trenches in places . . . about 150 men got through and raced for the town, they went up the street yelling like madmen.'[36] Dengate had ridden his luck: 'I never fired a shot, no one else did either I think, and was a huge bluff stakes, we put the wind up em properly. It's marvellous how we got through . . . I got a bullet through the leg of my breeches, just above the knee, grazed my leg but didn't make it bleed.'[37]

The main street in Beersheba leading to the mosque. Royal New South Wales Lancers Memorial Museum collection.

Other light horsemen under Lieutenant Rod Robey and Captain Jack Davies charged on into Beersheba itself. While Robey headed east, Davies, the only man in the regiment with a sword, rode up the main street holding the sword in one hand and his revolver in the other, swiping at the fleeing Turks with the former and firing with the latter until empty.[38] Meanwhile, one of the scouts, Thomas O'Leary, had charged out in front and jumped his horse across the trenches before galloping alone into Beersheba, where he helped capture a field gun and crew. Lieutenant Aubrey Abbott led his 12th Light Horse troop in, his clever bay mare following the track that wound through the barbed wire into the town.[39] David Harris wrote of riding on through the town despite 'falling beams from the fired buildings, exploding magazines and arsenals, and various hidden snipers'.[40]

The terrified Turkish defenders were in a state of chaos, many fleeing into the hills to the north and north-west. Arthur Adams, a man of few words, was with the 12th that day. His diary reads: 'Early morn arrived outside Beersheba. Poked around all day—went into action. Charged and took town—many prisoners, many guns, few losses.'[41] The light horsemen took 58 officers and 1090 men prisoner.[42] As Harold Mulder put it, 'Jacko seems to have got it fairly in the neck.'[43] Leo Hanly later helped collect the wounded Turks from the area in which the 4th Brigade had attacked. 'They left dead in trenches 3 thick,' he wrote.[44] General Allenby also recognised the crucial impact of the light horsemen. 'They galloped over two lines of trenches, 8 feet deep and 4 feet wide, full of riflemen; and put a neat finish to the battle,' he wrote.[45]

Many of the horses had been without water for some 30 hours, but as Gordon Cooper noted, the light horsemen 'Had a good deal of trouble in watering the horses.'[46] Though the shock of the light horse charge had prevented most of the wells from being blown, they could not provide enough water until the engineers could get them into proper working order. Only the pools of water formed from the storms six days earlier saved the day. The Turks had managed to destroy only two of the seventeen wells in Beersheba, and two reservoirs holding 400,000 litres of water were also left intact. Pumps were brought up by tractors to service the wells, while cattle were used to drive the waterwheels in the interim. By 4 November, 1,700,000 litres were being drawn per day.[47]

A light horseman looks over captured Krupp 77-mm field guns at Beersheba. Walter Smyth collection.

The 4th Light Horse had lost eleven men killed with another seventeen wounded, while the 12th had twenty killed and nineteen wounded. The effect of the charge galvanised Allenby's army. Everything had rested on the fall of Beersheba that day. Chetwode's infantry corps was ready and waiting to advance north of Beersheba but could not do so until the town fell and a water supply was guaranteed. A captured German staff officer thought the light horsemen were only making a reconnaissance and could not believe the charge was pushed home. 'They are not soldiers at all,' he said. 'They are madmen.'[48]

'It is quite a small place; with the exception of two big buildings and a mosque there is nothing of any size,' Maurie Evans wrote of Beersheba. 'All around was a mass of papers in Turkish.'[49] 'The town is not very big but is much more swanky than anything we have yet seen out here,' Harold Mulder added.[50] But it was clear that the Turks had expected to lose Beersheba and had prepared for it. In the same vein as other diarists, Maurie Pearce wrote that 'as we entered the town many explosions occurred, the enemy having mined most of the wells, water supplies, pumping plants etc'.[51] 'The whole place was a mass of cunningly contrived mines and I had to be very discreet in my search for horse feed,' Maurie Evans added.[52] As Lloyd Corliss noted, the Turks had plans to destroy the place. He wrote that 'there was a train left on the railway station loaded with many mines'.[53]

'I have not heard what our casualties in all are as yet but our regiment only had two men killed,' Lloyd Corliss wrote in one of his last entries.[54] Pat Hamilton was with the 4th Light Horse Field Ambulance when seven cartloads of wounded arrived. 'Each man to his job everything went like clockwork,' he wrote. 'First patient on table in about 20 minutes. Carts arriving all the time.' His field ambulance dealt with 46 patients that day.[55]

❖

On 1 November a bomb landed about 30 metres from the Anzac Dressing Station, despite a Red Cross flag being laid out on the ground. The stretcher-bearer lines were later bombed. 'Horses rearing and neighing, men running and

Beersheba railway station. Godfrey Burgess collection.

A field ambulance on the move. Fred Horsley collection.

shrieking,' Pat Hamilton wrote. Four men were killed, four wounded and twelve wounded horses had to be shot. William Brownjohn had his left leg blown off but the bearers got a tourniquet on in about 90 seconds. The wounded were on the operating table less than 45 minutes after being hit, but the shock of such a scene even among experienced stretcher-bearers was profound. One poor man, overcome with shock, was 'sent away a knock kneed weeping idiot'. The four dead ambulance men were among the 30 casualties buried the next day at Beersheba. 'Each one had an Australian red gum sapling [planted] at head and base.'[56]

The 3rd Brigade also had their losses. A German aircraft bombed the 9th Light Horse lines, killing thirteen men and wounding twenty more, along with 32 horses killed and 26 wounded. Aircraft also bombed the 8th Light Horse while the regiment was in close formation, and Colonel Leslie Maygar and his horse were hit, the horse bolting with its rider. When found, Maygar had lost a lot of blood and he later died. According to Pat Hamilton, the bomb 'blew Col Maygar's arm off and his horse bolted with him before they could get him . . . strange ending for a VC DSO'.[57] Tom Baker wrote that after Maygar had been hit by bomb shrapnel, 'they amputated his arm at once' then 'as they were bringing him in to the field hospital in a sand cart, the latter slipped over in the rocky hills and he lost a lot of blood, and that settled him'.[58] Henry Gullett wrote that due to the rough terrain 'he was afterwards thrown out of ambulance wagon and died a little later'.[59] Harold Mulder summed up the opinion of many: 'He was a grand old chap and the gamest man I ever saw.'[60] Next day, Maygar's men had some measure of revenge when they shot down one of the German planes.

On 5 November, Murray Bourchier sent off a short letter to his parents. 'I led my regiment in a cavalry charge,' he wrote. 'Australians will do me.'[61]

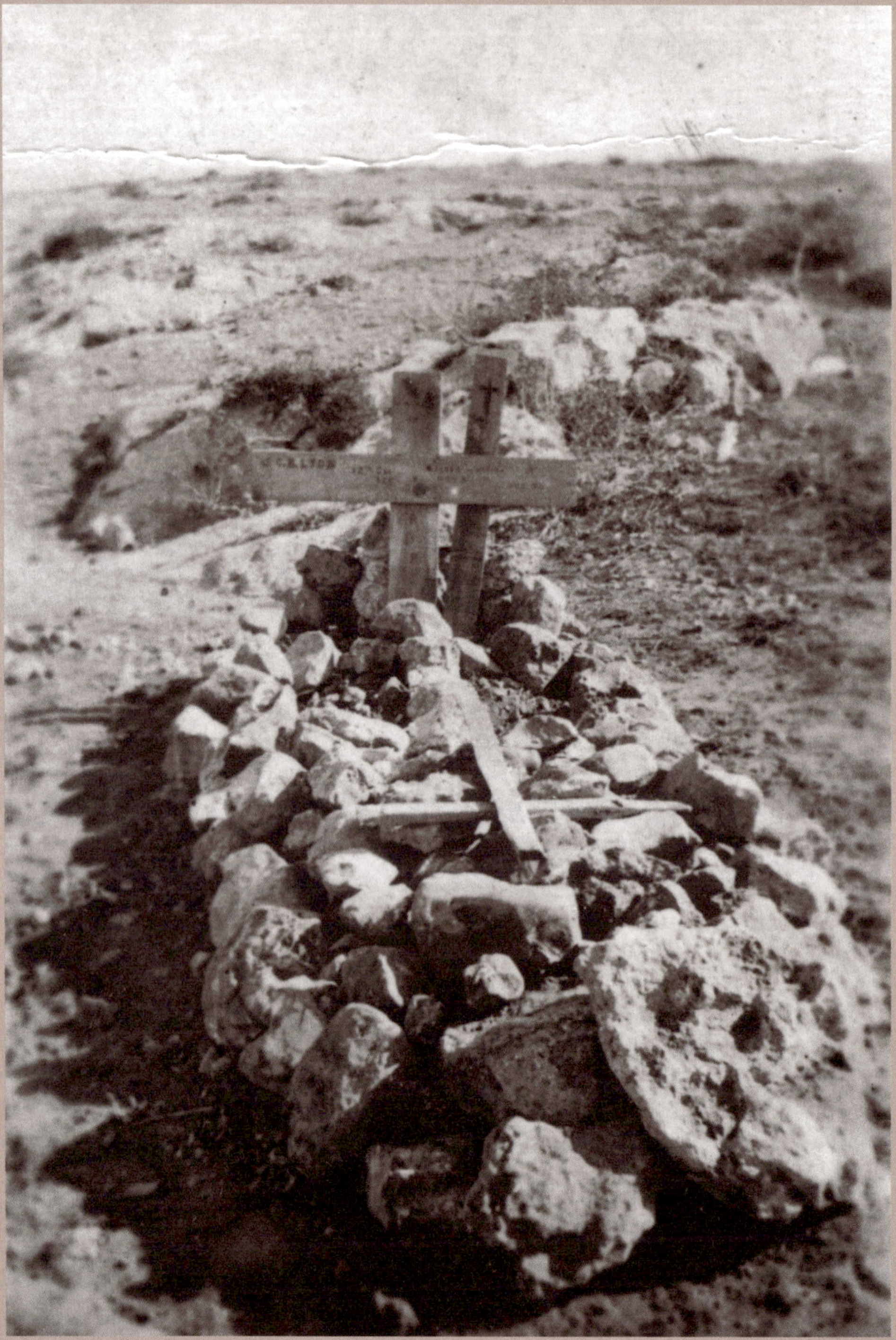

CHAPTER 9
'IN CHASE OF JOHNNY'
November 1917

The fall of Beersheba had opened the road to Hebron. As General Allenby had foreseen, von Kressenstein had moved troops across from Gaza to shore up his defences north of Beersheba. But Allenby did not want to draw too many troops east, so the 52nd Division attacked the Gaza outpost position of Umbrella Hill on the night of 1–2 November 1917. Allenby had to continue to confuse von Kressenstein because his main attack further west was delayed until the water supply at Beersheba could be consolidated. Meanwhile, one of the Turkish divisions in Gaza had been replaced, having first lost one-third of its strength due to the heavy bombardment.[1] Once Allenby's forces broke through at Tel el Sheria, Gaza would be in danger of isolation, making its final fall inevitable.

Meanwhile, Ryrie's brigade moved on Dhaheriye, on the road to Hebron. 'The country is something awful,' Ryrie wrote. 'Big gorges with steep hills & covered with flat rock very slippery, so here we are shelling them & they shelling us.'[2] On 2 November, Joe Burgess was with the 6th Light Horse in Ryrie's brigade advancing north on either side of the Hebron road. Once the light horsemen came under fire, they dismounted and headed up into the hills. 'We sighted the Turkish possie [position] on the hills and dismounted for action,' he wrote. 'Gosh, I'll not soon forget the climb over those hills, it was soon mafeesh [without] water.' Captain Alfred Thompson was killed at the head of his troop. 'I saw him fall,' Burgess wrote.[3]

Charles Livingstone was also with the 6th. 'I was posted on one side of the ravine with my Hotchkiss gun,' he wrote of the action on 3 November. His three-man gun section was isolated for more than two hours by enemy snipers. During the fight, Livingstone's No. 1 man, Geoff Warren,

'Poor old Charlie Lyon.' The grave of Lieutenant Charles Lyon, 3rd ANZAC Battalion of the Imperial Camel Corps. Lyon died on 9 November 1917 following the battle for Tel el Khuweilfe. His battalion had 22 men killed and 54 wounded in the fighting. John Davidson collection.

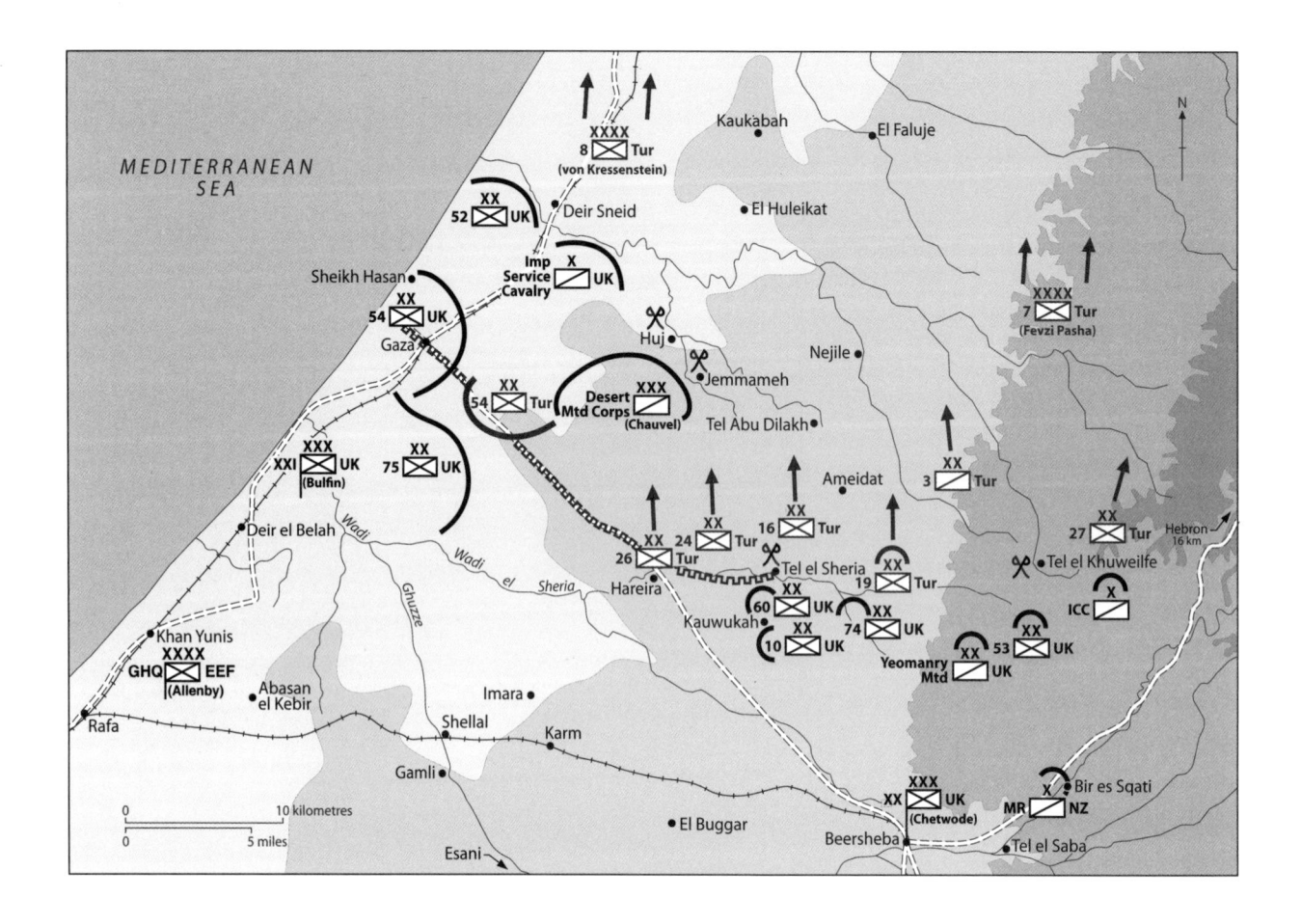

Map 5: The drive north

was killed by a bullet to the head and the No. 2 man was also killed, but Livingstone kept firing his gun, finally driving off the snipers. Meanwhile, on the other side of the ravine, Geoff Warren's brother, Ralph, had his leg broken by a bullet. As he was brought back he heard of Geoff's fate. Charles Livingstone was awarded a Distinguished Conduct Medal for his staunch bravery.[4]

Ion Idriess was with the 5th Light Horse moving up the Hebron road when the leading troop came under artillery fire from hill positions that commanded the road. 'That troop scattered like startled sheep,' Idriess wrote. Next day the dismounted light horsemen made their way up through the deep gullies to occupy hills on one side of the Hebron road along the valley, with the Turks entrenched atop the hills on the other side. Ion Idriess wrote of a section of four 6th Light Horsemen moving out ahead of the main force. 'At thirty yards range snipers opened out on them. One man got away.' The Ayrshire battery moved up in support but a black cloud rose around them as the Turkish guns got their range. 'But out of the black cloud came the gun flashes of the two little guns in reply,'

The type of barren hill country over which the advance on Dhaheriye took place. Harry Mattocks collection.

Idriess wrote. 'Then shell after shell burst above the guns . . . vicious hail . . . their screaming fragments striking the gun shields and wheels.'[5]

Next day, Idriess's section came under similar fire: 'Some men down, some horses were down, others rearing on their hind legs, one poor brute stood on head for seconds before it collapsed and rolled down the hill . . . screaming shells and a hail of jagged iron and lead . . . the Turkish guns were right onto us . . . the leaden hail just splashed down amongst us . . . one horse had his neck cut clean in half. Looking up the hill that evening, with its bloodstained rocks and dead horses, made a man think what a miserable, rotten thing this war is.' On 6 November, Ryrie's brigade moved back towards Beersheba with 'the almost paralysing wish for sleep'.[6]

Other mounted troops moved against the bare and dominating feature that was Tel el Khuweilfe, 15 kilometres north of Beersheba. On 2 November, Brigadier General John Wigan's 8th Mounted Brigade with Lieutenant Colonel Arch McLaurin's 8th Light Horse attached, moved on Khuweilfe. The light horsemen galloped up to the defences, but after coming under heavy fire took shelter among the rocks of the foothills. The 8th Light Horse kept at it until the men ran out of water and ammo. Harold Mulder was at Beersheba when the regiment rode in from the front after dark on 3 November. 'Dead beat and in an awful state for water,' he

Turkish forces watching the fighting near Tel el Sheria. George Francis collection.

wrote. 'Men and horses were out for 40 hours without a drop to drink and fighting all the time.'[7]

On 3 November, the infantry of the 53rd Division plus Cox's 1st Brigade were sent in against Khuweilfe. The light horsemen from Lieutenant Colonel Cecil Granville's 1st Light Horse dismounted and moved up on the Turkish left flank, where they found themselves isolated and many were wounded. 'Position very exposed & casualties heavy but hung on all day,' wrote Jim Greatorex, who was one of the wounded. 'Bullet cut through puttee on right leg,' was how he put it. Greatorex noted that these were the 'Heaviest casualties in regiment since 7 Aug on Gallipoli & hardest fight since Rafa'.[8] The regiment lost sixteen men killed, including three officers, while 43 men were wounded.[9]

'We were given no supports and only about two thirds of the Regt went into action,' Maurie Pearce wrote. 'The position proved to be far too extensive and formidable for us to take and we suffered a severe reverse. It was the most severe fighting I have ever been in. All our A Squadron officers were either killed or wounded.' Half of Pearce's troop were killed or wounded. 'I lost some of the best pals I have ever had,' he wrote of Oliver Hind and John Martin.[10] Les Horder, who was with A Squadron, found that the regiment was unable to get closer than 1000 metres to the Turkish redoubt. 'A good many horses hit,' he wrote. 'Had a job retiring at night.'[11] Maurie Evans, who was with the field ambulance, wrote, 'We were kept very busy all day under an intermittently heavy and fortunately erratic shellfire . . . the Turks have held us up.'[12] Jim Greatorex thought the shellfire was intentional: 'Turks fired deliberately on Red Cross causing considerable casualties in men & horses.'[13]

The infantry of the 54th Division plus the 3rd Australian Camel Battalion attacked Tel el Khuweilfe again on 6 November. They were supported by the 2nd Brigade Machine Gun Squadron, which had eight men killed and sixteen wounded in the unsuccessful attack. The Turks only evacuated the position after Tel el Sheria had fallen.

❖

With more Turkish forces moving east against the mounted troops, Allenby now let loose General Chetwode's XX Corps to strike north-west for Tel el Sheria and Hareira. Chetwode struck at Kauwukah at dawn on 6 November with three infantry divisions and the Mounted Yeomanry on the right flank. By 2.30 p.m. Chetwode's divisions had broken through and the Tel el Sheria railway station was captured late in the day. 'We set out for a five mile gallop to outflank the Turks,' Les Horder wrote. 'Took a good many prisoners all the way but had to pull up as the shells were too thick.'[14] John MacNamara went through later and wrote, 'there are any amount of dead lying about and they are all swollen and black from the sun . . . There were hundreds of rifles and bayonets lying about including same saw-edged ones.'[15]

With the loss of Tel el Sheria, the Tel el Khuweilfe fortress was now isolated and the way to the north was open to Chauvel's mounted brigades. They moved through, heading for water at Jemmameh and then Huj. Before dawn on 8 November, the 8th Light Horse left camp near Tel el Sheria and headed north. 'We left that morning and went in chase of Johnny,' Bill Smyth wrote.[16]

On 7 November, Major Percy Bailey's 11th and Colonel Don Cameron's 12th Light Horse crossed a wadi under fire north of Tel el Sheria. With difficult terrain ahead, Cameron dismounted his men while two squadrons of the 11th rode on before halting. But a troop of light

Getting water from a well near Tel el Sheria on 8 November 1917. Royal New South Wales Lancers Memorial Museum collection.

horsemen under Lieutenant Alwyn Brierty remained mounted as they advanced into heavy Turkish fire. All horses were hit and eleven men were killed, while all but one of the remaining ten men was wounded. Another 11th troop leader, Lieutenant John Bartlett, went out with a Hotchkiss gun and nine riflemen, and opened fire on the Turks before they too were targeted. Four of the ten were killed and three wounded. The two regiments hung on all day before being relieved by infantry at dusk.[17] The horses had had no water for 40 hours.[18]

❖

Following Chetwode's breakthrough, General Bulfin's XXI Corps had attacked a weakened Gaza on 7 November, taking Ali Muntar on the east side and advancing along the coast to the west. British troops finally entered the shattered town later that day. 'All day long large shells were bursting all along ridge from Gaza and further down towards Bir Sheba,' Edwin Brown wrote.[19] 'The sky is all aglow, the Turks have set fire to their dumps,' was how Maurie Pearce saw it.[20]

When George Hunt passed through Gaza a month later he wrote, 'Scene of desolation everywhere . . . In places cactus was torn out by roots with big shells . . . Holes made by monitor shells 10 feet deep, 12 feet across . . . Most houses half down.'[21] Robert Fell rode through two months later: 'Place in ruins and deserted. Shell holes everywhere. Buildings smashed and houses demolished. Went over to Turkish trenches at Umbrella Hill. They are blown to pieces.'[22] Frank Hurley, the Australian official photographer who had seen recent service on the Western Front, later wrote, 'Gaza is the Ypres of Palestine.'[23]

Maurie Evans noted that 'a never ceasing stream of big motor lorries with stores and munitions, batteries of guns, long lines of motor ambulances have been passing by.'[24] Pat Hamilton watched the same scene: 'Everyone pushing on, rushing on, hurrying on—staff cars, wireless, transports, camels, mounted troops. Turks retiring fast.'[25] Bill Smyth observed that all the transport

A mounted column moves under the demolished railway bridge across the Wadi el Sheria. George Francis collection.

114 AUSTRALIAN LIGHT HORSE

created dust 'six times as thick as any dust storm we had seen. In fact, the dust did not move . . . you could not see your hand in front of you.'[26]

When Cox's 1st Brigade advanced on the rail centre of Ameidat, north of Tel el Sheria, on 7 November, nearly 400 men plus significant stores and transport were captured. Cox wrote that 'although the enemy shell fire from both flanks was very persistent, this dashing move was carried out at the gallop until the objective was attained'.[27] Maurie Pearce was with the 1st Light Horse in the attack: 'We had a five mile gallop into the main Turkish dump. Had only slight skirmishing but succeeded in bagging nearly 250 prisoners.' The advance of the mounted troops had caused chaos. 'We passed hundreds of the enemy's transport wagons today abandoned by the roadside,' Pearce wrote. 'We had ample proof of the Turk's demoralisation today.'[28]

❖

Eager to interdict the Turks now pulling out of Gaza, Chaytor sent Ryrie's 2nd Brigade to attack Tel Abu Dilakh on 7 November. 'Away the whole brigade went full gallop out on to the plain,' Ion Idriess wrote. 'Presently up came the old Brigadier at a hard gallop, pipe alight.' The 5th Light Horse spread out behind the railway line and then, as Idriess wrote, 'away we went, full gallop towards the guns . . . it was a grand gallop'. Under heavy small-arms fire, the light horsemen found shelter in a gully before renewing the charge. 'In a dense cloud of black smoke and dust we spurred our horses up the bank,' Idriess wrote. 'The tearing whistle of machine-gun bullets at high pressure, straining hold on our maddened horses.' When the men and horses found shelter, Idriess wrote, 'At last panting horses and straining men out of the inferno into cover. Pools of blood were lying about.'[29]

It was getting dark as the men moved up the ridges towards the guns, which were withdrawn that night. On the following day the light horsemen chased after the guns until they were abandoned and captured. 'Squat solid little brutes they looked,' Idriess wrote of what were probably 4.7-inch howitzers. The light horsemen, including Idriess, stopped to fire at the retreating Turks: 'How great it was to see the spiteful spurts of dust kick the ground around their desperately moving legs.'[30]

It was not all one way; later that day the Turks counterattacked. 'We saw advancing towards us a long line of Turkish infantry,' Ion Idriess wrote. 'We just stood up and fired as fast as we could.' The Turks moved to outflank the 5th Light Horse on the right. 'Bullets were now coming

Troopers from C Troop, B Squadron, 6th Light Horse, advancing on Esdud. Reg Dixon collection.

like hail from two directions,' Idriess continued. His troop pulled back under fire, bullets 'whizzing past, kicking the dust in front all around and behind us'.[31]

All morning the light horsemen moved back as the Turks advanced until the 5th Mounted Brigade arrived about midday. Idriess watched as 'a long line of blue clad Turkish infantry' came steadily on, with other lines some 200 metres behind them: 'They looked simply grand those chaps, big blue men coming to push us off the face of the earth.' But the defence held. The 500 light horsemen held off about ten times their number. Idriess watched a textbook light horse attack on the Turkish infantry. 'Saw a squadron of our fellows gallop right up to the Turks, jump off their horses,' he wrote, 'swing their machine gun and rifle fire into the enemy while their horse holders galloped the horses back to cover.'[32]

The 3rd Light Horse entered Jemmameh on the afternoon of 9 November. Of most value there was a reservoir and pumping station, both captured intact. The horses of the two Australian brigades had now been without water for 50 hours and were taken to Jemmameh and Nejile to be watered.

❖

Hodgson now moved on Huj, where the 9th and 10th Light Horse came up against heavy opposition. Perhaps inspired by the Australian charge at Beersheba, a squadron of mounted yeomanry under Lieutenant Colonel Hugh Gray-Cheape charged an enemy gun position. As Captain Alan Alan-Williams wrote to his father, however, with the gun position protected by machine guns and infantry, 'it was like charging into hell.' The guns 'continued to fire until we were within 20 yards of them,' he wrote. Of the 50 men in the squadron, 33 were casualties, including Alan-Williams. More telling of the ferocity of the defence was the loss of 46 of the 50 horses that took part. The charging yeomanry captured four Krupp field guns, four 10-pound mountain guns, two 5.9-inch howitzers, three machine guns and more than 100 prisoners.[33] Arthur Mills went through Huj four months later and looked over the former Turkish stronghold. 'He was very strongly entrenched & had a wonderful field of fire,' Mills wrote. 'How we ever took it I don't know.'³⁴

On 9 November, Robert Fell wrote from Jemmameh of, 'Turks in full retreat. Saw fires of the dumps burning.' As the regiment moved to Huj, Fell saw 'Debris everywhere. Wagons along the road.'³⁵ 'We saw some awful things on the road,' Granville Ryrie added. 'Dead & wounded Turks and bullocks & horses in hundreds just killed & left in the teams harness & all.'³⁶ Despite the debris, the bulk of the Turkish Army had escaped. The lack of water and heavy Turkish resistance had kept their pursuers at bay. Most of the wells at Huj had been destroyed. The hardworking horses of the artillery batteries suffered the most. 'Some of the horses they have had to shoot for want of water,' Jeff Holmes wrote.³⁷

Out on the plain, thousands of Turks streamed north, but they were protected from cavalry charges by the German machine-gunners and Austrian artillerymen. Major Lewis Timperley noted that the Turks were in chaos but used their artillery and machine guns well. Without swords, Wilson's brigade could not ride down the Turkish soldiers, so his light horsemen had to stand off and pick them off with rifle fire. The 8th, 9th and 10th Light Horse harassed the retreating masses but could not stop them. Another 10th Light Horse troop, under Lieutenant Arthur Thompson, charged in; although stopped by machine-gun fire, the troopers were able to shoot up to 60 draught horses, denying the enemy the ammunition aboard the now-static wagons. A 5.9-inch and a 150-mm gun were captured by the brigade.³⁸

Chaytor moved his division out from Jemmameh on the morning of 9 November with Ryrie's brigade on the right flank. The 7th Light Horse was heavily shelled soon after leaving Nejile but moved on to Kaukabah, where 390 prisoners were captured along with 110 wagons. The Australian supply carts followed closely behind, ensuring the advance could continue. Among others who organised the supply network, Lieutenant Colonel William Stansfield, whom the official historian called 'the Queensland magician', had done his job very well.³⁹

Pumping water into horse troughs at Abasan el Kebir. A brigade of 2000 horses and camels could be watered in less than two hours using six spear point pumps each feeding a canvas trough. Claude Ballard collection.

During the drive north to Junction Station, Lieutenant Frank 'Towser' Nivison positioned his Vickers machine guns to shoot up 40–50 Turkish defenders, leading to the capture of the position. This photo shows Nivison's gun section in action during training. George Francis collection.

The German air arm was losing aircraft in the air and on the ground. At Huj the airfield hangars had been burned, along with seven aircraft—identifiable only by their frames. On 11 November, Leo Hanly passed through and 'saw skeletons of seven Taubes. Aeroplanes which had been destroyed by our airmen.'[40] 'Watered then lay down holding our horses and slept till daybreak,' Robert Fell wrote. 'Stench from dead Turks awful.'[41]

With only bucket and rope, it was difficult to get much water from the deep village wells. Reins and phone wire often had to be used to lower the buckets. The Turkish prisoners also suffered from the lack of water. Despite Chaytor's push, Ryrie got his brigade a day's break so they could water their horses before they began to drop. 'The water is very scarce and it is beginning to tell on the horses,' Robert Farnes wrote.[42] Ryrie moved his brigade to the coast, where spring water was found a metre down. For three days the men slept and swam in the ocean with their horses.

On 10 November, Cox's 1st Brigade moved on Esdud, the biblical Ashdod. 'I think they must have retreated in terrible disorder,' Jeff Holmes

A burned-out hangar and plane, probably at Huj. Harry Mattocks collection.

wrote. 'On one hill we saw the remains of a stubborn fight; dead bodies were strewed [*sic*] all over the ridge—all Jackos.' Holmes also passed about 30 abandoned gun limbers, all loaded with ammunition. 'This was a sad sight,' he wrote, 'as the enemy had shot all the limber mules through the head, and even some were knocked on the head by picks.'[43]

North of Esdud, the Wadi Nahr Sukereir was a formidable barrier, covered by Turkish positions in the hills beyond. On 11 November, Cox pushed his men across, Les Horder among them. 'Shrapnel fire very heavy but Scotties advance against it,' Horder wrote. 'By 4 Turks had been driven into one redoubt.'[44] Maurie Pearce was also there. His regiment teamed up with the Scottish infantry on their right and after 'having to advance over a thousand yards across flat country absolutely without cover ... attacked an entrenched ridge with redoubts'. Such actions took their toll. 'Our horses and men are getting worn out,' Pearce wrote on 11 November. 'Some of the horses are dropping dead.'[45]

The fluidity of the front meant the signallers were kept very busy. On 10 November, John Stephen, a 3rd Brigade signaller, wrote of how they

Watering horses from the village well at Esdud on 12 November 1917. Royal New South Wales Lancers Memorial Museum collection.

'IN CHASE OF JOHNNY' 119

'passed a long line of Bedouins running for their life with their belongings. Cause. Jacko put a couple of shells into their village.' The next day was 'dusty and windy resulting in hard work for visual signalling ... put through over 100 messages'.[46]

North of Balin, enemy reinforcements had arrived and there was a threat of a counterattack on the yeomanry there. The 8th and 9th Light Horse were sent in to support the yeomanry at nearby Burkusie Ridge, but about 4000 Turks finally drove the Australian regiments off. Harry Bostock wrote that 'the 3rd Brigade had a tough fight all day to hold it, and had to retire at night ... casualties in all regiments'.[47] Wilson pulled the brigade out and his light horsemen headed to the coast for a break.

On the coast north of Gaza, the infantrymen of the 52nd and 75th Divisions were almost level with Chauvel's mounted troops further inland. Air raids on the Turkish transport centres further hampered the enemy withdrawal. 'Yesterday we saw the finest sight we ever seen,' Jeff Holmes wrote on 9 November. 'At dinner time 20 of our planes passed over like a swarm of bees, to drop bombs on the enemy, and near dusk, 27 pass over on the same mission.'[48]

The Turks fell back on Katra and Junction Station on their right flank and Wadi Sunt south-west of Bethlehem on their left. The British infantry, led by Brigadier General John Pollock-McCall, attacked Katra. Brigadier General Charles Godwin's 6th Mounted Brigade then took over the attack towards El Mughar, charging on horseback from the coastal flank. Despite heavy losses, particularly among the horses, they took the position, along with 1100 prisoners and 22 machine guns. Harold Mulder went through Katra a few hours after the battle. 'The whole place was covered with dead bodies mostly Turks,' he wrote, 'tho we suffered pretty heavily.'[49]

A Rolls-Royce armoured car from the 11th Light Armoured Motor Battery. Ken McAulay collection. Courtesy of Margaret Smithers.

The infantry pushed on to Junction Station, where two armoured cars were the first into the town, capturing two trains and 45 motor vehicles. The railway line to Jerusalem was now cut, and on 14 November the 12th Light Horse entered a burning Et Tine (see Map 6) unopposed. Jerusalem lay beyond the hills to the east. Cox's 1st

Brigade headed for Ramleh via the Jewish village of Khurbet Deiran, with its red-tile-roofed houses, orange groves and abundant water. 'Locality very fine here & groves & orchards all over the landscape, truly a land flowing with milk & honey,' Jim Greatorex wrote. He also sampled the wine, which tasted like the 'nectar of the Gods'.[50] David Legge wrote that 'it's quite a shock to see pictures hanging on the wall and carpet on the floors again, especially out here'.[51] 'The streets are well kept and avenued with Australian gum trees,' Frank Hurley added.[52]

Lieutenant Colonel George Bourne's 2nd Light Horse entered Ramleh, on the main road from Jaffa to Jerusalem, on the morning of 15 November. 'A dirty sort of Gyppo [Egyptian] town,' was how Les Horder described it.[53] The 1st Light Horse headed further north to Ludd and then struck at the columns of retreating Turks. Two troops, led by Lieutenant William James, galloped along on either side of the fleeing Turks, braving rifle fire and shrapnel. 'We continued until we had headed the lot. Captured over 300 Turks,' James told Henry Gullett.[54] 'The Turks seemed absolutely tired out and too demoralised to show fight,' Maurie Pearce added.[55] Meanwhile, the New Zealand brigade captured Jaffa.

The capture of Junction Station had divided the Turkish 8th Army on the coast from the 7th Army further inland. Though the latter barred the way to Jerusalem through the Judean Hills, the loss of their supply line from Jaffa meant that their defence of Jerusalem would be a difficult task.

The barren country of the Judean Hills west of Jerusalem. 'The country is a series of great limestone hills, terribly rough and impassable but for the bridle tracks we have made,' Frank Hurley wrote. John Gorrell collection.

'IN CHASE OF JOHNNY'

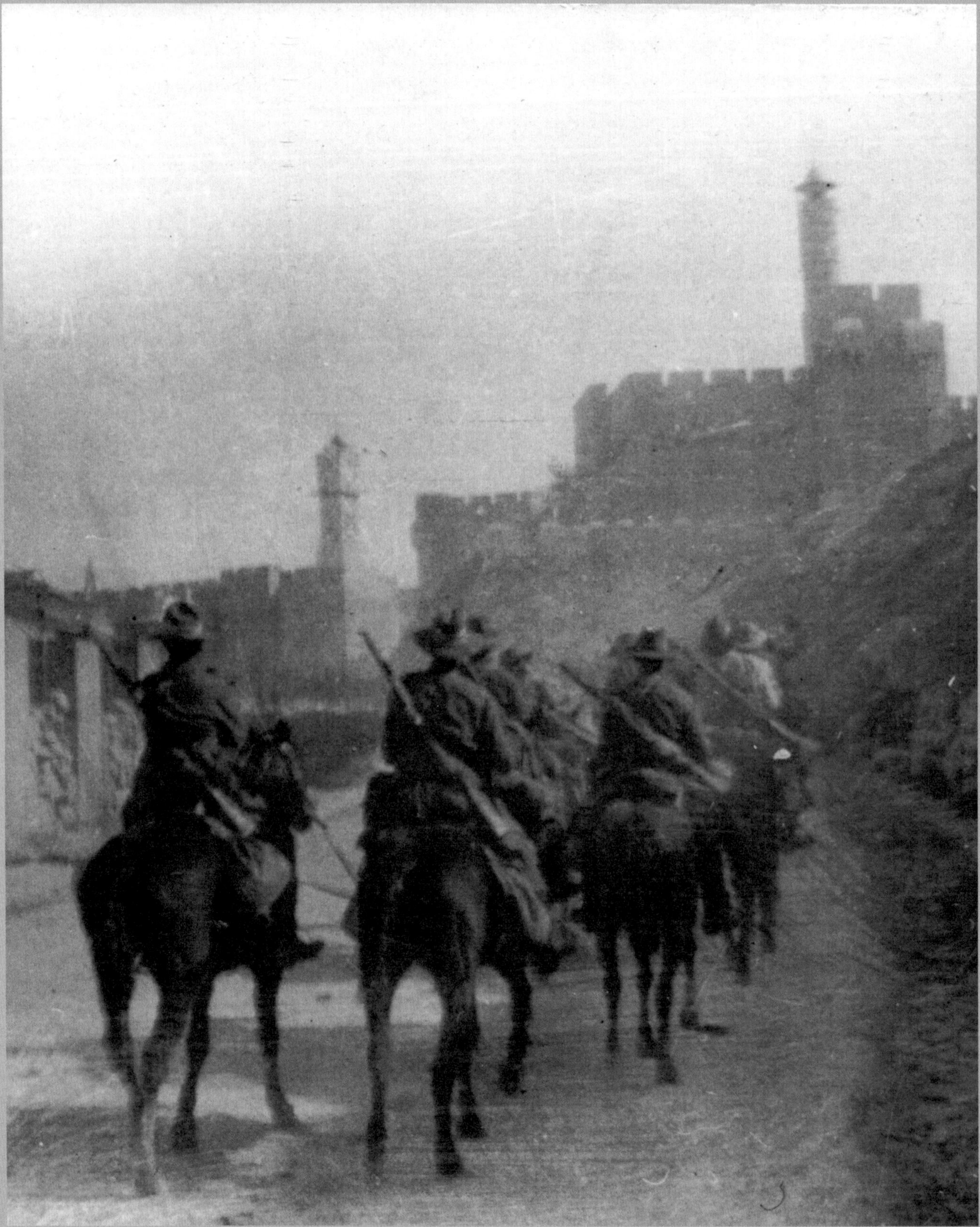

CHAPTER 10

JERUSALEM

November 1917 to January 1918

Although the British War Office supported General Allenby in his push for Jerusalem and beyond, the horrendous cost of the September–October Ypres offensive on the Western Front meant that he would soon be called upon to sacrifice some of his infantry divisions to that cause. Capturing Jerusalem would be no easy task.

On 18 November 1917, the Australian Mounted Division outflanked the enemy defences at Latron, 25 kilometres west of Jerusalem. While Grant's 4th Brigade made a direct assault, Wilson's 3rd Brigade advanced on the left, where the 8th and 9th Light Horse struggled forward over rough ground and, as the 8th's war diary noted, even the water cart broke to pieces and was abandoned.[1] But light horse patrols did get behind the Turkish lines and reach Yalo, about 6 kilometres east of Latron, causing the defenders at Latron to withdraw. On 21 November, the frustrated German staff officer Major von Papen wrote, 'now the VIIth Army bolts from any cavalry patrol'.[2]

For the final attack on Jerusalem, General Allenby's aim was to use the Yeomanry Mounted Division to cut the Nablus road north of the city and thus cut supply to the 7th Army defending the city. But the Turks took up strong positions astride the main road west of Jerusalem. 'The mountain where the Turks are, between here and Jerusalem, proved to be impassable for mounted troops,' Harold Mulder wrote, 'and we now have to wait for the infantry to come up . . . Jerusalem won't fall for a few days.'[3] The deteriorating weather did not help. On 19 November, the rains came and the nights got colder. That day Gordon Cooper wrote, 'Cruel night,

Light Horse troops enter Jerusalem. 'Every inch of the ground was interesting with some Biblical association and I sincerely regretted my lack of Testamental enlightenment,' Frank Hurley wrote of his visit there. John Gorrell collection.

Four wide-eyed Turkish officers strike a pose. Ralph Kellett collection.

rained incessantly.'[4] With the rain came the mud, slowing down operations and the vital supply lines that supported them.

Meanwhile, infantrymen from the 75th Division occupied Latron, but to the east the main road rose up into the mountains via narrow passes,

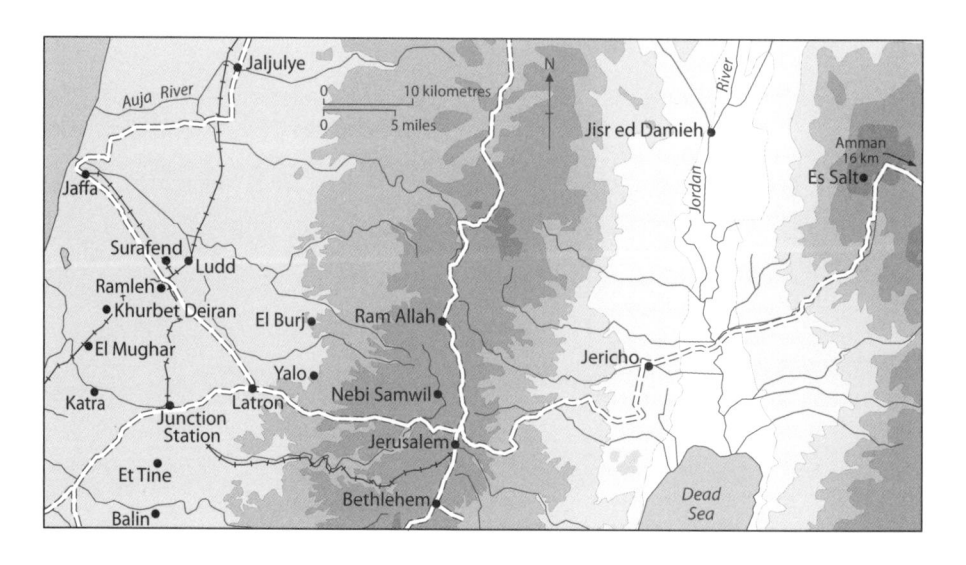

Map 6: Jaffa to Jerusalem

where any further advance could be readily stymied. North of the 75th, the Scots of the 52nd Division advanced into the hills over rough tracks that limited how many guns could be used. On the left flank of the Scots, the Yeomanry Mounted Division tried to reach the Nablus road but found the tracks near impassable and 'were held up alike by the difficulties of the terrain and the tenacity of the Turks'.[5]

The two infantry divisions kept at it and gradually forced the Turkish defenders back across the ridges towards Jerusalem, the 75th Division advancing under the cover of thick fog over the same country as King Richard I's crusaders in 1192. On 26 November the 60th Division, later joined by the 74th, relieved the 75th and 52nd on the front line. Though they had six infantry divisions in the line from Bethlehem to the Nablus road north of Jerusalem, the Turks were only just holding on while daily wasting away. Major von Papen wrote that 200 officers and more than 5000 men had been arrested in Jerusalem for desertion.[6] West of Jerusalem the Turks made three counterattacks on the British infantry at Nebi Samwil but each was held. On 30 November, Henry Langtip wrote, 'the Turks attacked at 3.00 this morning and the Scotties and Tommies knocked them back but suffered a good many casualties'.[7]

With the poor weather persisting, the British offensive stalled. 'A sea of mud and water all round,' Harold Mulder wrote on 21 November. Two weeks later, conditions were still dire. 'All our motor lorries and tractors are stuck all over the country and we're having a pretty bad time for supplies,' he added.[8] To keep supplies moving forward, 2000 donkeys were put into service. The decision was also made to switch the main focus of the offensive against Jerusalem from the north-west to the south-west.[9]

Meanwhile, north-east of Jaffa, Chauvel sent his forces across the Auja River on 24 November to prevent the Turkish forces on the coastal flank from moving to support Jerusalem. The desired outcome was achieved when Turkish forces counterattacked the Auja bridgehead that night. Further inland, the light horsemen

Leaving their mounts behind, the light horsemen move into the rugged Judean Hills, December 1917. Godfrey Burgess collection.

JERUSALEM 125

of the 3rd Brigade fought in the hills near El Burj as infantry, where the 8th Light Horse was prominent. On 1 December two officers—Captain George Fay and Lieutenant Vin Moore—were killed and another three wounded. As one of the men observed, 'there is no doubt the 8th is rough on officers'.[10] 'Jacko attacked in force . . . Our boys gave them hell,' John Stephen wrote of the attack. 'We appreciate this dismounted stunt as no horses to feed or water,' but 'it was hard work scrambling over rocks and boulders with all our gear and blankets slung around our shoulders'. Some days later, Stephen went back over the battlefield where some 65 Turks lay unburied, 'some with arms and legs blown off. Heads shattered, blood over everything. It was a sight not fit to be seen, but it brought to me the grimness and horror of war.'[11] Writing to his wife on 6 December, Granville Ryrie reflected the view of many of the troopers: 'I am sick of this fighting and goodness knows how much longer it is going to last.'[12]

The new push on Jerusalem began on 8 December. Again the British infantry was checked by the strong Turkish redoubts in the rugged hills west of Jerusalem. But with the capture of Bethlehem to the south on 9 December and mounting pressure from the north, the noose was tightened and the Turks pulled out of Jerusalem, the last troops leaving that same day. 'Gitmaya mejburuz,' was the cry across the city: 'We've got to go.'[13] As the Turks fled north for Nablus and east for Jericho, Governor Izzet Bey was one of the last to leave. Major General John Shea took the surrender of the city while the diverse population celebrated and welcomed the British Army, its presence ending some four centuries of Turkish rule. There were still Turkish troops on the Mount of Olives to the east, firing across the valley of Jehoshaphat, but they were soon cleared out at the point of British bayonets.

That afternoon, Major Charles Dunkley rode into the holy city at the head of his 10th Light Horse squadron. These light horsemen were the first Australian troops to enter Jerusalem. Robert Fell wrote of 'Great rejoicing at Jerusalem falling to us.'[14] Henry Gullett watched the 'amazing traffic' that had gathered on the Latron road up to Jerusalem: 'Caterpillars, motors, lorries, horses, donkeys, mules,

City parking lot, Jerusalem. Reg Dixon collection.

camels.'[15] These were all the trappings of an army in transition between different forms of horsepower.

General Allenby entered Jerusalem on 11 December, his path flanked by the wide variety of troops from all the countries under his command. 'Great masses of colour against the old grey stone walls,' Henry Gullett wrote. 'Troops very lean and worn but keen and exhilarated.'[16] Captain Hugo Throssell, the only light horseman to have been awarded the Victoria Cross in this war, commanded the ceremonial guard at the ancient Jaffa Gate. Eschewing any show of grandeur, Allenby dismounted and used the side entrance of the gate. Though the British Empire forces under his command had done all the fighting, no British flags were flown.

❖

Despite the onset of seasonal rains, Allenby was determined to push on north while the Turkish forces were still on the back foot. As always, the supply lines would be critical, and Egyptian labourers were immediately set to work on the Jaffa to Jerusalem road. Meanwhile, on the coastal flank, pontoon bridges were brought forward to help carry the advance

The 6th Light Horse passing through Jerusalem. Ralph Kellett collection.

A 12th Light Horse transport wagon stuck in the mud, Christmas 1917. Godfrey Burgess collection.

A group of 6th Light Horse troopers sits down to Christmas dinner in the holy land. Roy Millar collection.

over the Auja River. On the night of 20 December, following a very heavy bombardment that lasted more than seven hours, the Scottish Lowlanders of the 52nd Division crossed the pontoon bridges and advanced north.

On 27 December, Private James Duffy, an Irishman serving with the 6th Battalion, the Royal Inniskilling Fusiliers, went out with another stretcher-bearer to bring in a badly wounded man. The man with Duffy was then also wounded and his replacement was killed, leaving Duffy alone. Despite that, he was able to bring the first wounded man to cover and then the wounded stretcher-bearer, saving both lives. For his selfless bravery, Duffy was awarded the Victoria Cross.

With the onset of winter weather, the transport lines struggled to cope. With so much infantry in the line and supply difficult, the mounted divisions were withdrawn to obviate the need to supply fodder for the horses. On 22 December, Jim Greatorex wrote of 'country in very bad state mud and water everywhere'.[17] The 1st and 2nd Brigade moved to the railhead at Esdud, and at New Year the Australian Mounted Division was withdrawn back to Deir el Belah. On 6 January, Edwin Brown watched them march back: 'Black and wet mud, rain with water laying everywhere made it very miserable for them to travel.'[18] Stan Parkes wrote, 'When we marched out at 1000 it was pouring rain and almost a gale blowing which was bitterly cold, the roads were in an awful state and a number of wagons were stuck fast in the mud.'[19] There were also special moments that would never be forgotten. After a night when Frank Hurley was asked to talk of his Antarctic experiences to the men, he wrote, 'I felt, in the interest expressed on the faces around me, a reward for the tribulations of the South.'[20]

With the retreat of the Turkish forces to the north and the capture of Jerusalem, it was possible to resupply Colonel Lawrence's Arabs via a more direct route. Bert Inall was part of a camel convoy sent out to do just that. The camels were loaded up with ammunition and explosives and sent out, the convoy travelling by night and passing through rocky outcrops. The men made certain they had their Australian rising sun badges attached to their collars, and for good reason. When the last man in the line felt an arm around his neck during the night, a knife was held to his neck and a hand felt for the badge, thus confirming that the camel convoy was friendly. A tap on the head confirmed all was okay.[21]

When the camel convoy reached an oasis, the men in the convoy looked up at the sand hills around them and spotted groups of Arabs all around. With only one rifle between them, the men had no chance if the Arabs were hostile. 'We're fucked, we're fucked,' one cried out. Bert Inall, who was 26 years old and known as Pop, settled the men down as the Arabs advanced on them. It was Colonel Lawrence and a band of his Arab raiders. Their presence certainly made for a good photo.[22]

Some of Colonel Lawrence's Arab irregulars. Bert Inall collection. Courtesy of Barry Inall.

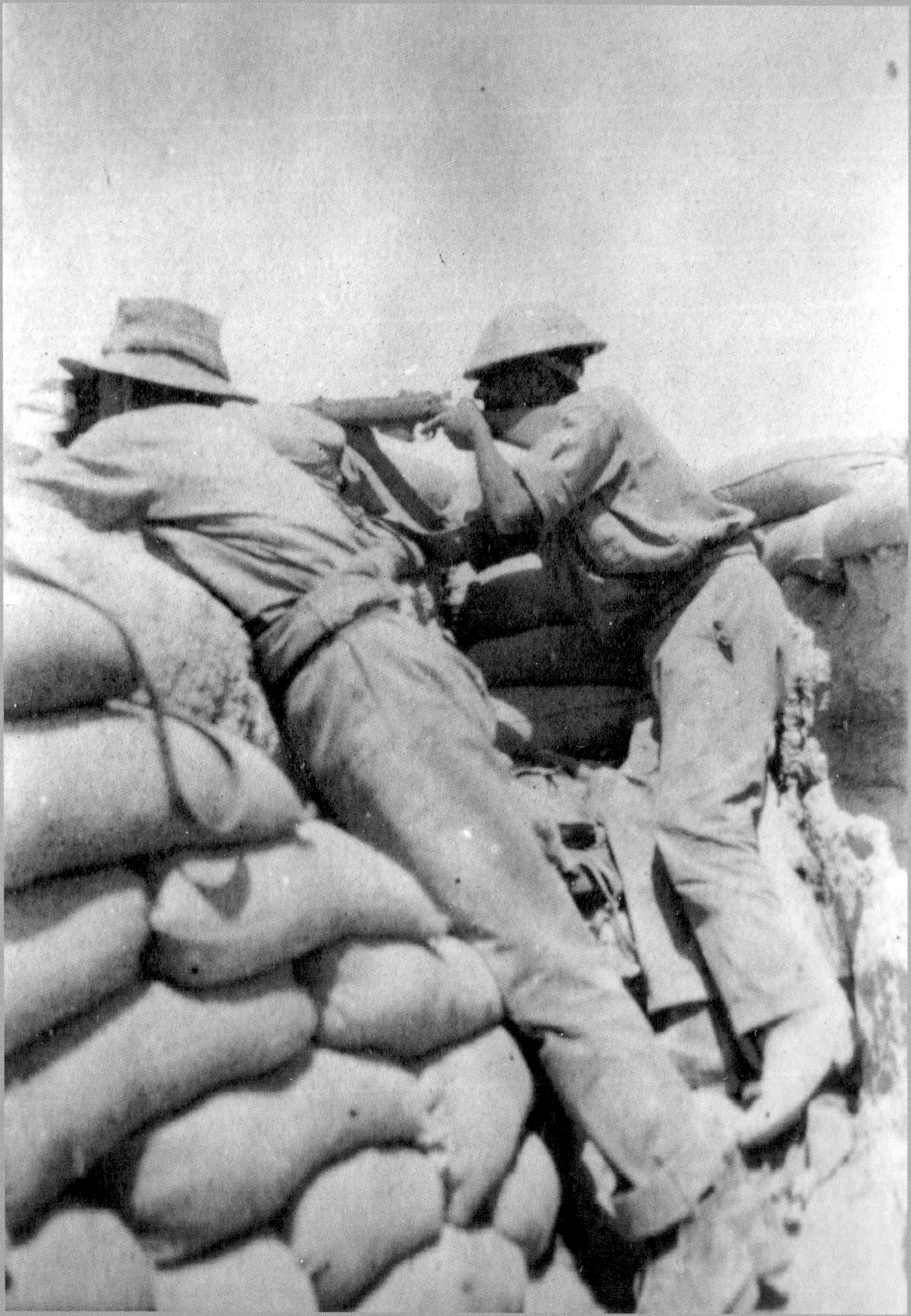

CHAPTER 11

'I CAN'T LOSE HALF MY MOUNTED TROOPS'

February to May 1918

After the fall of Jerusalem, General Allenby's next objective was to occupy the western side of the Jordan Valley from the Dead Sea to Wadi el Auja. General Chetwode's XX Corps was given the task, while the Anzac Mounted Division advanced from Bethlehem on the right flank heading for Jericho. The advance was via narrow valleys and mountain tracks, 'a gaunt place of fierce heat, strong winds, and blinding dust-storms, giving sustenance to neither man nor beast'.[1] The main enemy defences were astride the Jericho road, a 'track very rough and hilly' as Jim Greatorex described it.[2]

General Cox's 1st Brigade and the New Zealand Mounted Rifles Brigade concentrated at El Muntar some 10 kilometres from the Dead Sea. On 20 February 1918, the New Zealanders overran Turkish defences among the hills, thus opening the way for Lieutenant Charles Parbury's troop from the 1st Light Horse to move down the Wadi Kumran to the Dead Sea Plain. The rest of Cox's brigade followed and forced the Turks back from the Jericho road. Edwin Brown observed that 'Bridges blown away in several places caused a little delay.' At 8 p.m. the 1st Brigade was ordered to make a night march, 'passing down some very steep hills and gullies . . . and very windy till at last we come out on the flat side of the Dead Sea'.[3] Frank Hurley accompanied the brigade: 'At times the horses slid, more than walked down the steep rocky faces, and the only guide was the dim outline of the horseman ahead or the trail of sparks from the horseshoes.'[4]

The squalid town of Jericho was entered by the 3rd Light Horse on the morning of 21 February. 'A dirty little hole containing only one building

In the 6th Light Horse trenches defending the Jordan Valley bridgeheads. For sniping the men usually worked in pairs. Here Ralph Kellett is the rifleman on the right and Robert May is the observer. 'Our steel helmets were like ovens,' Sydney Barron wrote of his time in the valley. Ralph Kellett collection.

The Jerusalem to Jericho road winds its way through great waves of limestone at Talat ed Dumm. 'A bare barren place,' Granville Ryrie wrote. 'A sort of white chalky ground covered with stones, no grass or trees of any sort.' Walter Smyth collection.

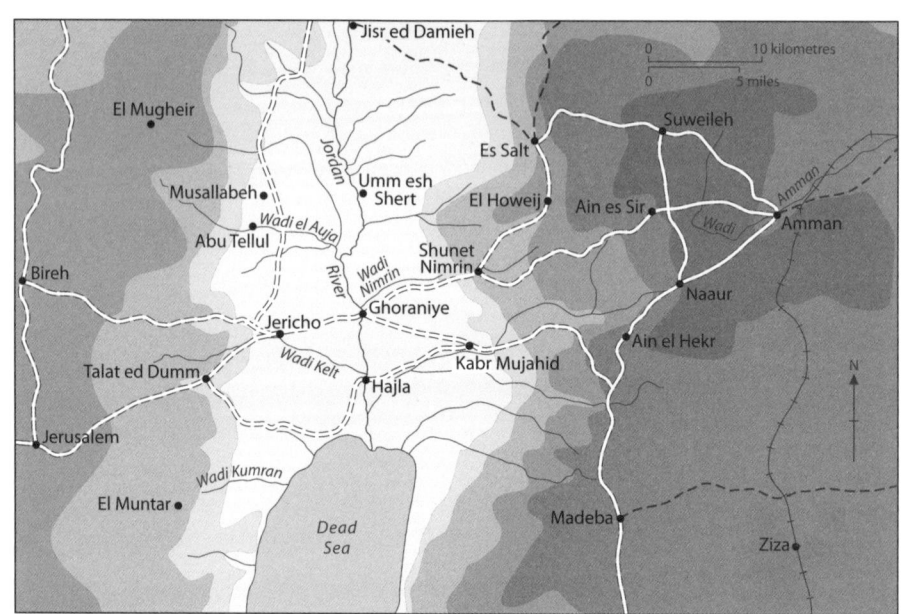

Map 7: Es Salt and Amman

Jericho locals. Reg Dixon collection.

132   AUSTRALIAN LIGHT HORSE

of any size ... the Jordan Hotel,' Maurie Evans wrote.[5] 'We captured only some 40 prisoners,' Frank Hurley added, 'wretched specimens of beings, unshaven, unkempt and hungry.'[6] Chetwode's infantry now moved forward to drive the Turks across the Jordan River. 'Their camps we could see at the foot of hills over the Jordan,' Edwin Brown wrote.[7] On the western side of the Jordan there were some imposing sights, such as the spectacularly sited Greek Orthodox Monastery of St George, hewn out of the cliffs of Wadi Kelt a few kilometres above Jericho. Nearby was the white Monastery of the Temptation, on Temptation Hill. Evans wrote that this was 'where JC was tempted by the devil and fasted 40 days etc'.[8]

On the night of 28 February, a Martinsyde aeroplane was transported to the western shore of the Dead Sea. The plane, which was nicknamed

The Monastery of the Temptation hewn out of the cliffs of the Mount of Temptation above Wadi Kelt. Reg Dixon collection.

Rushing a canteen in the Jordan Valley. Ralph Kellett collection.

'I CAN'T LOSE HALF MY MOUNTED TROOPS'

Mimi, the Martinsyde hydroplane on the Dead Sea. Wilfred Baker collection.

Mimi, was stripped of its wings and tail and fitted with floats, then launched before dawn to attack a fleet of enemy boats on the eastern shore. The hydroplane skimmed across the water until the rudder-yoke broke and it drifted ashore. The pilot then had the floats removed and converted to makeshift canoes, each to carry four men, but the men were unable to row close enough to the enemy boats to complete the mission.[9]

❖

A cart crosses the Jordan River on a barrel pontoon bridge. Six empty drums have been lashed into a wooden frame to create each pontoon. Reg Dixon collection.

Amman, 50 kilometres north-east of Jericho, was an important rail centre, with a rail tunnel and viaduct for the Hejaz railway nearby. Wanting to maintain the initiative, General Allenby ordered an operation against Amman to destroy the rail infrastructure and draw Turkish forces away from the coastal plain and the southern region. Major General John Shea would command a force based around his 60th Division, but floods delayed the crossing of the Jordan and the enemy rushed in reinforcements to hold the east bank.

By mid-March, the Anzac Mounted Division and the Imperial Camel Corps brigade had concentrated at Talat ed Dumm. The infantry of the 60th Division finally crossed the Jordan at Hajla on the night of 21 March, via a pontoon bridge constructed by the Australian engineers of the 1st Field Squadron. One of the engineers, Fred Bell, had swum downstream under heavy fire to position the stay cables of the bridge.

The New Zealanders crossed the Jordan and headed north up the east bank to clear the Ghoraniye crossing point, while other troops landed east of the Jordan estuary on the Dead Sea shore. In response, the Turks pulled back to the foothills around Shunet Nimrin, blocking the main road to Es Salt. The 6th Light Horse was the first Australian regiment to cross the Jordan, and the rest of Ryrie's 2nd Brigade followed. 'It is only a few yards wide and a couple of feet deep, bridged by a pontoon, and the banks, and even the stream itself was dense with foliage and made a pretty sight,' Jeff Holmes wrote.[10] The track that Ryrie's men followed to the east was barely suitable for led horses. Ryrie 'had to turn all limbers and carts back & it was soon evident that it was an almost impassable goat track'.[11] Rain made progress even more difficult, particularly for any camels. 'We climbed a hill, and slid down precipices and it beats me to this day how some of us never got killed,' Jeff Holmes wrote. 'We travelled awful slow, standing for hours in the cold rain.'[12]

A line of light horsemen bound for Es Salt. John Gorrell collection.

Cox took his 1st Brigade north but the supposed road really was 'a mere goat track'. Moving in single file, it took Lieutenant Colonel George Bell's 3rd Light Horse three hours to cover the first 5 kilometres. 'At one stage it was as much as we could do to get the pack horses along the narrow ledge,' Major James Clerke wrote. 'The ammunition panniers on the inside were scraping the rocky wall, while those on the off side hung over a precipice, from which was a sheer drop of hundreds of feet. Fortunately, the Turks did not expect us.'[13]

No opposition was encountered until mid-afternoon, by which time Bell's regiment had crossed the formidable range.[14] It may have been rough but, as Jim Greatorex wrote, the wildflowers gave the country the appearance of 'a veritable garden of Eden in places'.[15] Late on the afternoon of 25 March, Bell's 3rd Light Horse reached Es Salt, an old mountain town of 15,000 inhabitants west of Amman. Bell sent 80 of his dismounted light horsemen around the Turk lines at night, and when daylight broke they opened fire with Hotchkiss guns on three Turkish machine-gun crews. As a result, some 1000 defenders fled in panic and Es Salt was secured.[16] The light horsemen were particularly welcomed by some 4000 Christian residents of the town. 'The inhabitants seemed very pleased to see us, firing off rifles in the air and running amok generally,' Greatorex wrote.[17] British infantry arrived soon thereafter to occupy the town, while the light horsemen moved out to cover the approaches.

A Turkish machine-gunner dead at his gun. 'Out of time,' Godfrey Burgess wrote as the caption. Godfrey Burgess collection.

Meanwhile, Ryrie's brigade and Chaytor's New Zealanders headed for Amman. Arthur Mills led the 4th Battalion of cameleers across the hills. 'The track got slipperier, wetter and steeper,' he wrote. 'Lost quite a lot of camels, broken legs dislocated joints etc.'[18] Major Arch Bolingbroke led the 5th Light Horse in the absence of Colonel Cameron, and the regiment captured enemy motor lorries along the Es Salt to Amman road. But although the New Zealanders and cameleers were able to cut the railway line south of Amman, the 5th Light Horse could not do the same north of the town. The Turks held a strong position at Amman, with good observation for their artillery from the other side of Wadi Amman, alongside which the railway line ran. 'Very heavy machine gun fire,' George Hunt wrote of the enemy response. With 'no artillery to shift them from dominating position', Amman would not fall easily.[19]

When the 2nd Brigade, the New Zealand brigade and the cameleers advanced on 27 March, the Turkish fire was devastating. The attacks continued the next day and the casualties mounted. Granville Ryrie's brigade attacked dismounted and his cousin, Major Harold Ryrie of the 6th Light Horse, was badly wounded; within two years he would die of those wounds. Of the 58 men in Major Ryrie's squadron, 40 were killed, wounded or missing. Trooper Bert Scurrah was one of the wounded, shot through the spine and right foot, 'dangerously ill' as his service record put it.[20] 'It was a poor lot who lined the ridge just in front of our lines last night,' Joe Burgess wrote. Such dismounted infantry attacks were a long way from the glories of the mounted charges. 'Jacko is obstinate,' Burgess added.[21] The 7th Light Horse also suffered heavily—by the end of the day only 50 men were in the firing line. Arthur Mills's cameleers took part in an assault that night alongside the New Zealanders. 'At 0200 my boys fixed bayonets and charged the Jacko lines,' he wrote. 'We with NZ cleared enemy out of his sangar possies ... our boys did wonders they are all heroes.'[22] But the attackers were up against Turkish reinforcements that had arrived by rail from the north, and Amman remained in Turkish hands. General Shea ordered a withdrawal.

Cacolets were used to bring some of the wounded men from Amman back to Es Salt. Of these swaying platforms slung either side of a camel, the official historian wrote that 'It would be scarcely possible to devise a more acute torture for a man with mutilated limbs than this hideous form of ambulance-transport.'[23] 'The damnedest thing ever invented,' was how

Arthur Mills described them.²⁴ As an alternative, eleven wounded men were strapped face down on the backs of horses on a bed of greatcoats and got out that way. 'We put them on a horse back to front,' Mills wrote, 'put the man's feet in a water bucket hung from the horse's neck, laid the man's belly on the saddle and tied the man's hands together under the horse's flank.'²⁵ 'That night was the worst I had ever put in,' Granville Ryrie wrote. 'The cold was simply awful, we rode all night & got to Es Salt.'²⁶

There were a number of Circassian villages in this area. Many Circassians, who had been displaced from the northern Caucasus region by Russian forces in the 1860s and been resettled by the Turks, had strong sympathies towards the Turkish forces. 'The Circassians are openly hostile to our people,' Arthur Mills wrote. Emboldened Circassian villagers at Ain es Sir fired on the New Zealand rearguard, killing four or five.²⁷ In response, 36 Circassians were driven from their houses and killed. As the official historian observed, 'The retreat was not again molested.'²⁸

The Turks also increased pressure on Es Salt. The 3rd Light Horse fought hard to hold it, but although Colonel Bell thought it a mistake, the town was evacuated on 1 April. 'We imshied to near Es Salt today and

Refugees from Es Salt gather following the arduous trek to the Jordan Valley. 'All along we passed the poor unfortunate refugees trekking, walking, dragging themselves along,' Arthur Mills wrote. 'Men, boys, girls, women, old men, babies.' John Gorrell collection.

we were glad,' Joe Burgess wrote that day.[29] The Christians trudged back with the Allied forces in the wet and cold. Some of the light horsemen carried women and children up on their saddles. 'There were 3 or 4000 of all sorts and sizes and ages trying to carry all their worldly possessions and walk the 20 odd miles to the Jordan,' Granville Ryrie wrote.[30] 'It's crook to see the poor old folk struggling back,' Joe Burgess observed.[31] 'We did our best for the travelling myriads,' Ted Woods wrote. 'Our first two passengers were baby girls . . . we finished up with more civvies than soldiers on the transport.[32] 'Many of the boys had kiddies on their camels,' Arthur Mills noted.[33]

Though a stretch of the Hejaz railway had been destroyed during the operation, the Amman tunnel and viaduct remained intact; the operation had been a failure, with 1200 officers and men as casualties.[34] Jeff Holmes summed it up for most: 'It was by far the worst time I spent in my life.'[35] Granville Ryrie concurred: 'I never had anything like as rough a time since the day I was born.'[36]

❖

Utilising the natural hills and swamps, the light horsemen had added trenches, wire and cleared firing positions to form a strong defence around the three Jordan River bridgeheads, which now came under considerable Turkish pressure. 'Johnny has any amount of guns here now and nearly every morning wakes us up with his early morning drum fire,' John MacNamara wrote.[37] On 11 April, the Turks made a pre-dawn attack down the Wadi Nimrin against the Ghoraniye and Musallabeh bridgeheads. 'In the half light (0400) each burst could be seen like a small stroke of lightning,' Arthur Mills wrote. 'The echo booms and rolls along the rocky wadi.'[38] 'All through the day the artillery kept going,' Edwin Brown noted. 'About a thousand Turk troops had come down from the hills.'[39]

At Ghoraniye, the 2nd Light Horse defenders allowed the attackers to get within 100 metres of their positions before opening fire with their Vickers and Hotchkiss guns. Most of the attackers fell under this fire, and the few that reached the wire got no further. Colonel Cameron's 5th Light Horse also took a toll, as did the supporting artillery. General Cox wrote that the artillery dropped 'a perfect hail of shrapnel on the thick scrub', under the cover of which the enemy troops advanced.[40] The Turks withdrew that night.

At the Musallabeh bridgehead, Colonel George Langley's 1st Australian Camel Battalion was using stone sangars in lieu of trenches due to the

A German despatch rider makes room for a native cart on the road from Amman to Es Salt. Royal New South Wales Lancers Memorial Museum collection.

rocky terrain. The Turkish assault troops worked their way up the wadis while artillery fire kept the defenders' heads down, but the cameleers held them off. The bridgeheads remained secure.

❖

To support the Arab army operating to the south, General Allenby now decided to make a second attack on Es Salt and Amman. General Chauvel would command the force, which was based around his two mounted divisions with two infantry brigades, two Indian cavalry regiments and considerable artillery resources in support. Chauvel had been ordered by Allenby to make 'bold and rapid marches'. Under pressure to release up to 23 of his infantry battalions to France following the German spring offensive, Allenby wanted to gain the Amman–Es Salt area with a view to pushing on to Deraa and beyond before he lost most of his infantry.[41]

Chauvel moved the Australian Mounted Division across the Jordan on the evening of 29 April, covering the Londoners of the 60th Division in dust as the infantrymen prepared to attack the Turks at Shunet Nimrin. Sydney Barron later wrote, 'We moved off just after dusk, leaving our fires burning to deceive the enemy.'[42] Barron was with Grant's 4th Brigade as it advanced across the Jordan plain, attracting artillery fire once day dawned. 'Just on daylight Jacko discovered us and started to shell us from the opposite side,' Barron wrote.[43] Arthur Mills watched 'the mounted men working up the flat under the enemy big gun fire. Wave after wave in extended order galloping and trotting along as though on parade.'[44]

Continuing at the gallop, Grant's brigade suffered 23 casualties during the charge across the plain, six of them fatal. Wilson's 3rd Brigade followed Grant's and headed for Es Salt. 'Turks had the wind up. Star shells everywhere and heavy artillery opened at random,' Robert Fell wrote. 'We were white with dust after our night ride.'[45] 'We had climbed four thousand feet in the ten miles from the river,' Ron Kemp wrote of the subsequent move to Es Salt.[46] 'Words cannot describe that climb up, it seems a nightmare,' Stan Parkes added.[47]

There was no opposition until 3 kilometres west of Es Salt, where the Turks held hill positions, but these were soon taken by the dismounted troopers of the 9th and 10th Light Horse, before Lieutenant Charles Foulkes-Taylor of the 10th led the first troops into the town. They surprised a Turkish transport column trying to evacuate, forcing the carts off the track down into the wadi and taking 200 prisoners plus considerable material, including 28 new German machine guns.

Dawn in the Jordan Valley at Jisr ed Damieh on 30 April 1918. 'Just before battle,' Joe Bradshaw wrote as the caption. Joseph Bradshaw collection.

❖

Back down in the Jordan Valley on the night of 30 April, a force of some 4000 Turks crossed the Jordan River at Jisr ed Damieh and attacked Grant's 4th Brigade, threatening to cut the supply lines of the force at Amman and Es Salt. 'They looked like ants crawling along the white banks of the Jordan,' Bill Smyth wrote.[48] Grant was forced to pull his brigade back to defend the track to Es Salt, abandoning nine guns as he went. 'Breech blocks and sights removed, guns abandoned,' Henry Gullett wrote. 'A wild galloping chaos, every man for himself.'[49] Chauvel ordered up reinforcements.

Meanwhile, Ryrie's 2nd Brigade and a brigade of mounted yeomanry had also reached Es Salt. But the Turkish breakthrough at Jisr ed Damieh compelled Chauvel to concentrate on opening the Es Salt road at Shunet Nimrin rather than pushing on towards Amman. Shunet Nimrin had proved impregnable from the valley side, so the yeomanry, supported by part of Ryrie's brigade, were directed to attack the stronghold from the rear. Infantry from Shea's 60th Division also moved up to support the operation, and for five days in stifling heat the Londoners battered at the defences without success. 'The road wound through a gorge between hills which rose tier upon tier in rear, making a most effective position for observation and gun fire,' James Clerke wrote.[50]

The road through Wadi Nimrin. John Gorrell collection.

Meanwhile, Wilson's brigade adopted defensive positions around Es Salt. The 10th Light Horse was attacked on the night of 2 May but cut down hundreds with minimal loss. It was now three days since the crossing of the Jordan, but supplies were plentiful in Es Salt and there was good grazing country around the town. The 5th Light Horse, with the 8th and 10th alongside, now came under attack but drove the Turks back, capturing 319 prisoners. Some 200 more attackers were left dead in front of the Australian positions. Robert Fell was in the thick of the fighting with the 10th: 'Fighting very close. I do some bombing, crawled out in front and settled a machine gun and crew.'[51]

But with Shunet Nimrin still in Turkish hands, Chauvel, after conferring with Allenby, ordered a withdrawal late on the afternoon of 3 May. 'I can't lose half my mounted troops,' Allenby conceded.[52] 'We withdrew at night and got out through the pass,' Granville Ryrie wrote. 'It took some doing to get 5000 horses & men out in single file, if you allow 3 yds per horse it makes a column 8 miles long or more.'[53] Once again, the wounded suffered greatly during the retreat. Of two badly wounded men who were left behind at Es Salt, one later died but the other, Corporal William Simms, was found alive in a hospital at Aleppo five months later. Arthur Mills watched the light horsemen return. 'They came as fast as their tired animals could carry them,' he wrote. 'We could see them scurrying down the mountain track and across the flat.'[54] Back down in the Jordan Valley, Grant's men took a hammering but, with timely reinforcements, they kept the Turks at bay.

As with the first Es Salt 'raid', this second operation, despite the extraordinary dash of Grant's and Wilson's brigades, had ended in apparent failure. When General Allenby motored down to the valley to see Chauvel after the action, Chauvel expressed his regret at the operation's failure. 'Failure be damned. It has been a great success!' Allenby replied and said he would explain later.[55] He did so in a letter to a friend in London: 'Nothing much doing here, for the moment, but my big raids beyond the Jordan have drawn Turks against me, and have eased pressure on the Arabs further south.'[56] The two operations would prove crucial to the outcome of the war in the Middle East. As Allenby observed, they had the effect of forcing the Turkish command to direct more attention to the Amman area, and Allenby would subsequently exploit this in dramatic fashion.

❖

A ship ablaze at Port Said. John Gorrell collection.

In this war there were many ways to die, such as at Port Said on 10 January 1918. 'Explosion on ship laden with Benzene, soon on fire,' Alf Sly wrote. 'One poor unfortunate caught up in port hole—terrible death.'[57] Norm Garden also watched. 'The flames were mountains high and the smoke black as ink,' he wrote. 'Her stern was blown away.'[58]

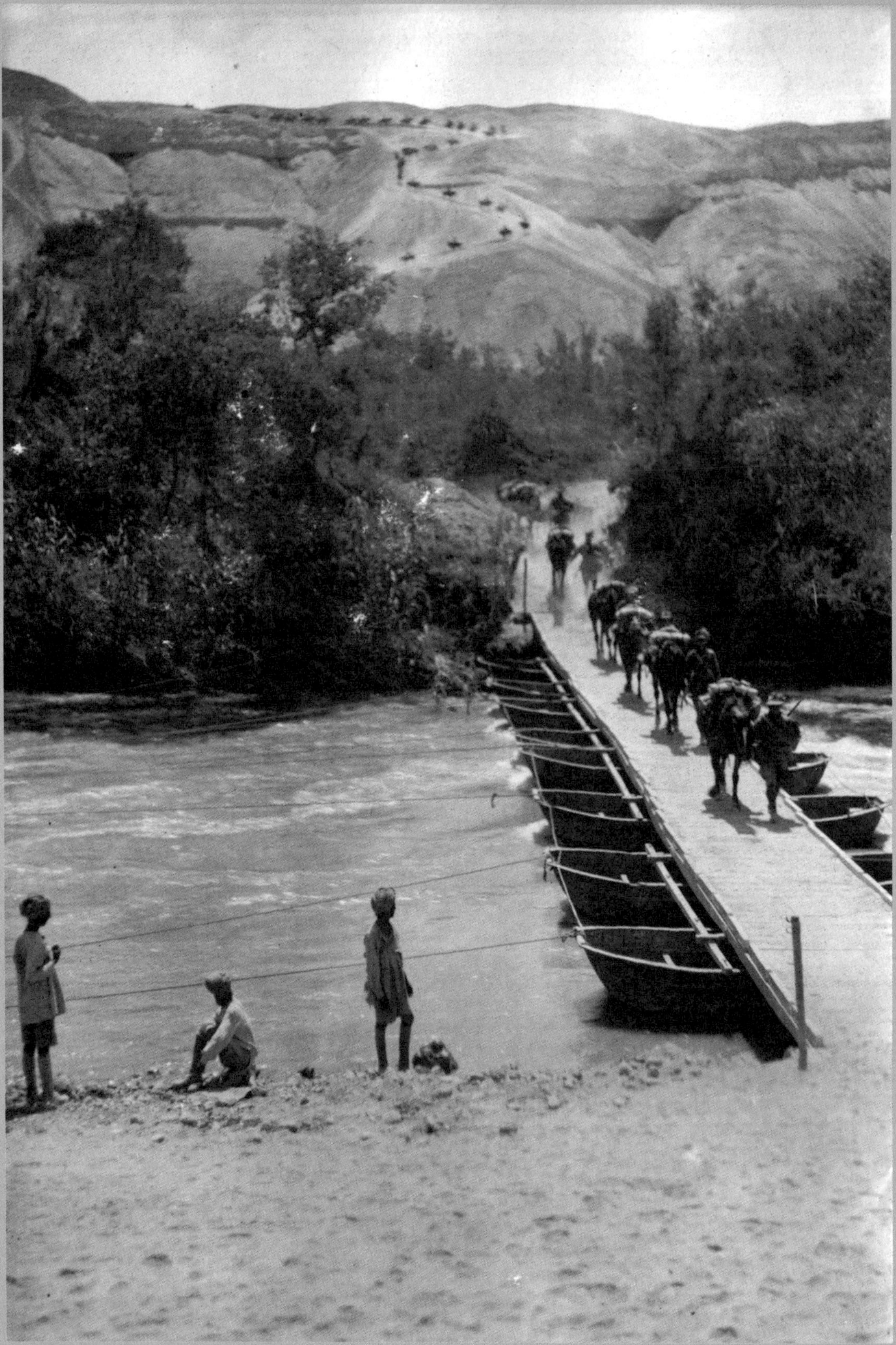

CHAPTER 12

FROM HELL TO ARMAGEDDON

May to September 1918

The lower reaches of the Jordan Valley were near uninhabitable in summer. 'Hell's Lid' was an apt description. William Cameron later wrote of 'a windless, mountain-walled world of dust and desolation, a thousand feet below sea level'. The dust, 'as fine as flour . . . rose in choking clouds with the slightest breath of wind . . . and when there was no dust there was the terrible blinding sunlight . . . Nightfall brought the mosquitoes. They came in battalions, in divisions and in army corps.'[1] Sydney Barron reported that 'During the day we were pestered with sand flies and at night by myriads of mosquitoes.'[2] The men worked hard to reduce any standing water and drain the swamps to limit the malaria menace.

The dilemma facing General Allenby in giving up the east-bank bridgeheads and withdrawing from the valley was that such a move would put at risk his plans for his next campaign. 'I must keep troops all the summer in the Jordan as I have to control the crossings and to secure command of the Dead Sea otherwise my Arab allies on the Hejaz railway would be abandoned to the Turks,' he wrote.[3] It would take the toughest of troops to survive a summer in the Jordan Valley, and therefore General Chauvel and his light horsemen got the job.

The Australian cameleers of the Imperial Camel Corps were now given horses and formed into the 14th and 15th Light Horse regiments, part of the 5th Brigade. The third regiment in the brigade would be of French colonial cavalry. After a training period, the brigade came under the command of Brigadier General George Macarthur-Onslow. 'Camel corps finish,' Arthur Mills noted on 4 June.[4] Mills wasn't finished; he would be given command of the 15th Light Horse.

A line of light horsemen descends the distant hills to cross a pontoon bridge over the River Jordan. Ralph Kellett collection.

A light horse camp in the Jordan Valley. The river runs below the cliffs. Ralph Kellett collection.

The onset of May 1918 brought a more intense heat and a finer dust. 'It's been a terrible day, wind and dust, our eyes are nearly cut out of our heads,' Joe Burgess wrote on 4 May.[5] It got worse. On 11 May, Robert Farnes added, 'The worse [sic] day we have had so far, very hot and the dust something terrible.'[6] Henry Gullett called it 'this threshold of hell'.[7]

As summer progressed through May into June, the suffering continued. Stan Parkes called it 'the worst place I have ever been in, heat, rocks, flies, dust'.[8] 'For heat, mosquitoes, dusts and pests of all nature I do not believe the Jordan Valley has any parallel,' Maurie Pearce added.[9] 'Eating, living and sleeping in dust and dirt,' Robert Fell wrote on 22 May, 'eaten alive with mosquitoes every night. Men going away with malaria every day . . . Jordan Valley an absolute nightmare.'[10] 'Spare me days, they are murderous,' Ted Dengate wrote. 'I never saw anything like it, they can sting one through the pants.'[11] 'One after another went down to malaria,' Sydney Barron observed, 'till there were only a handful of us left.'[12] General Allenby did what he could. 'I am draining, clearing and burning, under expert direction,' he wrote on 7 June, 'and I hope to improve things greatly.'[13]

The summer heat didn't let up. 'The hottest day we have had, 120 degrees [49 degrees Celsius] in shade,' Robert Fell wrote on 13 June.

'Felt absolutely knocked out with the heat.'[14] Two days later it was 52 degrees Celsius. 'There's no wonder they didn't keep the promise and stick to it,' Ron Kemp wrote of the fabled Promised Land.[15]

When it became obvious that the horrendous conditions would not force Chauvel's men out, the enemy tried force. Following heavy artillery fire, German troops attacked at Abu Tellul before dawn on 14 July. 'The Turks opened up all their guns and put it into us as hard as they could,' Robert Farnes wrote.[16] But the Turkish troops apparently didn't follow their German allies. 'When the Germans got well in the Turks left them to it & didn't support them,' Granville Ryrie wrote. 'It is good to have bad blood between them.'[17] There were heavy attacks on the outposts of Colonel Bourne's 2nd Light Horse, and Vale Post fell as the 'enemy swarmed into position', but the other outposts held despite three of them being cut off.[18] Daylight revealed some excellent enemy targets for the light horse machine guns. 'When the Germans looked behind them for

Jordan Valley dust. 'The ground was like flour by the time we had been there a few weeks, and our faces were covered with a white dust,' Charles Livingstone wrote. Ralph Kellett collection.

FROM HELL TO ARMAGEDDON

Inside a dugout at Vale Post in the Jordan Valley. Royal New South Wales Lancers Memorial Museum collection.

their supports they saw the 1 Brigade charging from behind them,' Maurie Evans wrote.[19] Bourne's light horsemen were magnificent, and Henry Gullett later noted that their effort was 'never excelled in the career of the light horse'.[20] General Cox then sent in Colonel Granville's 1st Light Horse, simply telling the commander, 'Get to them, Granny.' The charge broke the Germans, who 'ran about like a lot of mad rabbits'.[21] Slashing work with the bayonet finished the affair. 'A decisive win for the LH,' Edwin Brown wrote. 'Terrible punishment was dealt out by the artillery & MG. About six hundred prisoners were taken.'[22]

❖

Most of General Allenby's infantry divisions had now gone to France, replaced in the main by Indian reinforcements. Nonetheless, he had been able to gather seven complete infantry divisions and a strong artillery arm. 'There is a huge concentration of artillery going on along this sector of the front,' John MacNamara wrote on 13 September.[23] General Chauvel now had four mounted divisions under his command. As with the infantry, those British mounted troops that had departed for France had been replaced by Indian cavalry. His two Anzac divisions had suffered the horrors of the Jordan Valley summer and both the men and horses were in poor condition, but with his troops rested, good lines of communication and superiority in the air, Allenby looked on the upcoming campaigning season with confidence. The 135,000 men of the Egyptian Labour Corps had done a sterling job building up the railways, roads and other infrastructure to a state that could support the deployment of his force.

Three armies under General Otto Liman von Sanders, who had replaced von Falkenhayn, opposed Allenby—the 4th, 7th and 8th Armies, the latter two west of the Jordan. Von Sanders had more than 75,000 Turkish troops under his command, interspersed with German and Austrian artillery and machine-gun units. But this force was in poor shape. The railway system was overburdened by carrying supplies for both the

Indian troops moving up. Wilfred Baker collection.

Palestinian and Mesopotamian fronts, while the road system was very poor, exacerbated by a lack of motor transport. Troops invariably had to be marched rather than transported. General von Sanders had barely the equivalent of a brigade of cavalry available, some 3000 mounted troops in all. This lack of mounted troops and the immobility of his infantry would severely hamper von Sanders' response to Allenby's coming offensive.

Allenby's plan was to breach the Turkish line on the Plain of Sharon with his infantry and then move Chauvel's mounted corps through. As at Beersheba in the previous campaign, an effective deception plan would be integral to success. This time Allenby would feint in the west towards Es Salt and Amman, convincing the enemy that the troops in the Jordan Valley were being increased for such a move when in fact they were being reduced. Meanwhile, Colonel Lawrence also stepped up raids by his Arab army to the south of Amman, and this ensured that significant Turkish forces would remain in that area. As part of the deception in the Jordan Valley, 15,000 dummy horses were built, while dust was stirred up by day and camp fires lit at night. 'They keep moving the brigades from place to place, in each case leaving wooden horses standing on the old horse lines,' Maurie Evans observed.[24] 'The idea was to fool the enemy planes, flying over, by making as much dust as possible by galloping our horses between

FROM HELL TO ARMAGEDDON

German repair works at El Afule. Royal New South Wales Lancers Memorial Museum collection.

the rows of dummies, dragging bushes,' Charles Livingstone wrote.[25] On 16 September, General Chauvel moved his headquarters from Talat ed Dumm to Jaffa, though the old camp was left standing and the camp fires still burned at night. The deception plan worked. A captured German intelligence map from 17 September showed Chauvel's mounted force still concentrated in the Jordan Valley. A strong Royal Flying Corps presence helped deny von Sanders vital intelligence on Allenby's movements. 'Our air superiority is overwhelming,' John MacNamara wrote on 19 September.[26]

Allenby's great offensive began on 19 September. Four

150   AUSTRALIAN LIGHT HORSE

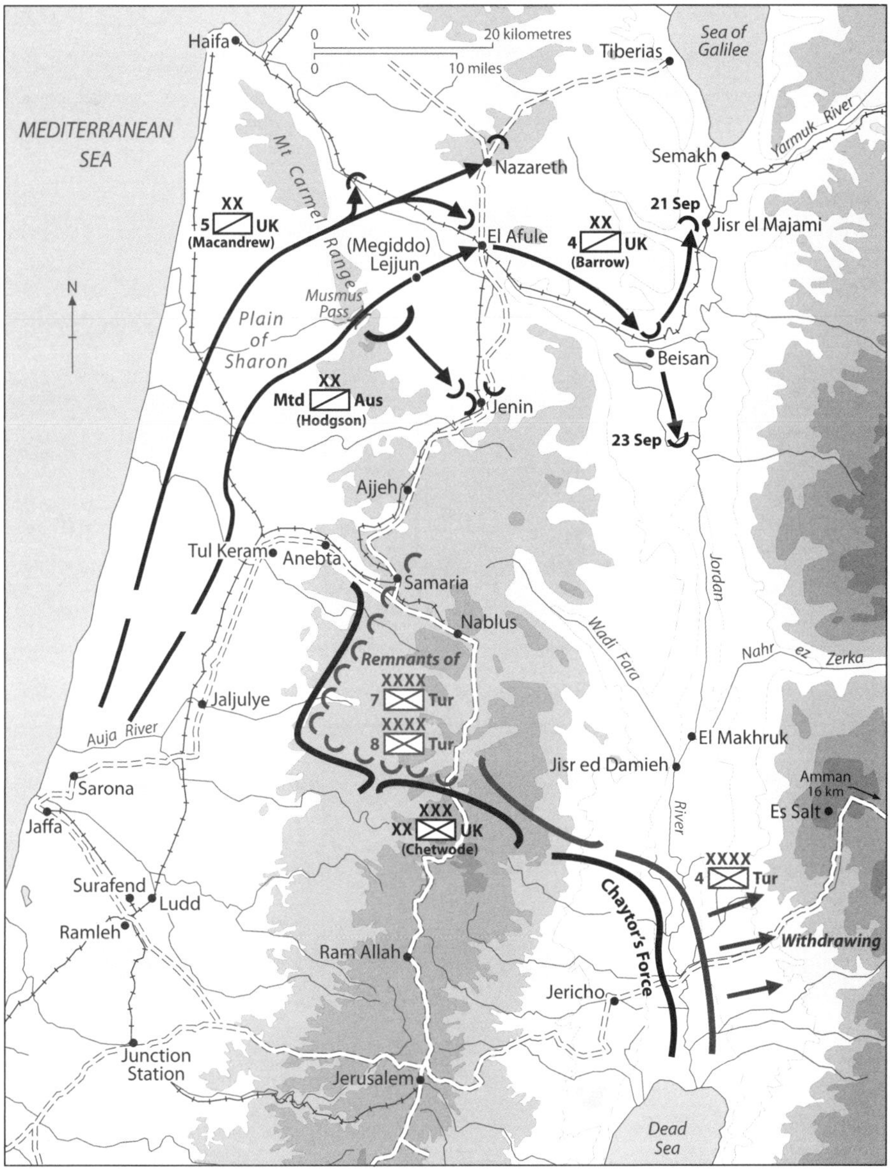

Map 8: The battle of Megiddo

infantry divisions made the initial attack, with three mounted divisions waiting to exploit any breach. Heavy air attacks hit the enemy headquarters, railway junctions and aerodromes in the rear, while 300 artillery pieces battered the forward enemy defences with a short yet sharp pre-dawn barrage. 'This barrage held Jacko to his ground and enabled the infantry to get right up with very few casualties,' Arthur Mills wrote. 'We followed on behind.'[27] The shaken defenders found the Indian infantrymen already upon them as the barrage lifted, and the first line of trenches was rapidly taken. The second line soon followed, the defences shattered.

OPPOSITE, BOTTOM
A line of dummy horses set up in the Jordan Valley. 'We used to take turns camping in a dummy camp made up out of sticks, bags and straw to represent rows of horses,' Charles Livingstone wrote. John Gorrell collection.

FROM HELL TO ARMAGEDDON

The Australian Mounted Division moved up from Ludd to Sarona and then passed through the Londoners of the 60th Division. Further inland, Major General George Barrow's 4th and Major General Henry Macandrew's 5th Cavalry Division moved unimpeded in parallel columns towards the vital mountain passes. Barrow's division passed through Musmus Pass in the night onto the Esdraelon Plain at Megiddo, the ancient battlefield site of Armageddon. Macandrew's division got through further north and headed for Nazareth. It was a stunning coup, securing the two mountain passes where even a single machine gun could have held up the advance for days. An enemy force sent to close the passes was too late and was caught out in the open by the Indian lancers, losing 46 men killed before the remaining 470 surrendered.[28]

El Afule fell and Nazareth, where Liman von Sanders had his headquarters, came under imminent threat as the advance continued through the night. Next morning a convoy of 70 trucks was overtaken and captured before it could enter Nazareth. 'Yeomanry galloped through narrow Nazareth streets before sunrise awakening amazed population,' Henry Gullett wrote.[29] Von Sanders managed to escape down the Tiberias road,

A ten-minute rest for the horses during the advance. John Gorrell collection.

An abandoned German vehicle near Beisan. George Francis collection.

but some 2000 rear-area personnel were captured. Meanwhile, General Chauvel moved up to Megiddo by motor car and ordered Barrow's division to head south-east to Beisan. Its capture had seen Barrow's men cover 130 kilometres in 34 hours of constant riding, an extraordinary achievement.

With the cavalry now in their rear cutting communications and supplies, the Turkish armies in the west would soon wither. They began to withdraw. Macarthur-Onslow's 5th Brigade moved through onto the plain west of Tul Keram in the wake of the Indian infantry. 'The horses in front of me swerve to the right to clear some object on the ground,' John Lowe wrote. 'An enemy shell has exploded in a group of our infantry. They are Indians—eight of them . . . I steel myself to meet what lies ahead . . . I can still hear the shrapnel screaming . . . small groups of Jackos pop up from the long grass waving dirty white rags.'[30] Three kilometres west of Tul Keram, Lieutenant Colonel Arthur Mills's 15th Light Horse came across some 300 Turks deployed across a line of hills blocking the advance. 'As soon as they saw us line up to charge they fled in all directions,' Mills wrote.[31]

By 6 p.m. on 19 September, Macarthur-Onslow's brigade had captured fifteen guns and 2000 prisoners. Ajjeh was next to fall to Macarthur-Onslow's light horsemen, following a night ride across rugged country. 'Rough roads, loose stones, steep hills and narrow goat tracks all helped to string the brigade out and delay the march,' Arthur Mills wrote.[32] Two squadrons from the 14th Light Horse under Colonel Langley reached Ajjeh at 7 a.m. on 20 September, cutting the railway line between Nablus and Jenin. The two farriers with the 15th Light Horse 'worked 36 hours without a break attending to horses that had lost their shoes in this

A group of light horsemen leaves a group of resting Turkish prisoners in their dust near Megiddo. 'Poor devils are footsore, tired and hungry,' Arthur Mills wrote. Ralph Kellett collection.

march'.[33] Such men were as vital to victory as any rifleman. Meanwhile, two divisions of Chetwode's infantry moved on Nablus. On 21 September, Macarthur-Onslow's brigade supported by armoured cars moved up the Vale of Barley through Anebta to support the attack. The Turks soon evacuated Nablus, and Macarthur-Onlsow was then directed to join up with the rest of the division at Jenin.

Chauvel had sent the 3rd Brigade to Jenin on 20 September. The 9th and 10th Light Horse led out and reached Jenin in the late afternoon. The 10th attacked an enemy camp during the approach, capturing 1800 enemy troops plus 400 horses and mules. With only 23 men from his machine-gun squadron, Lieutenant Reg Paterson captured a column of 2800 troops and four guns that were moving along the Nablus road, while another 8000 prisoners were taken in Jenin. 'Great stores of champagne, wine, rum, spirits, food and gold,' Robert Fell wrote. 'Scarcely a shot fired.'[34] Next day the 8th Light Horse marched the mass of prisoners back to Megiddo. Those retreating columns that were untouched by the ground forces suffered destruction from the air.

On 20 September, John Lowe was on the Nablus road just outside Tul Keram, where Allied aircraft had caught and attacked a Turkish convoy. 'Motor lorries, mules and bullock wagons lie there in shapeless heaps,' he wrote. 'Some of the drivers have not had time to leave their vehicles and lie in huddled heaps amongst the wreckage.'[35] The damage had been done on the afternoon of the previous day, when the Tul Keram to Anebta road was packed with retreating Turks. Lieutenant Howard Bowden Fletcher, formerly of the 12th Light Horse, was one of the Australian pilots above the packed road, which 'reminded us of a busy city street'. With empty cartridge cases attached to the bombs, the scream as they fell was frightening. 'Like huge vultures we swooped until the Turks became a demoralised rabble, cringing in terror beneath a hail of bombs and lead.'[36] Arthur Mills wrote of 'dead men, dead animals & smashed vehicles everywhere from Tulkeram to Nablus'.[37] 'A jumble of every sort of war gear,' John Davidson added, 'smashed to pieces and rolled off the road by advancing troops.'[38]

On 22 September, on entering Jenin, Arthur Mills wrote, 'It is in an awful mess.'[39] John Lowe, also in the area, wrote that 'the atmosphere is thick with decaying Turk'.[40] By 24 September, the Turkish 7th and 8th Armies had been effectively destroyed. Howard Bowden Fletcher watched the retreat from his aircraft above the narrow mountain pass at the upper reaches of Wadi Fara north-east of Nablus. The pass was completely blocked 'with a hideous shambles of dead horses, mules and oxen, smashed transport wagons and guns,' he wrote, 'making escape for the terrified Turks by this road absolutely impossible'.[41]

Shoeing a horse in the field. Ralph Kellett collection.

KILLED
484
29.9.18
SGT BROOK. L.S. MM
1ST ALH
AGE 25
RECT
CE
KILLED
29.9.18
TPR RADBURN. C.W
1ST ALH
AGE 28
RECT
PRES

CHAPTER 13

'TERRIFIED OF THE BEDOUINS'

September 1918

With Deraa and even Damascus now under threat in the north, the Turkish 4th Army west of Es Salt and Amman was in a precarious position. Turkish forces further south in the Hejaz were under an even darker cloud, and had begun the long withdrawal north harried by the emboldened Arab army. In the Jordan Valley, General Chaytor's mounted force secured the right flank of Allenby's offensive and waited for the anticipated withdrawal of the Turkish 4th Army to open the way to Amman. 'Our job to watch the Jordan flank,' Les Horder wrote on 20 September 1918.[1] Jericho Jane, a long-range Turkish gun positioned in the Wadi Nimrin (see Map 7), fired on the light horsemen around Jericho but with little effect. 'Jane has just sent over two dud shrapnel near the dump at Jericho from Shunet Nimrin in the hills opposite us,' Maurie Evans wrote.[2]

With most of the experienced British infantry battalions now shifted to France, new troops from the dominions took their place. On the morning of 21 September, a battalion of British West Indian troops seized two Turkish-occupied spurs north of Wadi el Auja before coming under heavy shelling. That evening, General Meldrum's New Zealand Mounted Rifles Brigade made a night approach and, helped by the West Indians, seized the bridge over the Jordan at Jisr ed Damieh the next day, 22 September. The New Zealanders captured 724 prisoners, 70 vehicles and considerable stores at El Makhruk.

The Indians supplied the bulk of the new units from the dominions. Risaldar Badlu Singh was an Indian cavalryman serving with the 14th Murray's Jat Lancers, part of the 29th Lancers fighting on the west bank of the Jordan south of Beisan. After his squadron took casualties from

'Killed by Circassians.' Sergeant Louis Brook and Trooper Clarence Radburn, both from the 1st Light Horse, were killed on 29 September 1918. Unbelievably, it was not until 1922 that the recovery of the bodies was attempted, and neither was ever found. **John Gorrell collection.**

an enemy hill position, Singh gathered up six other men and charged and captured the position. As he reached the crest of the hill, however, he was mortally wounded. Badlu Singh was posthumously awarded the Victoria Cross.

❖

Before dawn on 23 September, General Chaytor let loose Meldrum's, Ryrie's and Cox's brigades across the Jordan against the withdrawing Turks. The foothills were soon secure and once more the advance to Amman began. Maurie Evans, who had been on the receiving end of the Turkish artillery only days before, moved up the road through the Wadi Nimrin. 'On turning a corner in the wadi we were delighted to see Jericho Jane lying on her side in the stream with a dead Turk alongside her,' he wrote. 'She was just what I thought she was—a 5.9 naval gun.'[3]

Meldrum's New Zealand brigade reached Es Salt in the early evening of 23 September and boldly despatched a fighting patrol that finally blew the railway north of Amman, severely disrupting Turkish plans for withdrawal. Cox's 1st Brigade followed the New Zealanders into Es Salt, this time to stay.

'Jericho Jane', the 150-mm gun that had been positioned to fire down the Wadi Nimrin into the Jordan Valley. Here it lies overturned and abandoned. John Gorrell collection.

Taking a break on the way to Amman. John Gorrell collection.

Meanwhile, General Granville Ryrie's 2nd Brigade closed in on Amman, with Lieutenant Colonel Don Cameron's 5th Light Horse prominent in the attack. Lieutenant Archibald Currie took a party forward over open ground under heavy fire to attack an enemy post, and when they were within 75 metres a white flag was raised from the position. Currie and his men then stood up and advanced only to be cut down by enemy fire. All but two of Currie's men were hit, and Currie's wounds would prove fatal. Sergeant Patrick Kelly and two other men, one of whom was wounded, continued to advance and captured the post along with 33 prisoners.[4] The fact that any of the prisoners survived spoke volumes for the discipline of these light horsemen.

At 10.40 a.m. a support aircraft dropped a message to Ryrie's headquarters stating that the Turks were evacuating Amman, and three hours later troopers from the 5th Light Horse were fighting their way into the streets of the town. By 3.20 p.m. the troopers were through the town and headed for the high ground to the east. The resistance ahead of the 7th Light Horse was greater, but by 4 p.m. all of Amman had been captured.[5] George Hunt was with the 7th. 'Dismounted for action and tore into retreating enemy,' he wrote.[6] At Amman, Maurie Evans saw 'an enormous quantity of guns and material at the station' plus 'an almost perfect old Roman amphitheatre'.[7]

Granville Ryrie wrote of 'the remains of a huge Roman amphitheatre with some fine carved stone columns' at Amman. Harry Mattocks collection.

The 1st Light Horse cut off any retreat from Amman and 2360 prisoners were captured as well as six guns. 'We encountered the Turks ... escaping along the railway line,' Les Horder wrote. 'After knocking a few the remainder surrendered, 76 of them.'[8] Maurie Evans saw the carnage along the Es Salt to Amman road: 'For the first time in the war the scene sickened me. It was too much like butchery.'[9]

❖

Some 190 kilometres south of Amman, the 5000–6000 Turkish forces at Maan were now all but isolated. At dawn on 29 September, Cameron's 5th Light Horse headed south from Amman, and Cameron soon received information that significant numbers of Turks had reached Ziza, 32 kilometres south of Amman. As Cameron's men approached the town, it was obvious that the Turks were trapped there by a large force of local mounted Arabs, who could be seen on the hills to the east and west of the town. A Turkish officer and four men under a white flag then came out of Ziza along the railway line on a rail trolley to meet the light horsemen. They had a message from the Turkish commander in Ziza—he wanted to meet with Cameron.[10]

The Turkish commander, Ali Housain, was unwilling to surrender to Cameron, as he feared that a regiment of light horsemen was not strong enough to protect his troops from the 10,000 Arabs once they surrendered their arms. Cameron sent one of his squadron commanders, Major John Boyd, to the town and he returned with a signed document surrendering the force but insisting that 'in so doing [I] claim your protection for the safety of my soldiers, wounded and sick'. Cameron would need to wait for the rest of the brigade to arrive, however, before the Turks felt secure enough to lay down their arms. A number of Arab moves on the town had already been stopped by the Turkish defenders. At 4 p.m. Cameron told the Arabs that if they attacked again he would attack them. The occasional sound of captured Turks screaming 'like dying pigs' convinced Cameron of the danger the Arabs posed to an unarmed garrison.[11]

General Ryrie moved up with the 7th Light Horse to reinforce Cameron, and the light horsemen moved into Ziza before dusk. On arrival, Ryrie 'found a wild mob of Arabs thousands of them round the position. They were very truculent and very cheeky and said they were Sheriff's men and it was their right to take the place.' Ryrie took three Sheik chiefs hostage and 'left the Turks in the trenches with their rifles and machine guns, and put them on to fight the Arabs and my word they did pour it into them'.[12]

George Hunt wrote of how '4000 Turks surrendered and were gathered in from their lines of defence into Ze Za [sic] Railway Station'.[13]

Turkish prisoners at Amman. Reg Dixon collection.

Colonel Cameron 'was greatly struck by the fact that the Turkish garrison . . . was terrified of the Bedouins'.[14] 'We formed a square round the whole of the Turkish force and kept the Arabs outside,' Robert Farnes wrote. 'It seemed very strange to have all the Turks round you with fixed bayonets and ball cartridge.'[15] It was a unique moment in the war.

Next day, the New Zealand brigade arrived to help escort the now disarmed Turkish force to Amman. Three trains were captured at Ziza station with some 30 wagons, loaded with fifteen field guns and at least 30 machine guns plus considerable ammunition and other stores. 'Only one of the engines fit to use,' Jeff Holmes wrote, 'and that engine was empty of water.'[16] For the cost of 139 casualties, Chaytor had unhinged the Turkish 4th Army east of the Jordan, taking 4060 prisoners at Ziza, including 216 officers, while another 600 sick and wounded remained in the town awaiting evacuation once the railway line was reopened.[17] 'I counted the prisoners along the railway line just like a lot of sheep,' Ryrie

A captured train at Samra. John Gorrell collection.

wrote. 'Some of them had their wives with them & one a young baby.'[18] Jeff Holmes later saw the prisoners outside Amman after they had made a waterless trek of 32 kilometres from Ziza. 'They rushed us for water,' he wrote. 'One fellow pulled out a bag full of money . . . several offered us rings and Gallipoli Stars.'[19] George Hunt got something: 'Gave one old man a ride and he gave me a ring.'[20]

On 28 September, Cox's 1st Brigade headed north. Major Geoff Harris's squadron from the 1st Light Horse reached the station at Samra north of Amman (see Map 9), where two trains were abandoned, along with another four at Mafrak. Eight kilometres north of Samra, the light horsemen found Bedouins looting and stopped them. The Bedouins then opened fire and killed two light horsemen. As Horder wrote, the reprisals were swift. 'So they round up all Bedouins in sight and shoot the lot of them,' he wrote.[21] Thirteen of them were killed. Jim Greatorex put it more simply: 'Had slight encounter with Bedouin on the way.'[22]

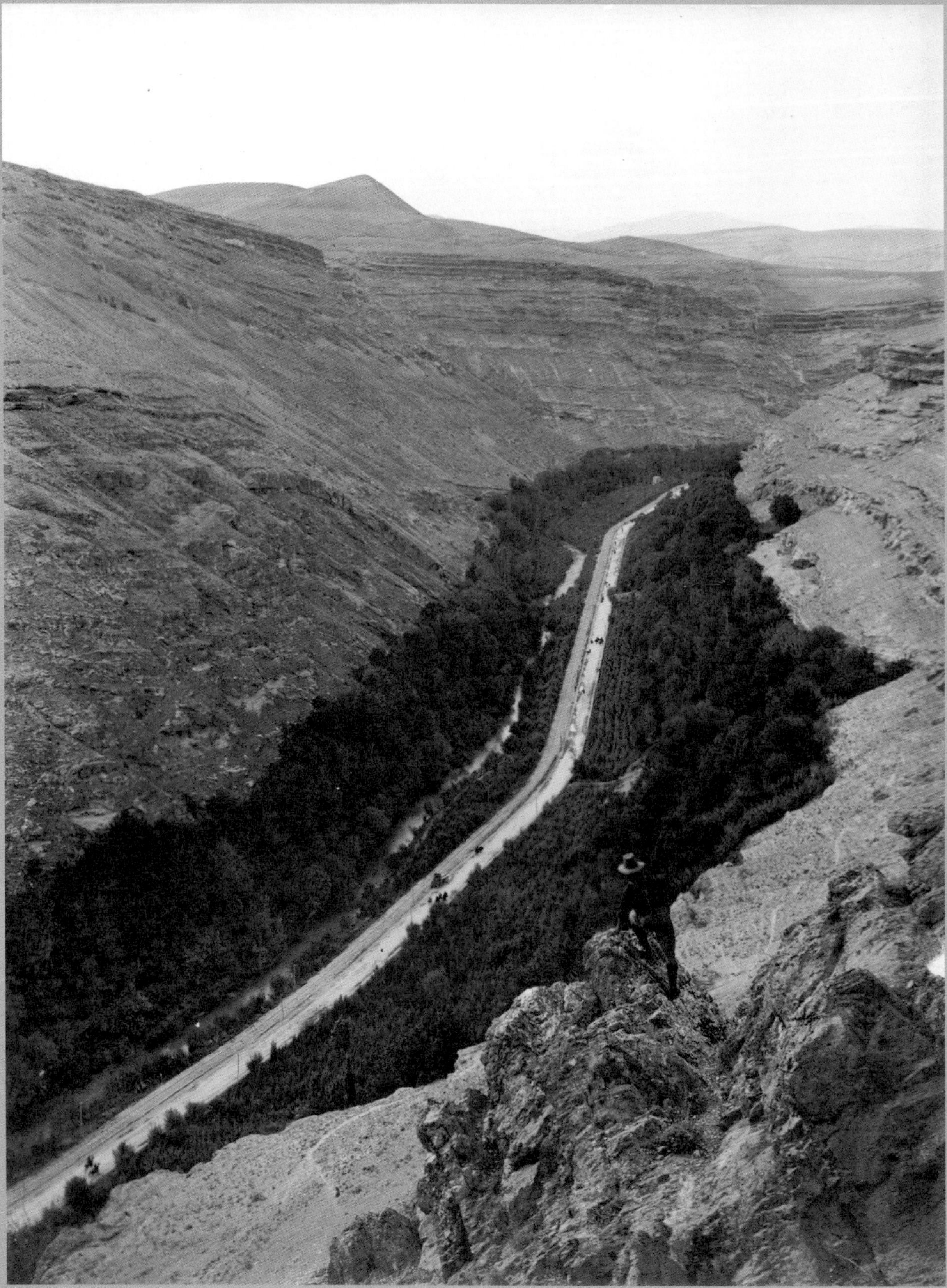

CHAPTER 14

'WE ARE GOING TO CHARGE THE TOWN'

September to December 1918

On 22 September 1918, General Allenby met with General Chauvel at Megiddo. Chauvel now had his eyes on Syria, in particular Damascus and then Aleppo, the loss of which would almost certainly end the war in the east for the Turks. Allenby's first objectives were Haifa and Acre on the coast, while inland Chauvel would drive for the Sea of Galilee at Tiberias and Semakh with General Hodgson's Australian Mounted Division.

Grant's 4th Brigade advanced on Beisan, clearing it on 24 September. Grant was then ordered to attack Semakh, on the southern edge of the Sea of Galilee, on the next day. That night the 11th Light Horse crossed the Jordan River just south of the Sea of Galilee and moved off in squadron columns. When the light horsemen came under fire, Colonel Harry Parsons called out 'we are going to charge the town, form squadron line'. Two squadrons under Major Edward Costello and Major Jim Loynes charged through the darkness at the German machine guns. Albert Donovan was with Loynes's A Squadron: '"Draw swords, charge!" came the command, and away we went, full gallop, straight for the line of spurting flame ... braving bullets, earth pits and trip wires.' Donovan watched as 'the wild sons of the Australian bush ... their swords gleaming in the moonlight, seemed to demoralise the Turks'. Donovan's horse leapt across a machine-gun position as it opened fire at point-blank range.[1]

One position was overrun and then the railway buildings, at a distance of 1600 metres, were charged, but heavy machine-gun fire split the advance some 700 metres out. Loynes's squadron went left towards the town while Costello swung his squadron to the right, heading for the railway station. His men came under heavy machine-gun fire and nearly

A light horseman perched on a crag of rock overlooking Barada Gorge. The road and railway follow the line of the river along the base of the gorge. Royal New South Wales Lancers Memorial Museum collection.

Two dead enemy machine-gunners and their well-used machine gun alongside the railway line at Semakh. Walter Smyth collection.

Map 9: Syria

50 horses went down. The squadron dismounted about 200 metres away from the station and took what cover it could. Eight light horse machine guns were quickly directed at the windows of the station building to keep the German machine-gunners from using them.[2]

Meanwhile, Loynes's men dismounted by the Galilee shore some 150 metres from the station. Sheathing their swords and fixing their bayonets, they closed in on the station buildings under the cover of Major Harold Harper's machine-gunners. Many of the light horsemen sheltered behind a wooden fence on top of a cutting about 20 metres from the station buildings.[3] Bert Donovan was with a group of men sheltering behind the railway line firing at the station building when a hand came out the door holding a white handkerchief. When Captain Wesley Whitfield ordered a ceasefire and went forward to take the surrender, however, he was shot down. The enraged light horsemen then attacked. 'Needless to say we took no prisoners from that joint,' Donovan later noted.[4] 'This action sent our boys mad. They rushed the station building,' Arthur Mills was told. He also offered a possible explanation. 'Unfortunately one part of the garrison in the railway station put up the white flag without letting the others in the building know.' When the light horsemen reached the building they 'could not force the doors and the enemy threw bombs at

Semakh railway station after the battle. 'The enemy was inside a stout brick building with plenty of ammunition and good cover,' Arthur Mills wrote of the two-storey building shown here. Reg Dixon collection.

'WE ARE GOING TO CHARGE THE TOWN'

them through the windows', but once the doors were forced, 'our men rushed in with the bayonette [sic] and that was the end of it'.[5]

One of the troopers later put the action to verse:

Victors and vanquished fight with eyes aflush,
While dawn breaks out with golden crimson flush,
Dust smeared and sweating, straining life for life,
Point blank the range, and hand to hand the strife.[6]

There were 'dead men and horses just outside the station yard, closer up more dead men and in the building more dead men,' Arthur Mills wrote. 'The walls were scored with bullets and splashed with blood ... blood from a wounded Turk upstairs was dripping through the ceiling into the room below.'[7] During the fight for Semakh, three Australian officers had been killed alongside eleven of their men. Another 29 men were wounded. In comparison, 98 enemy troops were killed and 364 captured, including 150 Germans.

When General Chauvel told Allenby of the fall of Semakh, Allenby made it clear that Damascus was now the objective. Tiberias soon fell and the road to Damascus beckoned. 'The road winds down the hills like a corkscrew,' John Lowe wrote, 'and we see Tiberias nestling on the shore of the Sea of Galilee at the foot of the hills.'[8] Meanwhile, General Barrow was directed east to Deraa, where he could link up with Colonel Lawrence's Arabs. If Deraa could be taken, the 20,000–30,000 men of the retreating Turkish 4th Army would be cut off. From Deraa, the plan was

The light horsemen enter Semakh. Walter Smyth collection.

German prisoners at Semakh. Walter Smyth collection.

that Barrow would also drive north for Damascus. Once he took Deraa, however, Barrow did not have the troops to capture the Turkish force that was withdrawing to Damascus. The columns were well protected by German machine guns and disinclined to surrender while the Arabs were on their eastern flank, baying for blood.

The 3rd Brigade moves along the road past the Sea of Galilee. Ralph Kellett collection.

'WE ARE GOING TO CHARGE THE TOWN'

On the morning of 27 September, the Australian Mounted Division moved out—with Macarthur-Onslow's 5th Brigade leading, followed by Wilson's 3rd. At Benat Yakub, a span of the stone bridge across the Jordan River had been blown and, under fire from the opposite bank, Wilson looked north and south for a fording point. Colonel Bourchier's 4th and Langley's 14th Light Horse scrambled across a ford about 3 kilometres south of the bridge, but harsh ground delayed a flanking move until daylight. 'Hats of light horsemen peeped above long dry grass at top of ridges,' Henry Gullett wrote of the attack at Benat Yakub, 'and in valleys behind were the horse holders restless for the gallop which so often followed dismounted fight.'[9]

Colonel Todd's 10th Light Horse got across to the north, and Lieutenant Colonel Arch McLaurin's 8th Light Horse followed as the 10th rolled up the enemy positions. Wilson's brigade kept moving, and later in the day captured the Circassian village of Kuneitra, 'a hungry little bluestone village' on the main road to Damascus.[10] Of the villagers, John Lowe wrote, 'the men wear a large black fur headgear similar to a British soldier's busby'.[11]

The 9th Light Horse led Wilson's brigade up the road to Damascus until stopped by machine-gun fire south of Sasa. This forced the troopers from the 9th and 10th Light Horse to dismount and advance over the rough terrain on either side of the road. Meanwhile, the 8th Light Horse advanced close to the road in the darkness and all six enemy machine-guns were captured, their locations given away by their gun flashes. When the 1500 defenders pulled out in motor vehicles, Grant's brigade took up the chase.

'The men, unshaven and dusty, thin from the ordeal of the Jordan, and with eyes bloodshot from the lack of sleep, rode with the bursting excitement of a throng of schoolboys,' Henry Gullett later wrote.[12] General Hodgson could see the Turkish column to the east trying to beat him to Damascus. With support from the ever-reliable Notts battery, Bourchier led the 4th and 12th Light Horse against Kaukab while Macarthur-Onslow's brigade crossed the Barbar River, which runs into Damascus from the south-west. The appearance of the French cavalry regiment moving around their right flank disturbed the German machine-gunners, and twelve machine guns were abandoned to Bourchier's men.

The Barada River brought water from the mountains through the Barada Gorge to Damascus, but what brought life to the city only brought death to the Turkish Army retreating north-west through the gorge. 'It was long and very narrow between very steep cliffs and only bare room for the stream, the railway line and a narrow road,' Ron Kemp wrote of the gorge. 'We had great difficulty in getting through the havoc and debris.'[13] The light horsemen had earlier set up machine guns covering the gorge and shot up the retreating enemy columns. 'Machine guns posted on the hills overlooking the gorge had the enemy at their mercy,' Arthur Mills later wrote.[14] The retreating Turks were cut off and some 4000 prisoners taken.

Damascus itself had few natural defences and could not long be held, despite significant numbers of Turkish troops in the city. Wilson decided that the chaotic state of those troops gave him the chance to march his light horsemen straight in. After some 400 years of Turkish rule, Damascus would fall to the Australians. In this they were helped by an act of treachery from the Turkish commander, Ali Riza, who met with General Barrow north of Deraa and handed over the plans for the city's defence. Djemal Pasha left the city on the afternoon of 30 September,

The destruction in the Barada Gorge. Royal New South Wales Lancers Memorial Museum collection.

and that night John Lowe watched from the hills as the Turks fired an ammunition and petrol dump. 'The explosions shake the ground like an earthquake and the flames make the night like day,' he wrote.[15]

At dawn on 1 October, Wilson's 3rd Brigade left its bivouac on the southern outskirts of Damascus and made its way towards the city, aiming to move through quickly and take the Homs road north. The 10th Light Horse passed the Turkish hospital and barracks, and soon thereafter Emir Said surrendered the city. 'We being the first troops to enter we got a great reception from the people who lined the streets and welcomed us with cheers and clapping,' Ron Kemp wrote.[16] Guided out of the city and onto the Homs road, Wilson was clear not long after 7 a.m. The Australians soon encountered German machine-gunners at Duma covering the retreating Turkish columns, but they rapidly broke through, taking 500 prisoners and 37 machine guns. Colonel Lawrence and his frenzied Arabs entered Damascus after Wilson had already left.

The light horsemen enter Damascus. Ralph Kellett collection.

Under Arab control, conditions in Damascus were soon chaotic. The population was starving, as were the many Turkish prisoners, but the Arabs were incapable of organising food supplies. Escorted by a squadron from the 2nd Light Horse, Chauvel rode through Damascus at noon on 2 October, followed by other units of his multinational force. Arthur Mills was there four days later. 'All day long and at night too rifles are being discharged,' he wrote. 'Street fights between the [Hejaz] troops and the Druses take place daily.' Conditions at the hospital were horrific. 'The job of burying the dead from the Turkish hospital is a big one,' Mills wrote on 11 October. 'Hundreds die daily.'[17] On 2 October, Arthur Mills noted, 'Our chief trouble is not from the enemy but from "friendly natives" who loot everything they can get their hands on and snipe at our despatch riders and [motor transport] drivers.' A captured sniper was executed in front of the local village sheiks as a warning. 'Shooting this man may put an end to this,' Mills wrote.[18] The final light horse action of the campaign came on 2 October, when Major Tom Daly's 9th Light Horse charged enemy positions and captured some 1500 troops, three field guns and 26 machine guns. Back in Egypt, Edwin Brown watched as 'Long train loads of Turkish prisoners still continue to go through.'[19]

❖

From 19 September to 2 October, the Australian Mounted Division had captured 31,355 prisoners, although more than 3000 of them would soon die of disease and starvation. The division lost only 21 men killed and 71 wounded,[20] but as Arthur Mills wrote on 5 October, 'the horses are looking played out and many of the men are sick but they must hang on a bit longer'.[21]

Chauvel now aimed for Aleppo, some 300 kilometres to the north. His 4th and 5th Cavalry Divisions headed in that direction while the Australian Mounted Division remained at Damascus. General Allenby already had his infantry moving up the coast with the aim of securing the port facilities at

Water for the horses.
Walter Smyth collection.

Beirut, from which Chauvel's mounted troops could be better supplied. Preceded by armoured cars, General Macandrew's 5th Cavalry Division moved through Rayak and Baalbek, then entered Homs on 15 October. But with the two cavalry divisions now drastically weakened by disease, Chauvel soon sent the Australian Mounted Division north to help. 'The boys are having a pretty rough time of it,' Arthur Mills wrote from hospital on 21 October. 'Most of them are sick [and] the others have 10 and 12 horses to attend to besides cooking and looking after their sick mates.'[22] Macandrew reached Aleppo on 22 October but did not have the troop strength to enter until 26 October. Captain Ernest James was with the armoured cars that first entered Aleppo. 'We entered without opposition,' he wrote. 'As the last train of Turkish troops was steaming out at one end, the armoured cars and light car patrols were driving into the other.'[23]

Thirteen kilometres north-west of Aleppo, 2500 Turks took up defensive positions, but as General Hodgson's Australian Mounted Division prepared to confront them, the Turks made their smartest move of the campaign and signed an armistice. 'I never saw such a change in men before,' Ron Kemp wrote of the weary light horsemen. 'They were like a lot of happy school boys, just let out of school.'[24] The Australian Mounted Division then marched across the mountains from Homs to Tripoli, where the camp conditions were superior. Meanwhile, the Anzac Mounted Division, badly affected by disease during the advance from the Jordan Valley, pulled back to their camps in Palestine. The light horsemen who had enlisted in 1914 were already on their way home. On 12 November, John MacNamara wrote of how 'all the 1914 men are down here now awaiting embarkation any day for Australia'.[25] Most of them sailed on 15 November and were home for Christmas.

The Australians lost 1397 men during the Middle Eastern campaigns. Although casualties on this scale were suffered on a number of occasions by Australians in a single day of fighting on the Western Front, it does not diminish the sacrifice of these brave men, whom some derided as 'cold-footed' for not being involved in France

The 6th Light Horse Regiment took 520 horses to war in 1914. The eighteen horses shown here were the only originals that remained at the end of the war. No horses returned to Australia after the war. The majority were either transferred to Indian mounted units or shot due to old age. Ralph Kellett collection.

and Belgium. Referring to the losses at Second Gaza, Ted Dengate wrote that 'if they could have seen the Battlefield after the 19th April last year, where the Light Horse and Camel Corps went into action, they would have seen the bones of "cold footed light horsemen", slowly bleaching in the hot summer sun'.[26] There the bones still lie, buried alongside so many others from conflicts past and present across this harsh land.

❖

The war was over but the killing was not. Surafend was a small town near Ludd around which the light horsemen had spent considerable time in camp. On 9 December, the Anzac Mounted Division was in camp there when an Arab thief shot a New Zealand soldier. The aggrieved New Zealanders, joined by some other troops, soon surrounded Surafend and demanded the murderer be handed over. The New Zealanders had previously had men killed by local Arabs, notably at Ain es Sir in March 1918. Their response on that occasion was immediate, but this time they waited throughout the day, giving the higher authorities the opportunity to take action. By nightfall no action had been taken so the troops, 'angry and bitter beyond sound reasoning', went into the village, evacuated the women and children and then burned down the village, killing many Arabs in the process. A nearby nomad camp was also razed.[27] 'They got all the women away and then burnt the village down,' Robert Farnes wrote. 'A lot of the Arabs were killed . . . there will be a terrible row about it.'[28] 'The Anzac Division are in great disgrace,' Granville Ryrie added.[29]

When General Allenby visited the Anzac Division a week later and 'spoke about the show on the Arab village he was very upset', Robert Farnes observed. 'He said he had been proud of us but was no longer.'[30] The official historian had earlier noted that 'British policy pandered foolishly' to the Bedouin and that 'Firm punishment for gross offences at the outset would have saved infinite trouble later on.'[31] Now that the trouble had arrived, 'the disciplinary machinery was as active as hitherto it had been tardy' and the whole division was held responsible.[32]

Nonetheless, the British command was still happy to have the light horse units kill Arabs when it suited their cause, such as to put down a revolt against British rule in Egypt in March 1919. The twelve light horse regiments that were still in Egypt awaiting repatriation were used to help suppress a rebellion that had turned violent. 'Christians in the country towns were attacked and murdered, particularly Armenians.

British officers and tourists proceeding to Upper Egypt on holidays were attacked in the train,' Brigadier General Lachlan Wilson wrote. 'Several of them were murdered and so mutilated with sticks that their bodies could not be identified.'[33] One of those casualties was Private Lawrence Redding, a South Australian serving with the Australian Army Medical Corps. He was aboard a Cairo-bound train that had left Luxor late on 17 March 1919 and was the object of boisterous stone-throwing Egyptian crowds as it passed through stations heading north. Next morning at Dairut, about 300 kilometres south of Cairo, the train was boarded by rioters and seven soldiers were murdered. Redding, who had been on a week's leave in Luxor and was returning to Cairo, was among them.

On that same day, at Minet el Qamh, north-east of Cairo near Zagazig, some 1000 stone-throwing rioters rushed a post held by Lieutenant Fred Macgregor and twenty men from the 10th Light Horse. The rioters got to within 10 metres of the post before Macgregor ordered his men to open fire; it was kill or be killed. The mob broke, leaving 39 rioters dead and another 25 wounded, but in the rush to flee, another 40 or so were drowned trying to cross a canal.[34] There were other clashes over the next two weeks, but the uprising petered out in early April and by July 1919 the last light horse units had embarked for Australia.

The train carriage in which seven soldiers, including Private Lawrence Redding, were murdered by rioting Egyptians. Godfrey Burgess collection.

❖

For some who returned to Australia the sacrifice went on. George Mitchell was a highly decorated war hero from the Western Front who appreciated the comradeship that war had engendered among the men of the 1st AIF. When he attended a light horse Anzac Day reunion in April 1936, Mitchell's eye was drawn to a group of light horsemen gathered around a man in a wheelchair. 'This cheerful looking youngster was shot in the spine during the fight at Amman, when a whole squadron of the Sixth was laid out,' Mitchell wrote.[35] The disabled youngster was

Bert Scurrah, the 6th Light Horse trooper who had been wounded at Amman and then carried out strapped across the back of a horse down the rugged mountain track to the Jordan Valley. That painful journey had been only the start of Bert Scurrah's struggle, and he was between life and death for three months before being evacuated back to Australia in July 1918. Things got no easier for him back home; though he had left the war behind, the war would never leave him. Following that Anzac Day reunion in 1936, Bert Scurrah would only see another two of them. May we ever remember his ilk, that tough breed of Australian horseman who had ridden into history.

Light Horse veterans at Randwick stables in Sydney on Anzac Day 1982. Left to right: Max Nichols, Eric Turner, Ted Pavel (7th Light Horse), Stan McColl, Jack Bowden (9th Light Horse), Duncan McKenzie (1st Remount Unit) and Jack Pollock (1st Light Horse). Tenterfield Museum collection.

WRITER BIOGRAPHIES

Private Sydney Barron served with the 12th Light Horse Regiment in the Sinai and Palestine campaigns. Barron, who was born in England, was a stock salesman from Perth in Western Australia. He enlisted in July 1915 and returned to Australia in June 1919.

Corporal Hubert Billings served as a signaller with the 1st Brigade in the Sinai campaign. In December 1916 he joined the Australian Flying Corps as a wireless mechanic. Billings was a clerk from Brighton Beach in Melbourne, Victoria. He enlisted in August 1914 and returned to Australia in December 1918.

Sergeant Henry 'Harry' Bostock served with the 10th Light Horse Regiment in the Sinai and Palestine campaigns. Bostock was a farmer from Pingelly in Western Australia. He enlisted in August 1915 and returned to Australia in August 1918.

Driver Edwin Brown served with the 1st Signal Squadron (attached to the 1st Brigade) in the Sinai and Palestine campaigns. Brown was a mattress-maker from Hurstville in Sydney, New South Wales. He enlisted in August 1914 and returned to Australia in October 1918.

Lieutenant Colonel Mick Bruxner served with the 6th Light Horse Regiment in the Sinai and Palestine campaigns. Bruxner was a grazier and stock agent from Tenterfield in New South Wales. He was made a member of the Distinguished Service Order and the French Legion of Honour. He enlisted in October 1914 and returned to Australia in July 1919.

Sergeant Joseph Burgess served with the 6th Light Horse Regiment in the Sinai and Palestine campaigns. Burgess was a tram conductor from Redfern in Sydney, New South Wales. He enlisted in September 1914 and returned to Australia in November 1918.

Trooper Gordon Cooper served with the 1st Machine Gun Squadron (attached to the 1st Brigade) in the Sinai and Palestine campaigns. Cooper was from Inverell in New South Wales. He enlisted in August 1914 and returned to Australia in November 1918.

Private Lloyd Corliss served with the 1st Light Horse Regiment in the Sinai and Palestine campaigns. Corliss was a labourer from Curlewis in New South Wales. He enlisted in January 1915 and died of wounds on 17 November 1917.

Trooper Edward Dengate served with the 12th Light Horse Regiment in the Sinai and Palestine campaigns. Dengate was a farmer from Molong in New South Wales. He enlisted in October 1916 and returned to Australia in August 1919.

Lance Sergeant Maurice Evans served with the 1st Light Horse Field Ambulance (attached to the 1st Brigade) in the Sinai and Palestine campaigns. Evans, who was born in England, was an agricultural student from Kyogle in New South Wales. He enlisted in August 1914 and returned to Australia in December 1918.

Lieutenant Robert Farnes served as a signaller with the 2nd Brigade in the Sinai and Palestine campaigns. He was awarded the Military Cross during operations at Jerusalem in December 1917. Farnes was a tea blender from South Melbourne in Victoria. He enlisted in August 1914 and returned to Australia in June 1919.

Lance Corporal Robert Fell served with the Imperial Camel Corps and the 10th Light Horse Regiment in the Sinai and Palestine campaigns. Fell was a traveller from Glebe in Sydney, New South Wales. He enlisted in July 1915 and returned to Australia in June 1919.

Lieutenant James Greatorex served with the 1st Machine Gun Squadron (attached to the 1st Brigade) in the Sinai and Palestine campaigns. Greatorex was a mechanical engineer from Coburg in Melbourne, Victoria. He enlisted in September 1914 and returned to Australia in May 1919.

Sir Henry Gullett was an official Australian war correspondent on the Western Front from 1915 to 1917. In 1917 he was put in charge of the War Records Section in Egypt, and in August 1918 was appointed as the official Australian war correspondent in the Middle East. After the war he wrote the volume of the official history covering the Australian forces in the Sinai and Palestine campaigns. Gullett, who was a Federal MP, was killed in an air accident at Canberra in August 1940.

Lance Sergeant Patrick Hamilton served with the 3rd and 4th Light Horse Field Ambulance in the Sinai and Palestine campaigns. He was mentioned in despatches in March 1917 for his actions at First Gaza. Hamilton was a university student from Kew in Melbourne, Victoria. He enlisted in March 1915 and returned to Australia in February 1919.

Driver Leo Hanly served with the 3rd Light Horse Field Ambulance (attached to the 3rd Brigade) in the Sinai and Palestine campaigns. Hanly, who was born in England, was a timekeeper from Elwood in Victoria. He enlisted in July 1915 and returned to Australia in February 1919.

Driver Jeff Holmes served with the 1st Field Squadron and the Engineers Training Unit in the Sinai and Palestine campaigns. Holmes was a farmer from Allora in Queensland. He enlisted in April 1916 and returned to Australia in April 1919.

Sergeant Leslie Horder served with the 1st Machine Gun Squadron (attached to the 1st Brigade) in the Sinai and Palestine campaigns. Horder was a grazier originally from Willoughby in Sydney, New South Wales. He enlisted in April 1915 and returned to Australia in September 1919.

Trooper George Hunt served with the 7th Light Horse Regiment in the Palestine campaign. Hunt was an orchardist from Parramatta in Sydney, New South Wales. He enlisted in December 1916 and returned to Australia in September 1919.

Captain James Francis 'Frank' Hurley was the official Australian war photographer on the Western Front in 1917. From October 1917 to May 1918 he served in that capacity in the Middle East. Hurley also served as an official photographer in the Second World War.

Private Ion Idriess served with the 5th Light Horse Regiment in the Sinai and Palestine campaigns. Idriess was a miner originally from Waverley in Sydney, New South Wales. He enlisted in October 1914 and returned to Australia in February 1918. He later became an important Australian author.

Trooper Pelham Jackson served with the 11th Light Horse Regiment in the Sinai and Palestine campaigns. Jackson was a clerk from Kynuna in Queensland. He enlisted in January 1915 and died of wounds on 19 April 1917. Although specific details of his grave location were recorded, his body was never recovered after the war.

Corporal Ronald Kemp served with the 3rd Signal Troop (attached to the 3rd Brigade) in the Sinai and Palestine campaigns. Kemp was a civil engineer from East Malvern in Melbourne, Victoria. He enlisted in February 1915 and returned to Australia in August 1919.

Corporal Verner Knuckey served with the 8th Light Horse Regiment in the Sinai campaign before transferring to the Australian Flying Corps as a mechanic in January 1917. Before the war, Knuckey was a clerk at the Commonwealth Treasury from East Malvern in Melbourne, Victoria. He enlisted in July 1915 and returned to Australia in September 1919.

Private Henry Langtip served with the 4th Light Horse Regiment in the Sinai and Palestine campaigns. Before the war, Langtip was a farmer from Port Albert in Victoria. He enlisted in January 1916 and returned to Australia in July 1919.

Corporal Charles Livingstone served with the 6th Light Horse Regiment in the Sinai and Palestine campaigns. He was awarded a Distinguished Conduct Medal during the fighting north of Beersheba in November 1917. Before the war, Livingstone was a tram conductor, originally from Harvey in Western Australia. He enlisted in October 1914 and returned to Australia in January 1919.

Sapper John Lowe served as a signaller with the 5th Signal Troop (attached to the 5th Brigade) in the Palestine campaign. Lowe, who was born in England, was a telegraphist from Brisbane in Queensland. He enlisted in March 1917 and returned to Australia in March 1919.

Lieutenant Stuart Macfarlane served with the 1st Light Horse Regiment in the Sinai and Palestine campaigns. He was awarded the Military Cross in September 1918. Macfarlane, who was born in New Zealand, was a grazier originally from Darling Point in Sydney, New South Wales. He enlisted in August 1914 and returned to Australia in May 1919.

Private John MacNamara served with the 1st Light Horse Brigade in the Palestine campaign before transferring to the Australian Flying Corps as a wireless operator in September 1917. MacNamara was awarded a Military Medal for bravery on 24 August 1917.

MacNamara was an agricultural student from Coffs Harbour in New South Wales. He enlisted in February 1916 and returned to Australia in March 1919.

Sergeant Gordon Macrae served with the 6th Light Horse Regiment in the Sinai and Palestine campaigns. Macrae was a farmer from Dorrigo in New South Wales. He enlisted in September 1914 and returned to Australia in December 1918.

Lieutenant Colonel Arthur Mills commanded the 1st Double Squadron AIF, the 4th Battalion of the Imperial Camel Corps and then the 15th Light Horse Regiment in the Sinai and Palestine campaigns. He was mentioned in despatches and made a member of the Distinguished Service Order. Mills was a dentist from Parramatta in Sydney, New South Wales. He enlisted in March 1915 and returned to Australia in July 1919.

Trooper Michael Minahan served with the Desert Column Headquarters and the 6th Light Horse Regiment in the Sinai and Palestine campaigns until he was wounded on 3 December 1917. Minahan was a drover from Tibooburra in outback New South Wales. He enlisted in September 1914 and returned to Australia in December 1918.

Captain Harold Mulder served with the 8th Light Horse Regiment in the Sinai and Palestine campaigns. Mulder was a grazier from Geelong in Victoria. He enlisted in August 1914 and returned to Australia in April 1918.

Captain Stanley Parkes served with the 3rd Light Horse Field Ambulance in the Sinai and Palestine campaigns and with the 8th Sanitary Section from June 1917. He was mentioned in despatches in March 1917 during First Gaza. Parkes was a draughtsman from Albert Park in Melbourne, Victoria. He enlisted in October 1915 and returned to Australia in March 1919.

Lieutenant Maurie Pearce served with the 1st Light Horse Regiment in the Sinai and Palestine campaigns. Pearce was a station overseer from Orange in New South Wales. He enlisted in March 1915 and returned to Australia in March 1919.

Sergeant William Peterson served with the 2nd Light Horse Regiment in the Sinai campaign. Peterson was a telephone serviceman from Warwick in Queensland. He enlisted in August 1914 and returned to Australia in May 1917 with a debilitating nervous condition.

Sergeant Ronald Ross served with the 8th Light Horse Regiment in the Sinai and Palestine campaigns. Ross was a blacksmith's striker from Maidstone in Victoria. He enlisted in September 1914 and returned to Australia in September 1919.

Major General Sir Granville Ryrie served as the commander of the 2nd Light Horse Brigade in the Sinai and Palestine campaigns. Ryrie was a farmer and politician from Michelago in New South Wales. He enlisted in September 1914 and returned to Australia in 1919.

Trooper William Smyth served with the 4th Signal Troop (attached to the 4th Brigade) in the Palestine campaign. Smyth was a postal assistant from North Carlton in Melbourne, Victoria. He enlisted in June 1916 and returned to Australia in August 1919.

Sapper John Stephen served with the 3rd Signal Troop (attached to the 3rd Brigade) in the Sinai and Palestine campaigns. He was mentioned in despatches on 18 March 1917 during First Gaza. Stephen was a public servant from Rochester in Victoria. He enlisted in June 1915 and returned to Australia in August 1919.

Sergeant Fred Tomlins served with the 1st Light Horse Regiment in the Sinai and Palestine campaigns. Tomlins was a farmer from Cowra in New South Wales. He enlisted in August 1914 and returned to Australia in November 1918.

Driver Frank Willis served with the 1st Light Horse Regiment in the Sinai campaign. Willis was a farmer from Crookwell in New South Wales. He enlisted in May 1915 and died of wounds on 4 August 1916.

Colonel J.W. Wintringham served as an officer in the Lincolnshire Yeomanry in Egypt and then with the 18th Machine Gun Squadron (attached to the 22nd Yeomanry Brigade) in Palestine. He was awarded the Military Cross and made a CBE during his service.

Lieutenant Colonel Frederick Wollaston commanded the 1/5th Battalion of the Suffolk Regiment (163rd Brigade, 54th Division) in Egypt and Palestine from August 1916 to January 1918. He was made a member of the Distinguished Service Order during his service. He was killed during a zeppelin raid on London on 7 March 1918.

PHOTO COLLECTION BIOGRAPHIES

Sapper Wilfred 'Tom' Baker served as a signaller with the 1st Signal Squadron in the Sinai and Palestine campaigns. Baker, who was born in England, was a labourer from South Yarra in Melbourne, Victoria. He enlisted in October 1914 and returned to Australia in July 1919.

Lance Corporal Claude Ballard served with the 2nd and the 7th Light Horse Regiments in the Palestine campaign. Ballard was a forest guard from Mallanganee in northern New South Wales. He enlisted in June 1916 and returned to Australia in August 1919.

Trooper Joseph Bradshaw served with the 4th Anzac Battalion of the Imperial Camel Corps and the 15th Light Horse Regiment in the Palestine campaign. Bradshaw was a labourer from Kogarah in Sydney, New South Wales. He enlisted in August 1916 and returned to Australia in August 1919.

Corporal Godfrey Burgess served with the 12th Light Horse Regiment in the Palestine campaign. Burgess was a produce merchant from Molong in New South Wales. He enlisted in November 1916 and returned to Australia in July 1919.

Lieutenant John Davidson served with the 3rd Anzac Battalion of the Imperial Camel Corps in the Sinai and Palestine campaigns. He also served with the 15th Light Horse in the Palestine campaign. He was awarded a Military Cross during Second Gaza and was later mentioned in despatches. Davidson, who was born in Scotland, was a farmer from Cowra in New South Wales. He enlisted in August 1914 and returned to Australia in January 1919.

Lance Corporal Reg Dixon served with the 6th Light Horse Regiment in the Palestine campaign. Dixon was a warehouseman from Centennial Park in Sydney, New South Wales. He enlisted in the AIF from the Royal Australian Naval Reserve in April 1917 and returned to Australia in August 1919.

Corporal Austin Edwards served with the 1st Light Horse Regiment in the Sinai and Palestine campaigns. Edwards was a joiner from Cundletown in New South Wales. He enlisted in February 1915 and returned to Australia in October 1919.

Wilfred 'Tom' Baker

Claude Ballard

Joseph Bradshaw

Godfrey Burgess

John Davidson

Reg Dixon

Austin Edwards

George Francis

Arthur Hitchcock

Bert Inall

Harry Mattocks

John Gorrell

Fred Horsley

Ralph Kellett

Lieutenant George Francis served with the 12th Light Horse Regiment and the 4th Machine Gun Squadron in the Sinai and Palestine campaigns. Francis was a station overseer from Neutral Bay in Sydney, New South Wales. He enlisted in March 1915 and returned to Australia in August 1919.

Trooper John Gorrell served with the 1st Light Horse Regiment in the Palestine campaign. Gorrell was a bank officer from Unanderra in New South Wales. He enlisted in March 1917 and returned to Australia in March 1919.

Private Arthur Hitchcock served as General Chauvel's batman in the headquarters of the Australian Mounted Division in the Sinai and Palestine campaigns. Hitchcock was a ship steward from Sydney in New South Wales. He enlisted in May 1915 and returned to Australia in September 1919.

Private Fred Horsley served with the 4th Light Horse Regiment in the Palestine campaign. Horsley was a teamster from Leichhardt in Sydney, New South Wales. He enlisted in November 1916 and returned to Australia in August 1919.

Private Bert Inall served with the 1st Anzac Battalion of the Imperial Camel Corps in the Palestine campaign. Inall was a postal linesman from Richmond in New South Wales. He enlisted in March 1916 and returned to Australia in May 1919.

Sergeant Ralph Kellett served with the 6th Light Horse Regiment in the Sinai and Palestine campaigns. Kellett was a clerk from Mudgee in New South Wales. He enlisted in December 1915 and returned to Australia in June 1919.

Private Ken McAulay served with the 2nd Light Horse Regiment in the Sinai and Palestine campaigns. McAulay was a teacher from Chatsworth Island in New South Wales. He enlisted in August 1915 and returned to Australia in September 1918.

Sergeant Harry Mattocks served with the 2nd Light Horse Brigade supply train in the Sinai and Palestine campaigns. Mattocks was a carpenter from Maitland in New South Wales. He enlisted in September 1914 and returned to Australia in December 1918.

Private Roy Millar served with the 6th Light Horse Regiment in the Palestine campaign. Millar was a horse breaker from Leichhardt in Sydney, New South Wales.

He enlisted in May 1917 and returned to Australia in July 1919.

Lieutenant Edwin Mulford served with the 12th Light Horse Regiment in the Sinai and Palestine campaigns. He was awarded a Distinguished Conduct Medal and was mentioned in despatches before joining No. 1 Squadron, Australian Flying Corps, in January 1918. Mulford was an electrician from Waverley in Sydney, New South Wales. He enlisted in August 1914 and returned to Australia in January 1919.

Lieutenant Colonel Hugh Poate served with the Australian General Hospital in Egypt and England. Poate was a surgeon from Sydney in New South Wales. He enlisted in August 1914 and returned to Australia in October 1917.

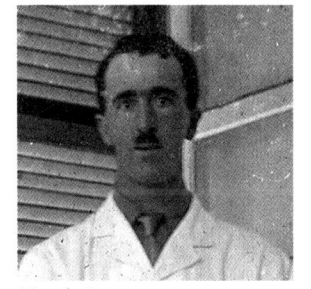

Sergeant Clarence Reid served with the 1st Light Horse Regiment in the Sinai and Palestine campaigns. Reid was a labourer from Gunnedah in New South Wales. He enlisted in August 1914 and returned to Australia in July 1919.

Sergeant Arthur Reynolds served with the 6th Light Horse Regiment in the Sinai and Palestine campaigns. Reynolds was a station manager from Merriwa in New South Wales. He enlisted in July 1915 and returned to Australia in June 1919.

Driver Walter Smyth served with the Australian Mounted Division divisional train in the Palestine campaign. Smyth was an apprentice from Woollahra in Sydney, New South Wales. He enlisted in March 1917 and returned to Australia in August 1919.

Private Horace Taberner served with the 1st Remount Unit in Egypt. Taberner was a farmhand from Kensington in Victoria. He enlisted in December 1915 and returned to Australia in August 1919.

Lieutenant Colonel William Maitland Woods was the senior chaplain to the Anzac Mounted Division and then the Desert Mounted Corps. He was decorated with the Order of the British Empire. William Woods, who was English-born, had been a chaplain to the forces since 1893. He enlisted in August 1915 and returned to Australia in February 1919. His son, **Temporary Sergeant Francis Maitland Woods** served with the 7th Light Horse Regiment and later with the Camel Transport Corps in the Sinai and Palestine campaigns. Francis Woods was an engineer fitter originally from Thursday Island. He enlisted in September 1914 and was discharged from the AIF in March 1918.

Edwin Mulford

Hugh Poate

Arthur Reynolds

Walter Smyth

William Maitland Woods

Francis Maitland Woods

PHOTO COLLECTION BIOGRAPHIES

ACKNOWLEDGEMENTS

Thanks to all the diarists and correspondents whose stories make up the text. Though all have long since left us, their words can still inspire us. Thanks to the staff at the Australian War Memorial, the State Library of New South Wales, the National Library of Australia, the Imperial War Museum and the UK National Archives for facilitating my research into their collections.

Thanks to those people who provided access to family photo and diary collections: Kay Alliband, Cameron Archer, Paul Batman, Colin Beaton, Robert Burgess, Lyndall Caldwell, Joan and Eleanor Cupit, Rob Davidson, Kerrie Ferguson, John Francis, Angela Glover, Richard Gorrell, Cliff Horsley, Barry Inall, Alan Kellett, John McFarlane, Russ Mattocks, Pat Murphy, Wendell Peacock, Jim Poate, Joan Scott, Bob Smith, Margaret Smith, Margaret Smithers, Kay Stacy, Laurie Taberner, Robyn Thompson, Carol Whiteside, Elizabeth Woods and Merrien Wrighter. Thanks also to Ross Brown and John Howells at the Royal New South Wales Lancers Memorial Museum and to the Tenterfield Museum for access to their photo archives. Thanks to Keith Mitchell for his outstanding work on the maps.

A special thanks to the people at Allen & Unwin—Sue Hines for instigating the project, and Angela Handley, Nicola Young and Philip Campbell for their editorial and design work.

BIBLIOGRAPHY

PRIMARY SOURCES

Baker, Wilfred 'Tom', diary, courtesy of Joan Cupit
Davidson, John, *The Dinkum Oil of Light Horse and Camel Corps*, Robina, Queensland: Bruce and Richard Davidson, 1996 (written circa 1934)
Hogan, Arthur, postcard album, author's collection
Inall, Bert, notes, courtesy of Barry Inall
McAulay, Ken, diary, courtesy of Margaret Smithers
Murphy, Patrick, 'Austin William Edwards'
Wallis, George, notes, <www.mamisa.net/Reference/Transcriptions/Wallis GL 54 R(T) 001.htm>
Woods, William Maitland, letters, courtesy of Elizabeth Woods

AUSTRALIAN WAR MEMORIAL

Official records

AWM4	AIF unit war diaries, 1914–18 War
AWM8	Unit embarkation nominal rolls, 1914–18 War
AWM22	AIF Headquarters (Egypt), Central registry files, 1914–18 War
AWM25	Written records, 1914–18 War
AWM27	AWM Library records
AWM28	Recommendation files for honours and awards, AIF, 1914–18 War
AWM38	Official History, 1914–18 War, Records of C.E.W. Bean, Official Historian
AWM40	Official History, 1914–18 War, Records of H.S. Gullett
AWM46	Captured German documents, 1914–18 War
AWM133	Nominal roll of AIF who left Australia for service abroad, 1914–18 War

Private records

PR86/300	Aubrey Abbott letters		3DRL/6595	Leslie Horder diary
1DRL/0005	Arthur Adams diary		PR91/140	George Hunt diary
PR89/179	Heinrich Römer-Andreae letter		1DRL/0373	Ion Idriess diary
3DRL/6060	Hubert Billings diary		1DRL/0380	Pelham Jackson papers
PR83/110	Harry Bostock diary		3DRL/3747	Ronald Kemp diary
2DRL/0444	Murray Bourchier letters		PR03193	Verner Knuckey diary
2DRL/1285	Edwin Brown diary		PR00053	Henry Langtip diary
PR00991	William Burchill diary		PR01457	David Legge diary
1DRL/0211	Gordon Cooper diary		2DRL/0211	Stuart Macfarlane diary
PR01906	Lloyd Corliss diary		PR02017	Harry Maddrell letters
PR00870	Charles Cox diary		PR00696	Leslie Maygar letters
3DRL/7678	Edward Dengate letters		1DRL/0501	Arthur Mills papers
PR00469	Roy Dunk papers		3DRL/3400(B)	Harold Mulder diary
PR83/106	Robert Farnes diary		PR01571	Stanley Parkes diary
PR03456	William Fraser diary		PR01032	Ronald Ross diary
PR00836	Norman Garden diary		PR01268	Alfred Sly diary
3DRL/6776	James Greatorex diary		PR00633	William Smyth diary
3DRL/7521	Patrick Hamilton diary		3DRL/3584	John Stephen diary and letters
PR05366	Leo Hanly diary		PR01058	Henry Sullivan diary
PR85/289	John Hobbs diary		PR01168	Frank Willis letters
PR00740	Jeff Holmes diary		PR02088	Edward Woods diary

NATIONAL LIBRARY OF AUSTRALIA

MS 883, 1, 5	Frank Hurley diary		MS 986	Granville Ryrie letters

STATE LIBRARY OF NEW SOUTH WALES

MLMSS 584	John Antill diary		MLMSS 2876	John MacNamara diary
CY 4132 (MLMSS 1219)	Joseph Bolger diary		CY 2417 (MLMSS 958)	Gordon Macrae diary
CY 4947	Joseph Burgess diary		MLDOC 1360	Michael Minahan diary
CY 4960 (MLMSS 1576)	Maurice Evans diary		MLMSS 2940	Maurice Pearce diary
CY 4893	Robert Fell diary		CY 2472 (MLMSS 2942)	William Peterson diary
MLMSS 2873	John Lowe diary		CY 587 (MLMSS 1002)	Fred Tomlins diary

IMPERIAL WAR MUSEUM, LONDON, UNITED KINGDOM

4082	Alan Alan-Williams papers		6759	J.W. Wintringham papers
203	C.W. Battine papers		12702	F.H.A. Wollaston papers
13560	C.H. Livingstone papers			

NATIONAL ARCHIVES, LONDON, UNITED KINGDOM

WO 95	First World War unit war diaries
CAB 44/12	A brief record of the advance of the Egyptian Expeditionary Force

NATIONAL ARCHIVES OF AUSTRALIA

B2455	1st AIF service records
A1194, 33.68/ 15152	Harry Chauvel, 'The Australian Light Horse in the Great War: A Short Story of the Desert Mounted Corps'

SECONDARY SOURCES

Bean, C.E.W. & Gullett, H.S. (eds), *Official History of Australia in the War of 1914-18*, vol. XII, *Photographic Record of the War*, Sydney: Angus & Robertson, 1938 (first published 1923)

Bou, J., *Australia's Palestine Campaign*, Sydney: Australian Army History Unit and Big Sky Publishing, 2010

Dennis, P., Grey, J., Morris, E., Prior, R. & Bou, J. (eds), *The Oxford Companion to Australian Military History*, 2nd edn, Melbourne: Oxford University Press, 2008

Gullett, H.S., *Official History of Australia in the War of 1914-18*, vol. VII, *Sinai and Palestine*, Sydney: Angus & Robertson, 1941 (first published 1923)

Lawrence, T.E., *Seven Pillars of Wisdom: A triumph*, Harmondsworth: Penguin, 1962 (first published by Jonathan Cape, 1935)

Returned Sailors and Soldiers' Imperial League of Australia (NSW branch), *Reveille* (magazine), 1929-1939

Thomas, Lowell, *With Lawrence in Arabia*, London: Arrow, 1962 (first published by the Century Co., 1925)

NOTES

INTRODUCTION
1 Chauvel notes, AWM, 2DRL/0793.
2 Gullett, *Official History of Australia in the War of 1914–18*, vol. VII, *Sinai and Palestine*, p. 20.
3 Hurley diary, NLA, MSS 883, 1, 5.

CHAPTER 1: 'SOLDIER'S HELL'
1 Light horse brigades are designated Brigade only—e.g. 1st Brigade; light horse regiments are designated Light Horse—e.g. 1st Light Horse.
2 Gullett notes, AWM40, 60; Gullett, *Sinai and Palestine*, p. 62.
3 Chauvel, 'The Australian Light Horse in the Great War', NAA: A1194, 33.68/15152.
4 Gullett, *Sinai and Palestine*, p. 49.
5 Ibid., pp. 81–4.
6 Gullett notes, AWM40, 76.
7 Gullett, *Sinai and Palestine*, pp. 85–8; Sullivan diary, AWM, PR01058.
8 Burgess diary, SLNSW, CY 4947.
9 Macrae diary, SLNSW, CY 2417.
10 Tomlins diary, SLNSW, CY 587.
11 Billings diary, AWM, 3DRL/6060.
12 Evans diary, SLNSW, CY 4960.
13 Peterson diary, SLNSW, CY 2472.
14 Fell diary, SLNSW, CY 4893.
15 Knuckey diary, AWM, PR03193.
16 Burgess diary, SLNSW, CY 4947.
17 Mulder diary, AWM, 3DRL/3400(B).
18 Evans diary, SLNSW, CY 4960.
19 Sullivan diary, AWM, PR01058.
20 Knuckey diary, AWM, PR03193.
21 Tomlins diary, SLNSW, CY 587.
22 Evans diary, SLNSW, CY 4960.
23 Gullett notes, AWM40, 62 and 76.
24 6th Light Horse War Diary, AWM4, 10/11/18, Pt 1.
25 Macrae diary, SLNSW, CY 2417.
26 Burgess diary, SLNSW, CY 4947.
27 Ryrie letters, 19 June 1916, NLA, MS 986.
28 Peterson diary, SLNSW, CY 2472.
29 Tomlins diary, SLNSW, CY 587.
30 Peterson diary, SLNSW, CY 2472.
31 Ibid.
32 Evans diary, SLNSW, CY 4960.
33 Tomlins diary, SLNSW, CY 587.
34 Peterson diary, SLNSW, CY 2472.
35 Tomlins diary, SLNSW, CY 587.
36 Billings diary, AWM, 3DRL/6060.
37 Tomlins diary, SLNSW, CY 587.
38 Macfarlane diary, AWM, 2DRL/0211.
39 Tomlins diary, SLNSW, CY 587.
40 Billings diary, AWM, 3DRL/6060.
41 Burgess diary, SLNSW, CY 4947.
42 Tomlins diary, SLNSW, CY 587.
43 9th Light Horse War Diary, AWM4, 10/14/16, 2–4; Antill diary, SLNSW, MLMSS 584.
44 Peterson diary, SLNSW, CY 2472.
45 Tomlins diary, SLNSW, CY 587.
46 Burgess diary, SLNSW, CY 4947.
47 2nd Brigade War Diary, AWM4, 10/2/18, 6.
48 Pearce diary, SLNSW, MLMSS 2940.
49 Knuckey diary, AWM, PR03193.
50 Cooper diary, AWM, 1DRL/0211.

CHAPTER 2: 'COME ON, BOYS, WE ARE MAKING HISTORY'
1 McAulay diary.
2 Gullett notes, AWM40, 61.
3 AWM46, 157.
4 *Reveille*, March 1938, pp. 14–16.
5 Chauvel, 'The Australian Light Horse in the Great War', NAA: 1194, 33.68/15152.
6 Mulder diary, AWM, 3DRL/3400(B).
7 Macrae diary, SLNSW, CY 2417.
8 Pearce diary, SLNSW, MLMSS 2940.
9 Holmes diary, AWM, PR00740.
10 158th Brigade War Diary, NA, WO 95/4625.
11 Peterson diary, SLNSW, CY 2472.
12 1st Brigade War Diary, AWM4, 10/1/25, 12.
13 *Reveille*, August 1936, p. 24.
14 Cooper diary, AWM, 1DRL/0211.
15 *Reveille*, August 1936, p. 24.
16 Livingstone papers, IWM, 13560.
17 Cooper diary, AWM, 1DRL/0211.
18 Peterson diary, SLNSW, CY 2472.
19 Peterson diary, SLNSW, CY 2472.
20 Gullett, *Sinai and Palestine*, p. 147.
21 Hobbs diary, AWM, PR85/289.
22 Tomlins diary, SLNSW, CY 587.
23 Corliss diary, AWM, PR01906.
24 Willis letters, 3 August 1916, AWM, PR01168.
25 *Reveille*, August 1936, p. 24.
26 Farnes diary, AWM, PR83/106.
27 2nd Brigade War Diary, AWM4, 10/2/19, 4.
28 *Reveille*, August 1936, p. 24.
29 Holmes diary, AWM, PR00740.
30 Cooper diary, AWM, 1DRL/0211.
31 Evans diary, SLNSW, CY 4960.
32 Tomlins diary, SLNSW, CY 587.
33 Evans diary, SLNSW, CY 4960.
34 Murphy, 'Austin William Edwards', p. 5.
35 *Reveille*, August 1936, p. 24.
36 Farnes diary, AWM, PR83/106.
37 G. Cross, 'Romani', *Reveille*, August 1933, p. 46.
38 *Reveille*, June 1935, p. 8.
39 Fraser diary, AWM, PR03456.
40 *Reveille*, August 1936, p. 24.
41 *Reveille*, August 1933, p. 20.
42 *Reveille*, March 1938, pp. 14–16.
43 Greatorex diary, AWM, 3DRL/6776.
44 Römer-Andreae letter, AWM, PR89/179.
45 Gullett, *Sinai and Palestine*, pp. 151–2.
46 Billings diary, AWM, 3DRL/6060.
47 *Reveille*, March 1938, pp. 14–16.
48 Fraser diary, AWM, PR03456.
49 Peterson diary, SLNSW, CY 2472.
50 Macrae diary, SLNSW, CY 2417.
51 Burchill diary, AWM, PR00991.
52 Römer-Andreae letter, AWM, PR89/179.

53 Pearce diary, SLNSW, MLMSS 2940.
54 Farnes diary, AWM, PR83/106.
55 Wallis notes.
56 Tomlins diary, SLNSW, CY 587.

CHAPTER 3: 'JOHN TURK MUST PAY FOR HIS AUDACITY'

1. 2nd Brigade War Diary, AWM4, 10/2/19, 4.
2. Peterson diary, SLNSW, CY 2472.
3. Billings diary, AWM, 3DRL/6060.
4. McAulay diary.
5. Farnes diary, AWM, PR83/106.
6. *Reveille*, August 1936, p. 25.
7. Tomlins diary, SLNSW, CY 587.
8. Wellington Mounted Rifles War Diary, NA, WO 95/4547; Light Horse Field Ambulance War Diary, NA, WO 95/4530.
9. Corliss diary, AWM, PR01906.
10. Cooper diary, AWM, 1DRL/0211.
11. *Reveille*, August 1936, p. 25.
12. Pearce diary, SLNSW, MLMSS 2940.
13. 1st Brigade War Diary, AWM4, 10/1/25, 12.
14. Evans diary, SLNSW, CY 4960.
15. Corliss diary, AWM, PR01906.
16. Greatorex diary, AWM, 3DRL/6776.
17. Tomlins diary, SLNSW, CY 587.
18. Knuckey diary, AWM, PR03193.
19. 3rd Brigade War Diary, AWM4, 10/3/19.
20. 10th Light Horse War Diary, AWM4, 10/15/14, 3.
21. Knuckey diary, AWM, PR03193.
22. Evans diary, SLNSW, CY 4960.
23. Peterson diary, SLNSW, CY 2472.
24. Ibid.
25. Macrae diary, SLNSW, CY 2417.
26. Burchill diary, AWM, PR00991.
27. Evans diary, SLNSW, CY 4960.
28. Macfarlane diary, AWM, 2DRL/0211.
29. Pearce diary, SLNSW, MLMSS 2940.
30. Tomlins diary, SLNSW, CY 587.
31. Peterson diary, SLNSW, CY 2472.
32. Tomlins diary, SLNSW, CY 587.
33. Evans diary, SLNSW, CY 4960.
34. Holmes diary, AWM, PR00740.
35. Bostock diary, AWM, PR83/110.
36. Jackson letter, 30 August 1916, AWM, 1DRL/0380.
37. Knuckey diary, AWM, PR03193.
38. Ibid.
39. Hogan postcard, 8 Aug 1916, author's collection.
40. Knuckey diary, AWM, PR03193.
41. Tomlins diary, SLNSW, CY 587.
42. Billings diary, AWM, 3DRL/6060.
43. Farnes diary, AWM, PR83/106.
44. Peterson diary, SLNSW, CY 2472.
45. Tomlins diary, SLNSW, CY 587.
46. Greatorex diary, AWM, 3DRL/6776.
47. 1st Brigade War Diary, 10/1/25, 14.
48. Peterson diary, SLNSW, CY 2472.
49. Knuckey diary, AWM, PR03193.
50. Tomlins diary, SLNSW, CY 587.
51. Parkes diary, AWM, PR01571.
52. Knuckey diary, AWM, PR03193.
53. Parkes diary, AWM, PR01571.
54. Peterson diary, SLNSW, CY 2472.
55. Maddrell letters, 28 August 1916, AWM, PR02017.
56. Pearce diary, SLNSW, MLMSS 2940; Trooper George Nobbs was killed in action on 9 August 1916.
57. Bostock diary, AWM, PR83/110.
58. Knuckey diary, AWM, PR03193.
59. Langtip diary, AWM, PR00053.
60. Knuckey diary, AWM, PR03193; Ross diary, AWM, PR01032.
61. Cross, 'Romani', *Reveille*, August 1933, p. 46.
62. *Reveille*, March 1938, pp. 14–16.

CHAPTER 4: 'OH, YOU BEAUTIES'

1. Minahan diary, SLNSW, MLDOC 1360.
2. Gullett notes, AWM40, 68.
3. Gullett, *Sinai and Palestine*, p. 208.
4. Fell diary, SLNSW, CY 4893.
5. Pearce diary, SLNSW, MLMSS 2940.
6. Baker diary.
7. Corliss diary, AWM, PR01906.
8. Evans diary, SLNSW, CY 4960.
9. Baker diary.
10. *Reveille*, December 1933, p. 3.
11. Pearce diary, SLNSW, MLMSS 2940.
12. Holmes diary, AWM, PR00740.
13. Tomlins diary, SLNSW, CY 587.
14. Ibid.
15. Fraser diary, AWM, PR03456.
16. Mills report, AWM, 1DRL/0501.
17. Bolger diary, SLNSW, CY 4132.
18. Gullett, *Sinai and Palestine*, p. 221.
19. Bostock diary, AWM, PR83/110.
20. Tomlins diary, SLNSW, CY 587.
21. Holmes diary, AWM, PR00740.
22. *Reveille*, October 1934, p. 8.
23. *Reveille*, December 1933, p. 27.
24. Gullett notes, AWM40, 69.
25. Ibid.
26. Pearce diary, SLNSW, MLMSS 2940.
27. Ross diary, AWM, PR01032.
28. Tomlins diary, SLNSW, CY 587.
29. Baker diary.
30. Hanly diary, AWM, PR05366.
31. Tomlins diary, SLNSW, CY 587.
32. Hanly diary, AWM, PR05366.
33. Gullett notes, AWM40, 69.
34. Parkes diary, AWM, PR01571.
35. Holmes diary, AWM, PR00740.
36. Evans diary, SLNSW, CY 4960.
37. Tomlins diary, SLNSW, CY 587.
38. Peterson diary, SLNSW, CY 2472.
39. Tomlins diary, SLNSW, CY 587.
40. Fell diary, SLNSW, CY 4893.
41. Parkes diary, AWM, PR01571.
42. Holmes diary, AWM, PR00740.
43. New Zealand Mounted Rifles Headquarters War Diary, AWM4, 35/1/21.
44. 2nd Light Horse War Diary, AWM4, 10/8/26.
45. Corliss diary, AWM, PR01906.
46. Macfarlane diary, AWM, 2DRL/0211.
47. Greatorex diary, AWM, 3DRL/6776.
48. Cooper diary, AWM, 1DRL/0211.
49. Fell diary, SLNSW, CY 4893.
50. Stephen diary, AWM, 3DRL/3584.
51. Gullett, *Sinai and Palestine*, pp. 237–8.
52. Bostock diary, AWM, PR83/110.
53. Fraser diary, AWM, PR03456.
54. Minahan diary, SLNSW, MLDOC 1360.
55. New Zealand Mounted Rifles Headquarters War Diary, AWM4, 35/1/21; Auckland Mounted Rifles War Diary, NA, WO 95/4545.
56. Greatorex diary, AWM, 3DRL/6776.
57. Horder diary, AWM, 3DRL/6595.
58. 9th Light Horse War Diary, AWM4, 10/14/23; Stephen diary, AWM, 3DRL/3584.
59. Holmes diary, AWM, PR00740.
60. Davidson, *The Dinkum Oil of Light Horse and Camel Corps*, p. 75.
61. Bolger diary, SLNSW, CY 4132.

62 Gullett notes, AWM40, 73; Davidson, *The Dinkum Oil of Light Horse and Camel Corps*, p. 75.
63 Greatorex diary, AWM, 3DRL/6776.
64 Gullett notes, AWM40, 73.
65 Stephen diary, AWM, 3DRL/3584.
66 Corliss diary, AWM, PR01906.
67 Pearce diary, SLNSW, MLMSS 2940.
68 Fraser diary, AWM, PR03456.
69 Gullett, *Sinai and Palestine*, p. 242.
70 Ibid.
71 Fell diary, SLNSW, CY 4893.
72 Gullett, *Sinai and Palestine*, p. 244.

CHAPTER 5: 'BUT WE HAVE GAZA'

1 Gullett, *Sinai and Palestine*, p. 257.
2 Ibid., p. 246.
3 Parkes diary, AWM, PR01571.
4 Holmes diary, AWM, PR00740.
5 Gullett, *Sinai and Palestine*, p. 256.
6 Farnes diary, AWM, PR83/106.
7 Minahan diary, SLNSW, MLDOC 1360.
8 Burgess diary, SLNSW, CY 4947.
9 Parkes diary, AWM, PR01571.
10 Farnes diary, AWM, PR83/106.
11 Ibid.
12 Baker diary.
13 Burgess diary, SLNSW, CY 4947.
14 Tomlins diary, SLNSW, CY 587.
15 158th Brigade War Diary, NA, WO 95/4625.
16 Burgess diary, SLNSW, CY 4947.
17 Gullett, *Sinai and Palestine*, pp. 265–6.
18 Bostock diary, AWM, PR83/110.
19 The official history says the fog lifted at about 6 a.m. but the 158th Brigade War Diary, 160th Brigade War Diary and Chauvel's report all state that it didn't lift until 8 a.m.
20 Holmes diary, AWM, PR00740.
21 Macrae diary, SLNSW, CY 2417.
22 Parkes diary, AWM, PR01571.
23 Farnes diary, AWM, PR83/106.
24 Gullett, *Sinai and Palestine*, pp. 268–9.
25 Farnes diary, AWM, PR83/106.
26 Macrae diary, SLNSW, CY 2417.
27 Holmes diary, AWM, PR00740.
28 Burgess diary, SLNSW, CY 4947.
29 Farnes diary, AWM, PR83/106.
30 158th Brigade War Diary, NA, WO 95/4625.
31 Farnes diary, AWM, PR83/106.
32 Wollaston papers, IWM, 12702.
33 Bolger diary, SLNSW, CY 4132.
34 Burgess diary, SLNSW, CY 4947.
35 Tomlins diary, SLNSW, CY 587.
36 Chauvel report, AWM22, 739/4/101.
37 Farnes diary, AWM, PR83/106.
38 5th Light Horse War Diary, AWM4, 10/10/27.
39 Gullett notes, AWM40, 64.
40 Ryrie letters, 30 March 1917, NLA, MS 986.
41 Macrae diary, SLNSW, CY 2417.
42 Minahan diary, SLNSW, MLDOC 1360.
43 Chauvel report, AWM22, 739/4/101.
44 Gullett, *Sinai and Palestine*, pp. 293–4.
45 Gullett notes, AWM40, 64.
46 Farnes diary, AWM, PR83/106.
47 Burgess diary, SLNSW, CY 4947.
48 158th Brigade War Diary, NA, WO 95/4625.
49 Wintringham papers, IWM, 6759.
50 Farnes diary, AWM, PR83/106.
51 Baker diary.
52 Parkes diary, AWM, PR01571.
53 Burgess diary, SLNSW, CY 4947.
54 Gullett, *Sinai and Palestine*, p. 285.
55 Ryrie letters, 30 March 1917, NLA, MS 986.
56 Minahan diary, SLNSW, MLDOC 1360.
57 Macrae diary, SLNSW, CY 2417.
58 Bostock diary, AWM, PR83/110.
59 Ross diary, AWM, PR01032.
60 Chauvel report, AWM22, 739/4/101.
61 Holmes diary, AWM, PR00740.
62 Baker diary.
63 Gullett, *Sinai and Palestine*, p. 296.
64 Holmes diary, AWM, PR00740.
65 Parkes diary, AWM, PR01571.

CHAPTER 6: 'AN UNQUALIFIED FAILURE'

1 Wintringham papers, IWM, 6759.
2 Ryrie letters, 21 April 1917, NLA, MS 986.
3 Pearce diary, SLNSW, MLMSS 2940.
4 Fell diary, SLNSW, CY 4893.
5 Evans diary, SLNSW, CY 4960.
6 Baker diary.
7 Minahan diary, SLNSW, MLDOC 1360.
8 Burgess diary, SLNSW, CY 4947.
9 Evans diary, SLNSW, CY 4960.
10 Burgess diary, SLNSW, CY 4947.
11 Minahan diary, SLNSW, MLDOC 1360.
12 Pearce diary, SLNSW, MLMSS 2940.
13 Evans diary, SLNSW, CY4960.
14 Macrae diary, SLNSW, CY 2417.
15 Fell diary, SLNSW, CY 4893.
16 Adams diary, AWM, 1DRL/0005.
17 MacNamara diary, SLNSW, MLMSS 2876.
18 2nd Brigade War Diary, AWM4, 10/2/28.
19 Farnes diary, AWM, PR83/106.
20 MacNamara diary, SLNSW, MLMSS 2876.
21 Tomlins diary, SLNSW, CY 587.
22 Wollaston papers, IWM, 12702.
23 Ibid.
24 Bolger diary, SLNSW, CY 4132.
25 Gullett notes, AWM40, 45.
26 3rd Battalion Imperial Camel Corps War Diary, AWM4, 11/8/4.
27 Wollaston papers, IWM, 12702.
28 Davidson, *The Dinkum Oil of Light Horse and Camel Corps*, p. 82.
29 Gullett notes, AWM40, 64.
30 Davidson, *The Dinkum Oil of Light Horse and Camel Corps*, p. 83.
31 Farnes diary, AWM, PR83/106.
32 Gullett, *Sinai and Palestine*, p. 318.
33 Ibid., pp. 320–1.
34 Smyth diary, AWM, PR00633.
35 Hamilton diary, AWM, 3DRL/7521.
36 Maygar letters, 1 August 1917, AWM, PR00696.
37 Stephen letters, 4 May 1917, AWM, 3DRL/3584.
38 Fell diary, SLNSW, CY 4893.
39 Kemp diary, AWM, 3DRL/3747.
40 Parkes diary, AWM, PR01571.
41 Hanly diary, AWM, PR05366.
42 Parkes diary, AWM, PR01571.
43 Stephen letters, 4 May 1917, AWM, 3DRL/3584.
44 Loynes letter, 3 July 1917, Jackson papers, AWM, 1DRL/0380.
45 Gullett, *Sinai and Palestine*, p. 329.
46 Tomlins diary, SLNSW, CY 587.
47 MacNamara diary, SLNSW, MLMSS 2876.

48 7th Light Horse War Diary, AWM4, 10/12/19, Pt 1.
49 Farnes diary, AWM, PR83/106.
50 Baker diary.
51 MacNamara diary, SLNSW, MLMSS 2876.
52 Evans diary, SLNSW, CY 4960.
53 Holmes diary, AWM, PR00740.
54 Gullett, *Sinai and Palestine*, p. 335.
55 Woods, letter to Charles Bean, 27 April 1918.
56 Ibid.
57 Fell diary, SLNSW, CY 4893.
58 Woods, letter to Charles Bean, 27 April 1918.
59 Parkes diary, AWM, PR01571.
60 Horder diary, AWM, 3DRL/6595.
61 Langtip diary, AWM, PR00053.

CHAPTER 7: 'FIRST-RATE HORSE-MASTERS'

1 Dengate letters, 19 and 22 May 1917, AWM, 3DRL/7678.
2 Burgess diary, SLNSW, CY 4947.
3 Pearce diary, SLNSW, MLMSS 2940.
4 Burgess diary, SLNSW, CY 4947.
5 MacNamara diary, SLNSW, MLMSS 2876.
6 Evans diary, SLNSW, CY 4960.
7 Burgess diary, SLNSW, CY 4947.
8 Fell diary, SLNSW, CY 4893.
9 MacNamara diary, SLNSW, MLMSS 2876.
10 Gullett, *Sinai and Palestine*, p. 357.
11 Burgess diary, SLNSW, CY 4947.
12 Ryrie letters, 11 July 1917, NLA, MS 986.
13 Wintringham papers, IWM, 6759.
14 *Reveille*, March 1931, p. 12.
15 Gullett, *Sinai and Palestine*, pp. 365-7.
16 MacNamara diary, SLNSW, MLMSS 2876.
17 Brown diary, AWM, 2DRL/1285.
18 Pearce diary, SLNSW, MLMSS 2940.
19 Evans diary, SLNSW, CY 4960.
20 Gullett, *Sinai and Palestine*, pp. 370-2.
21 Ibid., p. 374.
22 Macrae diary, SLNSW, CY 2417.
23 Farnes diary, AWM, PR83/106.
24 Pearce diary, SLNSW, MLMSS 2940.
25 MacNamara diary, SLNSW, MLMSS 2876. MacNamara refers to the pilot as Dietmach.
26 Holmes diary, AWM, PR00740.
27 Burgess diary, SLNSW, CY 4947.
28 Lawrence, *Seven Pillars of Wisdom*, p. 352.
29 Ibid., p. 352.
30 Thomas, *With Lawrence in Arabia*, p. 104.
31 Lawrence, *Seven Pillars of Wisdom*, p. 353.
32 Ibid., pp. 367-8.
33 Ibid., pp. 370-5.
34 Ibid., pp. 376-7.
35 Thomas, *With Lawrence in Arabia*, p. 104.

CHAPTER 8: 'AUSTRALIANS WILL DO ME'

1 5th Mounted Brigade Headquarters War Diary, NA, WO 95/4507.
2 Stephen diary, AWM, 3DRL/3584.
3 Fell diary, SLNSW, CY 4893.
4 Horder diary, AWM, 3DRL/6595.
5 Evans diary, SLNSW, CY 4960.
6 Stephen diary, AWM, 3DRL/3584.
7 Bostock diary, AWM, PR83/110.
8 Mulder diary, AWM, 3DRL/3400(B).
9 Cooper diary, AWM, 1DRL/0211.
10 Evans diary, SLNSW, CY 4960.
11 Burgess diary, SLNSW, CY 4947.
12 Idriess diary, AWM, 1DRL/0373.
13 Holmes diary, AWM, PR00740.
14 Ryrie letters, 5 November 1917, NLA, MS 986.
15 Gullett, *Sinai and Palestine*, pp. 378-9.
16 MacNamara diary, SLNSW, MLMSS 2876.
17 Idriess diary, AWM, 1DRL/0373.
18 Mulder diary, AWM, 3DRL/3400(B).
19 Horder diary, AWM, 3DRL/6595.
20 Stephen diary, AWM, 3DRL/3584.
21 Ibid.
22 Hamilton diary, AWM, 3DRL/7521.
23 Idriess diary, AWM, 1DRL/0373.
24 Ryrie letters, 5 November 1917, NLA, MS 986.
25 Idriess diary, AWM, 1DRL/0373.
26 Gullett, *Sinai and Palestine*, pp. 390-1.
27 Dunk papers, AWM, PR00469.
28 Auckland Mounted Rifles War Diary, NA, WO 95/4545.
29 Gullett, *Sinai and Palestine*, p. 393.
30 W. Grant comments, AWM38, 7953-31.
31 4th Brigade War Diary, AWM4, 10/4/10.
32 D. Harris letter, Gullett notes, AWM40, 45.
33 Ibid.
34 Gullett, *Sinai and Palestine*, pp. 396-7.
35 Gullett, *Sinai and Palestine*, pp. 400-1; Gullett notes, AWM40, 59.
36 Dengate letters, 5 November 1917, AWM, 3DRL/7678.
37 Ibid., 17 January 1918.
38 Gullett notes, AWM40, 59.
39 Abbott letters, 8 October 1973, AWM, PR86/300.
40 D. Harris letter, Gullett notes, AWM40, 45.
41 Adams diary, AWM, 1DRL/0005.
42 4th Brigade War Diary, AWM4, 10/4/10.
43 Mulder diary, AWM, 3DRL/3400(B).
44 Hanly diary, AWM, PR05366.
45 Allenby letter, 20 November 1917, Battine papers, IWM, 203.
46 Cooper diary, AWM, 1DRL/0211.
47 Gullett, *Sinai and Palestine*, pp. 435-6.
48 Gullett notes, AWM40, 59.
49 Evans diary, SLNSW, CY 4960.
50 Mulder diary, AWM, 3DRL/3400(B).
51 Pearce diary, SLNSW, MLMSS 2940.
52 Evans diary, SLNSW, CY 4960.
53 Corliss diary, AWM, PR01906.
54 Ibid.
55 Hamilton diary, AWM, 3DRL/7521.
56 Ibid.
57 Ibid.
58 Baker diary.
59 Gullett notes, AWM40, 59.
60 Mulder diary, AWM, 3DRL/3400(B).
61 Bourchier letters, 5 November 1917, AWM, 2DRL/0444.

CHAPTER 9: 'IN CHASE OF JOHNNY'

1. Allenby report, NA, CAB 44/12.
2. Ryrie letters, 5 November 1917, NLA, MS 986.
3. Burgess diary, SLNSW, CY 4947.
4. Livingstone papers, IWM, 13560; Livingstone service record, NAA: B2455.
5. Idriess diary, AWM, 1DRL/0373.
6. Ibid.
7. Mulder diary, AWM, 3DRL/3400(B).
8. Greatorex diary, AWM, 3DRL/6776.
9. 1st Light Horse War Diary, AWM4, 10/6/31.
10. Pearce diary, SLNSW, MLMSS 2940.
11. Horder diary, AWM, 3DRL/6595.
12. Evans diary, SLNSW, CY 4960.
13. Greatorex diary, AWM, 3DRL/6776.
14. Horder diary, AWM, 3DRL/6595.
15. MacNamara diary, SLNSW, MLMSS 2876.
16. Smyth diary, AWM, PR00633.
17. Gullett, *Sinai and Palestine*, pp. 432–4.
18. Adams diary, AWM, 1DRL/0005.
19. Brown diary, AWM, 2DRL/1285.
20. Pearce diary, SLNSW, MLMSS 2940.
21. Hunt diary, AWM, PR91/140.
22. Fell diary, SLNSW, CY 4893.
23. Hurley diary, 6 February 1918, NLA, MS 883, 1, 5.
24. Evans diary, SLNSW, CY 4960.
25. Hamilton diary, AWM, 3DRL/7521.
26. Smyth diary, AWM, PR00633.
27. Cox diary, AWM, PR00870.
28. Pearce diary, SLNSW, MLMSS 2940.
29. Idriess diary, AWM, 1DRL/0373.
30. Ibid.
31. Ibid.
32. Ibid.
33. Alan-Williams letter, IWM, 4082.
34. Mills diary, AWM, 1DRL/0501.
35. Fell diary, SLNSW, CY 4893.
36. Ryrie letters, 15 November 1917, NLA, MS 986.
37. Holmes diary, AWM, PR00740.
38. Gullett, *Sinai and Palestine*, pp. 446–8.
39. Ibid., pp. 451–2.
40. Hanly diary, AWM, PR05366.
41. Fell diary, SLNSW, CY 4893.
42. Farnes diary, AWM, PR83/106.
43. Holmes diary, AWM, PR00740.
44. Horder diary, AWM, 3DRL/6595.
45. Pearce diary, SLNSW, MLMSS 2940.
46. Stephen diary, AWM, 3DRL/3584.
47. Bostock diary, AWM, PR83/110.
48. Holmes diary, AWM, PR00740.
49. Mulder diary, AWM, 3DRL/3400(B).
50. Greatorex diary, AWM, 3DRL/6776.
51. Legge diary, AWM, PR01457.
52. Hurley diary, NLA, MS 883, 1, 5.
53. Horder diary, AWM, 3DRL/6595.
54. Gullett notes, AWM40, 73.
55. Pearce diary, SLNSW, MLMSS 2940.

CHAPTER 10: JERUSALEM

1. 8th Light Horse War Diary, AWM4, 10/13/29.
2. Allenby report, NA, CAB 44/12.
3. Mulder diary, AWM, 3DRL/3400(B).
4. Cooper diary, AWM, 1DRL/0211.
5. Allenby report, NA, CAB 44/12.
6. Allenby report, NA, CAB 44/12.
7. Langtip diary, AWM, PR00053.
8. Mulder diary, AWM, 3DRL/3400(B).
9. Allenby report, NA, CAB 44/12.
10. Mulder diary, AWM, 3DRL/3400(B).
11. Stephen diary, AWM, 3DRL/3584.
12. Ryrie letters, 6 December 1917, NLA, MS 986.
13. Allenby report, NA, CAB 44/12.
14. Fell diary, SLNSW, CY 4893.
15. Gullett notes, AWM40, 65.
16. Ibid.
17. Greatorex diary, AWM, 3DRL/6776.
18. Brown diary, AWM, 2DRL/1285.
19. Parkes diary, AWM, PR01571.
20. Hurley diary, NLA, MSS 883, 1, 5.
21. Bert Inall notes.
22. Ibid.

CHAPTER 11: 'I CAN'T LOSE HALF MY MOUNTED TROOPS'

1. Gullett, *Sinai and Palestine*, p. 537.
2. Greatorex diary, AWM, 3DRL/6776.
3. Brown diary, AWM, 2DRL/1285.
4. Hurley diary, NLA, MS 883, 1, 5.
5. Evans diary, SLNSW, CY 4960.
6. Hurley diary, NLA, MS 883, 1, 5.
7. Brown diary, AWM, 2DRL/1285.
8. Evans diary, SLNSW, CY 4960.
9. *Reveille*, April 1939, p. 44.
10. Holmes diary, AWM, PR00740.
11. Ryrie letters, 10 April 1918, NLA, MS 986.
12. Holmes diary, AWM, PR00740.
13. *Reveille*, April 1937, p. 60.
14. Cox diary, AWM, PR00870.
15. Greatorex diary, AWM, 3DRL/6776.
16. Gullett notes, AWM40, 62.
17. Greatorex diary, AWM, 3DRL/6776.
18. Mills diary, AWM, 1DRL/0501.
19. Hunt diary, AWM, PR91/140.
20. Scurrah service record, NAA: B2455.
21. Burgess diary, SLNSW, CY 4947.
22. Mills diary, AWM, 1DRL/0501.
23. Gullett, *Sinai and Palestine*, p. 577.
24. Mills letters, 8 May 1918, AWM, 1DRL/0501.
25. Ibid.
26. Ryrie letters, 10 April 1918, NLA, MS 986.
27. Mills diary, AWM, 1DRL/0501.
28. Gullett, *Sinai and Palestine*, p. 580.
29. Burgess diary, SLNSW, CY 4947.
30. Ryrie letters, 10 April 1918, NLA, MS 986.
31. Burgess diary, SLNSW, CY 4947.
32. Woods diary, AWM, PR02088.
33. Mills diary, AWM, 1DRL/0501.
34. Gullett, *Sinai and Palestine*, p. 584.
35. Holmes diary, AWM, PR00740.
36. Ryrie letters, 10 April 1918, NLA, MS 986.
37. MacNamara diary, SLNSW, MLMSS 2876.
38. Mills diary, AWM, 1DRL/0501.
39. Brown diary, AWM, 2DRL/1285.
40. Cox diary, AWM, PR00870.
41. Gullett, *Sinai and Palestine*, pp. 599–600.
42. *Reveille*, January 1936, p. 21.
43. Ibid.

44 Mills diary, AWM, 1DRL/0501.
45 Fell diary, SLNSW, CY 4893.
46 Kemp diary, AWM, 3DRL/3747.
47 Parkes diary, AWM, PR01571.
48 Smyth diary, AWM, PR00633.
49 Gullett notes, AWM40, 62.
50 *Reveille*, December 1939, p. 30.
51 Fell diary, SLNSW, CY4893.
52 Gullett, *Sinai and Palestine*, p. 631.
53 Ryrie letters, 6 May 1918, NLA, MS 986.
54 Mills diary, AWM, 1DRL/0501.
55 *Reveille*, June 1936, p. 23.
56 Allenby letter, 22 August 1918, Battine papers, IWM, 203.
57 Sly diary, AWM, PR01268.
58 Garden diary, PR00836.

CHAPTER 12: FROM HELL TO ARMAGEDDON

1 *Reveille*, September 1929, p. 23.
2 *Reveille*, January 1936, p. 21.
3 Allenby letter, 7 June 1918, Battine papers, IWM, 203.
4 Mills diary, AWM, 1DRL/0501.
5 Burgess diary, SLNSW, CY 4947.
6 Farnes diary, AWM, PR83/106.
7 Gullett, *Sinai and Palestine*, p. 642.
8 Parkes diary, AWM, PR01571.
9 Pearce diary, SLNSW, MLMSS 2940.
10 Fell diary, SLNSW, CY 4893.
11 Dengate letters, 5 May 1918, AWM, 3DRL/7678.
12 *Reveille*, January 1936, p. 21.
13 Allenby letter, 7 June 1918, Battine papers, IWM, 203.
14 Fell diary, SLNSW, CY 4893.
15 Kemp diary, AWM, 3DRL/3747.
16 Farnes diary, AWM, PR83/106.
17 Ryrie letters, 17 July 1918, NLA, MS 986.
18 Greatorex diary, AWM, 3DRL/6776.
19 Evans diary, SLNSW, CY 4960.
20 Gullett, *Sinai and Palestine*, p. 671.
21 Ibid., p. 667–8.
22 Brown diary, AWM, 2DRL/1285.
23 MacNamara diary, SLNSW, MLMSS 2876.
24 Evans diary, SLNSW, CY 4960.
25 Livingstone papers, IWM, 13560.
26 MacNamara diary, SLNSW, MLMSS 2876.
27 Mills diary, AWM, 1DRL/0501.
28 Gullett, *Sinai and Palestine*, p. 695.
29 Gullett notes, AWM40, 70.
30 Lowe diary, SLNSW, MLMSS 2873.
31 Mills diary, AWM, 1DRL/0501.
32 Ibid.
33 Ibid.
34 Fell diary, SLNSW, CY 4893.
35 Lowe diary, SLNSW, MLMSS 2873.
36 *Reveille*, August 1930, p. 30.
37 Mills diary, AWM, 1DRL/0501.
38 Davidson, *The Dinkum Oil of Light Horse and Camel Corps*, p. 103.
39 Mills diary, AWM, 1DRL/0501.
40 Lowe diary, SLNSW, MLMSS 2873.
41 *Reveille*, August 1930, p. 30.

CHAPTER 13: 'TERRIFIED OF THE BEDOUINS'

1 Horder diary, AWM, 3DRL/6595.
2 Evans diary, SLNSW, CY 4960.
3 Ibid.
4 Gullett, *Sinai and Palestine*, p. 720.
5 2nd Brigade War Diary, AWM4, 10/2/45; 5th Light Horse War Diary, AWM4, 10/10/45.
6 Hunt diary, AWM, PR91/140.
7 Evans diary, SLNSW, CY 4960.
8 Horder diary, AWM, 3DRL/6595.
9 Evans diary, SLNSW, CY 4960.
10 5th Light Horse War Diary, AWM4, 10/10/45.
11 Ibid.
12 Ryrie letters, 1 October 1918, NLA, MS 986.
13 Hunt diary, AWM, PR91/140.
14 5th Light Horse War Diary, AWM4, 10/10/45.
15 Farnes diary, AWM, PR83/106.
16 Holmes diary, AWM, PR00740.
17 7th Light Horse War Diary, AWM4, 10/12/36.
18 Ryrie letters, 1 October 1918, NLA, MS 986.
19 Holmes diary, AWM, PR00740.
20 Hunt diary, AWM, PR91/140.
21 1st Light Horse War Diary, AWM4, 10/6/41; Horder diary, AWM, 3DRL/6595.
22 1st Light Horse War Diary, AWM4, 10/6/41; Greatorex diary, AWM, 3DRL/6776.

CHAPTER 14: 'WE ARE GOING TO CHARGE THE TOWN'

1 *Reveille*, September 1936, p. 12.
2 Gullett notes, AWM40, 75.
3 Ibid.
4 *Reveille*, September 1936, p. 12.
5 Mills diary, AWM, 1DRL/0501.
6 Smyth diary, AWM, PR00633.
7 Mills diary, AWM, 1DRL/0501.
8 Lowe diary, SLNSW, MLMSS 2873.
9 Gullett notes, AWM40, 59.
10 Gullett, *Sinai and Palestine*, pp. 743–4.
11 Lowe diary, SLNSW, MLMSS 2873.
12 Gullett, *Sinai and Palestine*, p. 747.
13 Kemp diary, AWM, 3DRL/3747.
14 Mills diary, AWM, 1DRL/0501.
15 Lowe diary, SLNSW, MLMSS 2873.
16 Kemp diary, AWM, 3DRL/3747.
17 Mills diary, AWM, 1DRL/0501.
18 Ibid.
19 Brown diary, AWM, 2DRL/1285.
20 Gullett, *Sinai and Palestine*, p. 772.
21 Mills diary, AWM, 1DRL/0501.
22 Ibid.
23 *Reveille*, October 1934, p. 21.
24 Kemp diary, AWM, 3DRL/3747.
25 MacNamara diary, SLNSW, MLMSS 2876.
26 Dengate letters, 30 March 1918, AWM, 3DRL/7678.
27 Gullett, *Sinai and Palestine*, p. 789.
28 Farnes diary, AWM, PR83/106.
29 Ryrie letters, 27 December 1918, NLA, MS 986.
30 Farnes diary, AWM, PR83/106.
31 Gullett, *Sinai and Palestine*, p. 242–3.
32 Ibid., p. 789.
33 *Reveille*, June 1938, p. 13.
34 Ibid., p. 20.
35 *Reveille*, May 1936, p. 6.

INDEX

Abasan el Kebir 85-6, 97, 117
Abu Tellul 147
Acre 165
Adams, Lt Arthur 74, 105
Ain es Sir 138, 175
Ajjeh 153
Akaba 1, 92-4
Alan-Williams, Capt Alan 116
Aleppo 143, 165, 173-4
Ali Muntar 61, 63-5, 71, 75, 114
Allenby, Gen Sir Edmund
   appointment of 81, 87-8
   and Beersheba 90, 99, 105, 109
   and Jerusalem 123, 127
   and Jordan Valley 131, 134, 140-6
   and Megiddo 148-50
   and Damascus 165, 168
   and Surafend 175
Ameidat 115
Amman 92, 134-43, 157-63, 176-7
Anebta 154-5
Antill, Maj Gen John 3, 12, 33
Asluj 4, 85, 87, 97-100
Atawineh 77-8
Auja River 125, 128
Austin, L Cpl Charles 80
Australian Flying Corps 60-1, 155
Australian Imperial Force
   Camel Battalions
   1st 76, 139
   3rd 54, 76, 109, 113
   4th 137
   LH Regiments
   1st 12, 51, 86, 100, 112, 121
      at Romani 18-24, 32, 38, 40
      in Jordan Valley 131, 148
      at Amman 160, 163
   2nd 48, 52, 121, 173
      at Romani 20, 28, 34, 38-9
      at Beersheba 101-2
      in Jordan Valley 139, 147
   3rd 46, 116
      at Romani 11, 20-1, 38
      at Beersheba 101-2
      in Jordan Valley 131, 136, 138
   4th 170
      at Beersheba 102-3, 106
   5th 8, 28, 65, 101, 110, 115
      in Jordan Valley 137, 139, 142
      at Amman 159-60
   6th 9, 68, 127-8, 174
      at Romani 18, 23-5
      on Hebron Road 109-10
      in Jordan Valley 135-7, 176-7
   7th 100, 117, 137
      at Romani 23-5, 31
      at Gaza 62, 66, 68, 80
      at Amman 159, 161
   8th 78, 97, 107, 117, 155, 170
      at Romani 36-40
      at Magdhaba 46, 48
      at Khulweilfe 111, 113
      in Judean Hills 120, 123, 126
   9th 12, 53, 107, 141, 154
      at Romani 33, 37
      at Magdhaba 46, 48
      at Gaza 68, 78
      at Huj 116-17
      in Judean Hills 120, 123,
      at Damascus 170, 173
   10th 12, 78, 97, 126, 154, 176
      at Romani 33, 40
      at Magdhaba 44-8
      at Huj 116-17
      in Jordan Valley 141-2
      at Damascus 170, 172
   11th 3, 35, 57, 102, 165
      at Gaza 76-8
      at Tel el Sheria 113-14
   12th 3, 15, 77, 85-6, 120, 170
      at Beersheba 102-6
      at Tel el Sheria 113
   14th 145, 153, 170
   15th 145, 153
   LH Field Ambulances
   1st 7
   2nd xi, 47, 80
   3rd 39, 49-50, 62, 78
   4th 106
   LH Field Squadrons
   1st 19, 135
   LH Machine Gun Squadrons
   1st 52
   2nd 113
   3rd 95
   4th x
Austrian army 23, 33, 117, 148

Baalbek 174
Bailey, Maj Percy 113
Baker, Spr Wilfred Tom 44-5, 48, 60, 68-9, 72, 80, 107, 181
Balin 120
Ballard, L Cpl Claude 181
Barada Gorge 165, 170-1
Barbar River 170
Barron, Pte Sydney 131, 140-1, 145-6, 178
Barrow, Maj Gen George 85, 152-3, 168-9, 171
Barry, Pte William 76
Bartlett, Lt John 114
Bean, Capt Charles 81
Beersheba 4, 57-8, 85, 109-11
   battle of 90-107
Beirut 174
Beisan 153, 157, 165
Bell, L Cpl Fred 135
Bell, Lt Col George 101, 136, 138
Benat Yakub 170
Benkwitz, Lt 15
Bethlehem 120, 125-6, 131
Bey, Izzet 126
Bey, Khadir 48
Bey, Tala 67
Billings, Cpl Herbert 11-12, 27, 31, 38, 178
Bir el Abd 6, 9-10, 16, 37-41, 57
Bir el Bayud 9, 41, 44
Bir el Hassana 57
Bir Nagid 39
Birkbeck, Maj Gilbert 48
Bolger, Pte Joseph 46, 64
Bolingbroke, Maj Arch 65
Bostock, Sgt Harry 35, 40, 46, 53, 62, 68, 98, 120, 178
Bourchier, Lt Col Murray 102-3, 107, 170
Bourne, Lt Col George 20, 38, 121, 147-8
Boyd, Maj John 161
Bradley, Pte Tom ix, 86
Bradshaw, Tpr Joe 77, 141, 181
Brierty, Lt Alwyn 114
British army
   Imperial Camel Corps 43, 59, 134, 145
   Royal Horse Artillery 3, 23-4, 37-9, 51, 74, 101-2, 139
   Divisions
   4th Cavalry 152, 173
   5th Cavalry 152, 173-4
   52nd 5, 10, 75, 109, 120, 125
   53rd 58, 62-3, 112
   54th 58, 62, 75, 113
   60th 125, 134, 140, 142
   74th 125
   75th 120, 124-5

INDEX   193

British army (*continued*)
   Anzac Mtd 1, 6, 18, 58, 65, 81, 131, 134, 174–5
   Australian Mtd 123, 128, 140, 152, 165, 170, 173–4
   Yeomanry Mtd 85, 97, 113, 123–5
   Brigades
   5th Mtd 4, 27, 52–3, 58, 77, 116
   6th Mtd 58, 120
   22nd Mtd 58, 67
Brook, Sgt Louis 157
Brook, Cpl Walter 92–5
Brown, Dvr Edwin 89, 114, 128, 131, 133, 139, 148, 173, 178
Brownjohn, Pte William 107
Bruxner, Lt Col Michael 20, 24, 31–2, 178
Bulfin, Lt Gen Edward 90, 114
Burchill, Dvr William 28, 33
Burgess, Cpl Godfrey 86, 181
Burgess, Sgt Joe 6, 8–9, 12, 59, 61, 63–4, 67–8, 72, 85–8, 91, 98, 109, 137, 139, 146, 178
Burkusie Ridge 120
Burton, Lt Frank 103

Cain, Capt John 65
Cairo 1, 29, 57, 81, 87–8, 176
Cameron, Lt Col Don 102–3, 113, 137, 139, 159–62
Cameron, William 145
Campbell, Lt Archie 76
Chambers, Tpr Arthur 39
Chauvel, Gen Sir Harry ix, 1, 3
   and Romani 17, 20, 27–8, 37
   and Magdhaba 43–6
   and Gaza 65–6, 68–9
   and Beersheba 97–9, 102
   and Jordan Valley 140–5, 148–50
   and Megiddo 153–4, 165
   and Syria 168, 173–4
Chaytor, Maj Gen Sir Edward 3, 27, 32, 46, 67, 81, 115–18, 162
Chetwode, Lt Gen Sir Philip ix, 44, 50, 113–14, 131, 154
   and Rafa 51–4
   and Gaza 62–3, 65–8, 71, 81
   and Beersheba 85, 88, 99, 106
Circassians 138, 157, 170
Clerke, Maj James 136, 142
Cooper, L Cpl Gordon 13, 20, 23, 32, 52, 98, 105, 123, 178
Corliss, Pte Lloyd 22, 32, 44, 52, 106, 178
Costello, Maj Edward 165
Cotter, Pte Albert 104
Cox, S Sgt Arthur 104
Cox, Maj Gen Charles 1, 3, 9, 15, 46, 67, 115, 119, 158, 163
   and Rafa 51–2, 54
   and Jordan Valley 131, 139, 148

Cox, Lt Fred 48
Cross, Maj Donald 25, 40
Currie, Lt Archibald 159

Dairut 176
Dallas, Maj Gen Alister 63–5, 67
Daly, Maj Tom 173
Damascus ix, 78, 92, 165, 168–73
Davidson, Lt John 51, 53–4, 76–7, 155, 181
Davies, Capt Jack 104
Dead Sea 131, 133–5, 145
Deir el Belah 61, 63, 68, 71–2, 85, 89, 128
Dengate, Tpr Edward 85, 104, 146, 175, 178
Deraa 92, 140, 157, 168–9, 171
Dhaheriye 109, 111
Dittmar, Lt Gustav 91
Dixon, L Cpl Reg xi, 181
Djemal Pasha 15, 89–90, 171
Dobell, Maj Gen Charles 43, 58, 66, 68, 71, 74, 80–1, 85
Donovan, Sgt Albert 165, 167
Dueidar 5, 33
Duffy, Pte James 128
Duma 172
Dunk, Cpl Roy 101
Dunkley, Maj Charles 126

Edwards, Cpl Austin 24, 181
El Afule 150, 152
El Arish 43–4, 48–52, 55–7, 60–1
El Buggar 97
El Burj 126
El Makhruk 157
El Mughar 120
El Muntar 131
Es Salt 132, 135–43, 149, 157–60
Esani 97
Esdraelon Plain 152
Esdud 116, 118–19, 128
Et Tine 120
Etmaler 25–6, 38
Evans, Cpl Maurice 7–8, 10, 23–4, 32–5, 44, 50, 72–4, 80, 89, 97–8, 112, 133, 148–9, 157–60, 178
Evans, Capt Wilfred 78

Falkenhayn, Gen Erich 89–90, 148
Farnes, Lt Robert 23, 28, 31, 38, 59, 62–3, 65, 67–8, 74, 77, 80, 91, 118, 146–7, 162, 175, 178
Fay, Capt George 126
Fell, L Cpl Robert 8, 44, 51–2, 55, 68, 71, 78, 86, 97, 114–18, 126, 141–2, 146, 155, 178
Ferris, Pte Cecil 57
Fetherstonhaugh, Maj Cuthbert 104
Fletcher, Lt Howard Bowden 155
Flockhart, L Sgt John 39

Foley, Pte Thomas 74
Foulkes-Taylor, Lt Charles 141
Francis, Lt George 182
Fraser, Chaplain William 25
Fulton, Lt Col David 20, 46

Galilee, Sea of ii, 15, 165–9
Gallipoli ix, 8, 16, 29, 44, 50, 74, 78, 80, 90, 103, 112, 163
Gamli 89
gas warfare 71–5, 89
Gaza 57–61, 88–92, 103, 109, 114
   first battle of 62–9
   second battle of 71–80, 175
German air detachment 6, 11–12, 62, 74, 79–80, 90–1, 106–7, 118
German army 15–18, 26–7, 31–3, 48, 89, 117, 123, 147–8, 165–72
Ghoraniye 135, 139
Godwin, Brig Gen Charles 120
Gorrell, Tpr John 182
Grant, Brig Gen William 77, 165
   and Beersheba 97, 102–3
   and Jordan Valley 141, 143
Granville, Lt Col Cecil 112, 148
Gray-Cheape, Lt Col Hugh 116
Greatorex, Sgt James 26, 32, 38, 52–4, 112–13, 121, 128, 131, 136, 163, 178
Green Hill 63, 65
Gullett, Sir Henry ix, 1, 13, 69, 79, 87, 152, 170, 178
   and Magdhaba 48–9
   and Rafa 54–5
   and Beersheba 102–3, 107
   and Jerusalem 126–7
   and Jordan Valley 141, 146, 148

Haifa 165
Hajla 135
Hall, Spr William 78
Hamilton, L Sgt Patrick 77, 99, 106–7, 114, 179
Hamisah 5–6
Hanly, Dvr Leo 48–9, 78, 105, 118, 179
Hareira 79, 85, 97, 113
Harper, Maj Harold 167
Harris, Sgt David 102–3, 105
Harris, Maj Geoff 163
Hassall, Lt Rowland x
Hebron 100, 109–10
Hejaz 134, 139, 145, 157, 173
Hejaz railway 92, 94–5
Hind, Tpr Oliver 112
Hitchcock, Pte Arthur 3, 182
Hobbs, Spr John 22
Hod ed Debabis 39
Hod el Enna 20
Hod Salmana 10, 13
Hodgson, Maj Gen Henry
   and Gaza 58–9, 62, 77

194   AUSTRALIAN LIGHT HORSE

and Beersheba 102
and Huj 116
and Syria 165, 170, 174
Hogan, Pte Arthur 36
Holmes, Pte Jeff 19, 35, 45-7, 50-3, 58, 62-3, 68-9, 91, 98, 117-20, 135, 139, 162-3, 179
Homs 172, 174
Horder, Sgt Les 53, 97-9, 112-13, 119-21, 157, 160, 163, 179
Housain, Ali 160
Huddleston, Maj Hubert 54
Huj 113, 116-18
Hunt, Tpr George 114, 137, 159, 161, 163, 179
Hurley, Capt Frank xi, 58, 103, 114, 121, 123, 128, 131, 133, 179
Hussein, Sherif Ali lbn 92, 161
Hyman, Maj Eric 103-4

Idriess, Tpr Ion 98-9, 101, 110-11, 115-16, 179
Imara 89
Inall, Pte Bert 129, 182
Indian army 140, 148-53, 157-8

Jackson, Tpr Pelham 35-6, 78, 179
Jaffa 121, 124-5, 127, 150
James, Capt Ernest 174
Jemmameh 113, 116-17
Jenin 153-5
Jepson, Sgt Christian 31
Jericho 126, 131-4, 157-8
Jerusalem 71, 78, 88, 120-32
Jifjafa 4, 12
Jisr ed Damieh 141, 157
Jordan River 133-5, 139-43, 145, 148, 157-8, 162, 165, 170
Jordan Valley 131, 133, 138, 143-51, 157-8, 170, 174, 177
Judean Hills 99, 121, 125
Junction Station 60, 89, 118-21

Kantara 1-7, 19, 27-9, 57, 71, 89
Katia 3-6, 8, 15-16, 18, 20, 31-5
Katra 120
Kaukab 170
Kaukabah 117
Kellett, Sgt Ralph 131
Kelly, Sgt Patrick 171
Kemkemian, Armenac 80
Kemp, Pte Ron 78, 141, 147, 171-2, 174, 179
Khalasa 97-8
Khan Yunis 59, 61-3, 71, 89
Khurbet Deiran 121
Knuckey, Pte Verner 8, 36-9, 179
Kressenstein, Gen Kress von 15-17, 27, 89, 109
Kuneitra 79, 170
Kut-el-Amara 6

Lahfan 45
Langley, Lt Col George
  with 1st Camel Bn 43, 139
  with 14th LH 153, 170
Langtip, Staff Sgt Henry 40, 83, 125, 179
Latron 123-4, 126
Lawrence, Gen Sir Herbert 18-19, 27, 43
Lawrence, Lt Col T.E. 92-5, 129, 149, 168, 172
Lawrence of Arabia see Lawrence, Lt Col T.E.
Lawson, Maj James 103
Legge, Cpl David 121
Lester, Pte Bruce 71
Livingstone, Cpl Charles 20, 109-10, 147, 150-1, 179
Lloyd-Baker, Capt Michael 5
Long, Lt Walter 18
Lowe, Spr John 153, 155, 168, 170, 172, 179
Loynes, Maj James 78, 165, 167
Ludd 121, 152, 175
Luxor 7, 176
Lyon, Lt Charles 109

Maan 94, 160
MacAndrew, Maj Gen Henry 152, 174
McAulay, Tpr Ken 31, 182
McCook, Tpr Gordon 40
Macfarlane, Lt Stuart 12, 34, 52, 179
McGrath, Lt William 40
Macgregor, Lt Fred 176
McIntosh, Lt Col Harold 77
McKenzie, Duncan 177
McKenzie, Maj Ken 103
McLaurin, Lt Col Arch 111, 170
McMinn, Nurse Beulah 29
McNamara, Lt Frank 60-1
MacNamara, Pte John 74, 79-80, 86-91, 99, 113, 139, 148-50, 179
Macrae, Sgt Gordon 6, 9, 18, 28, 33, 62, 66, 68, 91, 180
Maddrell, Capt Harry 39
Mafrak 163
Magdhaba 44-51, 53, 55
Mageibra 5, 18
Magruntein 51
Martin, Lt Alex 48
Martin, Tpr John 112
Mattocks, Sgt Harry 182
May, Sgt Robert 131
Maygar, Lt Col Leslie 46, 78, 107
Mazar 43, 57
Mecca 92
Medina 92
Megiddo 151-5, 165
Meinertzhagen, Col Richard 90
Meldrum, Brig Gen William 23, 25, 32, 157-8

Meredith, Lt Ben 103
Meredith, Brig Gen John 15, 20, 32, 77, 97
Mesopotamia 6, 149
Millar, Pte Roy 182-3
Mills, Lt Col Arthur 46, 75, 79, 116-17, 137-45, 151-5, 167-8, 171, 173-4, 180
Minahan, Tpr Michael 43, 53, 59, 66, 68, 72, 74, 180
Minet el Qamh 176
Minia 1
Mitchell, George 176
Moore, Lt Vin 126
Mudawwarah 94
Mühlmann, Maj Carl 17, 26-7, 41
Mulder, Capt Harold 8, 17, 98-9, 105-7, 111, 120, 123, 125, 180
Mulford, Lt Edwin 183
Murray, Gen Sir Archibald x, 1, 3, 6, 19, 43, 51
  and Gaza 57, 69, 71, 81
Musallabeh 139
Musmus Pass 152

Nablus 123, 125-6, 153-5
Nazareth 152
Nebi Samwil 125
Nejile 116-17
Nekhl 57
Nelson, Lt William 24
New Zealand Mounted Rifles ix, 3, 10
  at Romani 13, 18, 23, 27, 31-2, 37
  at Magdhaba 46
  at Rafa 51-3
  at Gaza 58, 66-7
  at Beersheba 101-2
  at Jaffa 121
  in Jordan Valley 131, 135-8
  at Amman 157-8, 162
Nile River 1, 7, 51
Nivison, Lt Frank 15, 118
Nobbs, Tpr George 40
Nutt, Maj Norman 72

Oghratina 5-6, 10-17, 19, 32, 39
O'Leary, Pte Thomas 105
Onslow, Brig Gen George M. 25, 100, 145, 153-4, 170

Papen, Maj von 123, 125
Parbury, Lt Charles 131
Parkes, Lt Stan 33, 39, 50-1, 57, 59, 62, 68-9, 78, 83, 128, 141, 146, 180
Parsons, Col Harry 165
Paterson, Lt Reg 154
Paul, Cpl Carrick 25
Pearce, Capt Maurice 13, 18, 28, 32-4, 40, 44, 71, 74, 86, 89-91, 106, 112-15, 119-21, 146, 180

Peterson, Pte William 7–12, 20–1, 28, 31, 33–4, 38–9, 50, 180
Plain of Sharon 149
Playfoot, Pte Jeffery 27
Poate, Maj Hugh 29, 183
Pollock-McCall, Brig Gen John 120
Port Said 143

Radburn, Tpr Clarence 157
Rafa 1, 44, 59, 69, 81, 87, 89
 battle of 51–5
Ramleh 121
Rayak 174
Redding, Pte Lawrence 176
Reid, Sgt Clarence 183
Reynolds, Sgt Arthur 183
Righetti, Lt Alan 28, 31
Rinaldi, Sgt Francis 18
Riza, Ali 171
Robertson, Maj Horace 45, 47
Robey, Lt Rod 104
Romani 3–12, 17–19, 43, 57
 battle of 20–41
Römer-Andreae, Heinrich 26, 28
Roper, Tpr Walter 18
Rose, Cpl William 60
Ross, Sgt Ron 40, 48, 68
Royal Flying Corps 150
Royston, Brig Gen John 43, 97
 and Romani 15–16, 21, 24–5, 31
 and Magdhaba 46–8
 and Rafa 52–3, 55
 and Gaza 68, 77–8
Rutherford, Capt David 60–1
Ryrie, Maj Gen Sir Granville 3–6, 9, 15, 83, 126, 175, 180
 and Gaza 65–8, 71
 and Beersheba 88, 98–101
 and Hebron Road 109, 111
 and Tel Abu Dilakh 115, 117–18
 and Jordan Valley 132, 135–42
 and Amman 158–62
Ryrie, Maj Harold 137

Saint Quentin, Capt Count 48
Samra 162–3
Sanders, Gen Otto Liman von 148–52

Sarona 152
Sasa 170
Scott, Col William 46
Scurrah, Tpr Gordon 137, 177
Semakh 15, 165–9
Shanahan, Maj Michael 21–2
Shea, Maj Gen John 126, 134, 137, 142
Shellal 72, 74, 79–83, 89, 97
Shunet Nimrin 135, 140, 142, 157
Simms, Cpl William 143
Singh, Risaldar Badhu 157–8
Smith, Brig Gen Clement 46
Smyth, Dvr Walter 183
Smyth, Tpr William 77, 113–14, 141, 180
Sohag 7–8
Stansfield, Lt Col William 117
Stephen, Spr John 53–4, 78, 97, 99, 119, 126, 180
Suez Canal 1–4, 16–18, 99
Sullivan, Pte Henry 8
Surafend 175

Taberner, Pte Horace 1, 183
Talat ed Dumm 132, 134, 150
tank warfare 71–2, 75–7
Tel Abu Dilakh 115
Tel el Khuweilfe 109–13
Tel el Saba 101–2
Tel el Sheria 109, 112–15
Thomas, Lowell 93
Thompson, Capt Alfred 109
Thompson, Lt Arthur 117
Thomson, Sgt Robert 80
Thorpe, Pte Herbert 80
Throssell, Lt Frank 74
Throssell, Lt Hugo 74, 127
Tiberias 152, 165, 168
Timperley, Maj Lewis 117
Todd, Lt Col Thomas 12, 46–7, 170
Tomlins, Lt Fred 8, 10–12, 22–4, 29, 31, 33, 35, 38–9, 45–50, 60, 65, 74, 79, 180
Tripoli 174
Tul Keram 153, 155
Turkish army 89–90, 123–5, 148, 155–7

Divisions
3rd 16–17, 20
53rd 62

Ussher, Tpr Leo 80

Vale Post 147–8
Vernon, Brig Gen H.A. 67

Wadi el Arish 44
Wadi el Auja 131, 157
Wadi Fara 155
Wadi Ghuzze 58, 62–3, 68–9, 72, 74, 81, 88–9, 98
Wadi Kelt 133
Wadi Kumran 131
Wadi Nahr Sukereir 119
Wadi Nimrin 139, 142, 157–8
Wadi Rum 94
Wadi Sunt 120
Wadi Um Muksheib 12
Waite, Lt Fred 65
Wallis, Lt George 29
Ware, Sgt Vernon 8
Warren, Tpr Geoff 109–10
Warren, Pte Ralph 110
water supply 3–4, 8–10, 12, 17, 69, 97–9, 105–6, 117–19
 Suez pipeline 43, 57, 71, 89
Wells, Sgt Colin 13
Whitfield, Capt Wesley 167
Wigan, Brig Gen John 111
Wiggin, Brig Gen Edgar 4–6, 27
Willis, Tpr Frank 22, 180
Wilson, Brig Gen Lachlan 8, 97, 117
 and Jordan Valley 141–3
 and Damascus 170–2
 and Egyptian uprising 176
Wintringham, Col J.W. 67–8, 71, 180
Wollaston, Lt Col Fred 64, 75–6, 180
Woods, Sgt Edward 139
Woods, Sgt Francis M. 183
Woods, Rev William M. 81, 83, 183

Yells, Sgt Charles 92–5

Zagazig 176
Ziza 160–3